MODERNIST CULTURE IN AMERICA

*paradox of "modern"
as history.
4 roots views*

*artistic digest
of Ang's dawn
th 19th
Cent*

MODERNISM IS OUR CLASSICISM

— WORLD VIEW
— AMERICAN DOMINATION?
— NATIONAL
— CONSCIOUSNESS
— ANTI CONVENTIONAL
— EXPLORATORY
— CULTURE ATTACHED
— MASS MEDIA
— REACTION TO PREVIOUS (VICTORIAN)
— NINETEENTH CENT. ROOTS
— REST

LIMITS of DESCRIPTION
NOT CONSCIOUS
"MODERN"

Modernist Culture in America

[handwritten: WHAT IS Art "term" - Kav is if Fact is Artist + AUDIENCE?]

Edited by
Daniel Joseph Singal
Hobart and William Smith Colleges

[handwritten: DECONSTRUCTION: SUBMITS INDIVIDUAL TO COLLECTIVE CONSCIOUSNESS? INDIVIDUAL MUSICAL REFLECTS SOCIAL (CULTURAL) VALUES. ISN'T THAT WHAT LITERALLY HISTORY or "HISTORY we IDEAS" WAS?

TEXT REFLECTS CULTURAL CONTEXT]

Wadsworth Publishing Company
Belmont, California
A Division of Wadsworth, Inc.

History Editor: Peggy Adams
Editorial Assistant: Tammy Goldfeld
Production Editor: Donna Linden
Designer: Andrew Ogus
Print Buyer: Barbara Britton
Permissions Editor: Peggy Meehan
Copy Editor: Thomas L. Briggs
Compositor: Scratchgravel, Auburn, Washington
Cover Design: Andrew Ogus

© 1991, 1987 American Studies Association. *Modernist Culture in America*, edited by Daniel Joseph Singal. Originally published as Volume 39, Spring 1987, Number 1, of *American Quarterly*.

Printed in the United States of America   49

1 2 3 4 5 6 7 8 9 10—95 94 93 92 91

Library of Congress Cataloging-in-Publication Data

Modernist culture in America / edited by Daniel Joseph Singal.
    p. cm. — (American society and culture series)
    "Originally published as volume 39, spring 1987, number 1 of
American quarterly"—T.p. verso.
    Includes bibliographical references.
    ISBN 0-534-14808-5
    1. Modernism (Art)—United States. 2. Postmodernism—United
States. 3. Arts, Modern—20th century—United States. I. Singal,
Daniel Joseph, 1944– . II. Series.
NX504.M6 1991
700'.973'0904—dc20   90-46974

Contents

Introduction

During the past decade or so, Americanists have finally joined those who study twentieth-century Europe in realizing the importance of Modernist culture. Prior to that time, the reigning assumption held that Modernism was, for the most part, an exclusively European phenomenon that somehow couldn't or didn't happen here. To be sure, those writing on specific fields of artistic endeavor like painting, literature, and architecture have fully recognized the dominant influence of Modernism within their bailiwicks from roughly 1900 onward. But there has been little sense that these developments might be related—that what has happened to the modern American novel, for example, might be part of the same underlying cultural movement that transformed the graphic arts.

A surge of recent scholarship has now demonstrated, however, that Modernism did happen here, and that its impact on American culture and society has been far greater than previously understood. The more the topic has been explored, the clearer it has become that an extensive research agenda still remains before us. Hence the need for this symposium, which originally appeared as a special issue of *American Quarterly* in the spring of 1987, and which is now being made more widely available through re-publication as a book. Its purpose is not only to provide a summary of what we have learned thus far about Modernism in the United States, but also to suggest the questions and issues that must be dealt with in the future.

In order to make sure that all major areas of Modernist influence were covered, each contributor to the symposium began with a particular assignment. My own was to provide a general overview of the subject, while that of Malcolm Bradbury was to set American Modernism in a transatlantic context. David Hollinger was asked to write on the relationship between Modernism and scientific thought, George Roeder on Modernism and twentieth-century American painting, and Houston Baker on Modernism and Afro-American culture. Carolyn Burke was to focus on the connections between Modernism and feminism, Daniel Bell was to explore the present status of Modernism in American society, and Jackson Lears was given the formidable task of sketching its impact on popular culture. Finally, John Carlos Rowe was to concern himself not only with Modernist influence on American literature, but with the literary and cultural movement that has come to be called "postmodernism."

The results, as the following pages will attest, read almost like a Modernist novel. One is immediately struck by the conflicting perspectives that are presented. Some writers see Modernism suffusing every realm of American life; others depict it as limited to high art. It is defined variously as an aesthetic style, an artistic credo, a body of philosophic doctrine, and a national culture. Its essence for some authors lies in a tendency toward alienation, fragmentation, and irrationalism; for others, in the pursuit of cohesion and integration.

These differences of perspective even extend to the issue of capitalization. Some authors spell Modernism with a capital "M," suggesting that they tend to view it as a major historical culture, while others prefer a lowercase "m," a usage appropriate to a far more circumscribed literary or artistic movement. Since the question of capitalization really does reflect a writer's basic approach to the subject, we decided to give each author free rein in this regard. Given the fact that so many of the great literary works written in the Modernist tradition pay little heed to stylistic consistency, this policy seems only appropriate for a symposium on Modernism.

Again, as with a good Modernist novel, the reader of this book is left to his or her own devices to discover the overlapping themes and common conclusions that exist among these different "voices." But that is exactly the way it should be, because this field of study is so new and our knowledge of it remains so tentative. Our hope, accordingly, is that the essays collected here will serve as a springboard for discussion about American Modernism, rather than as any sort of final word on the subject.

I would like to express my personal gratitude to the contributors for their willingness to join in this enterprise, and our collective thanks to both Janice Radway, the outgoing editor of *American Quarterly*, and Gary Kulik, the journal's new editor, for their invaluable support. We are also grateful to Shirley Wajda, the journal's former managing editor, for all her help.

MODERNIST CULTURE IN AMERICA

ॐ

Towards a Definition of American Modernism

Daniel Joseph Singal
Hobart and William Smith Colleges

"ON OR ABOUT DECEMBER 1910, HUMAN CHARACTER CHANGED." SO
declared Virginia Woolf in a statement that virtually all subsequent
writers on Modernism have felt obliged to quote. Though historians tracing the origins of Modernist culture have quarreled with
Woolf's exact choice of date, they have increasingly come to agree
that sometime around the turn of the century the intelligentsia in
Europe and America began to experience a profound shift in sensibility that would lead to an explosion of creativity in the arts,
transform moral values, and in time reshape the conduct of life
throughout Western society. Modernism, Peter Gay reports, "utterly
changed painting, sculpture, and music; the dance, the novel, and
the drama; architecture, poetry, and thought. And its ventures into

This essay was written during leave time provided by the John Simon Guggenheim
Foundation and by Hobart and William Smith Colleges; I am most grateful to
both. It has benefited significantly from the criticisms of David Hollinger, Michael
Ann Holly, and Janice Radway.

1

unknown territory percolated from the rarefied regions of high culture to general ways of thinking, feeling, and seeing." Indeed, notwithstanding the growing evidence that a new sensibility of "postmodernism" has recently made its appearance, many writers would contend that Modernism itself has served as the dominant culture of twentieth-century America from the period just after the First World War up to the present.[1]

Although there is assuredly no consensus on exactly what Modernist culture is, there does seem to be a growing accord on what it is not. Perhaps the commonest misconception is the practice of equating it with "modernization," a concept emanating from Max Weber and still fashionable among many social scientists. Put simply, Modernism should properly be seen as a *culture*—a constellation of related ideas, beliefs, values, and modes of perception—that came into existence during the mid to late nineteenth century, and that has had a powerful influence on art and thought on both sides of the Atlantic since roughly 1900. Modernization, by contrast, denotes a *process* of social and economic development, involving the rise of industry, technology, urbanization, and bureaucratic institutions, that can be traced back as far as the seventeenth century. The relationship between these two important historical phenomena is exceedingly complex, with Modernism arising in part as a counter-response to the triumph of modernization, especially its norms of rationality and efficiency, in nineteenth-century Europe and America. Despite that initial hostility, however, the Modernist stance toward modernization has typically been marked by ambivalence, with Modernists simultaneously admiring the vitality and inventiveness of technological progress while decrying the dehumanization it appears to bring in its wake. Thus, despite the etymological similarity, Modernism and modernization must be sharply differentiated; nor should "modern" and "Modernist" ever be treated as synonyms.[2]

Another problematic view of Modernism equates it exclusively with the philosophy and style of life of the artistic avant-garde at the turn of the twentieth century. "Modernism" in this sense usually connotes radical experimentation in artistic style, a deliberate cultivation of the perverse and decadent, and the flaunting of outrageous behavior designed to shock the bourgeoisie. The entire movement, according to this definition, was comprised essentially of a small number of highly talented poets and painters based in the bohemian quarters of certain large cities, such as Paris, New York, Vienna, and Berlin, culminating around the time of the First World War in the work of such "canonical" masters as Picasso, Pound, and Joyce. A variation on this definition, put forth by literary critics like Irving Howe and Lionel Trilling, allows Modernism slightly more range by viewing it as an "adversary culture" originating in bohemia but later adopted by twentieth-century intellectuals in their growing estrangement from mass society, and ultimately reappearing as a virtual parody of its earlier self in the form of the 1960s counterculture. In either case, this perspective sees Modernist thought as essentially negative and rebellious in character, and far too amorphous ever to be susceptible to definition.[3]

As the present essay will attempt to show, however, there is a more recent and far more satisfactory approach to Modernism that takes issue with the "bohemian" interpretation, contending that those writing in the Trilling tradition confuse the tip for the whole iceberg by focusing on the more visible and spectacular manifestations of the culture during its period of ascendancy while ignoring its underlying structure. Far from being anarchic, Modernist thought in this view represents an attempt to restore a sense of order to human experience under the often chaotic conditions of twentieth-century existence, and it most assuredly does contain a unifying principle if one knows where to look. Not just the plaything of the avant-garde, Modernism has assumed a commanding position in literature, music, painting, architecture, philosophy, and virtually every other realm of artistic or intellectual endeavor. Moreover, Modernism in this formulation has cast its influence well beyond the intellectual elite to encompass much of contemporary middle-class Western society. Its values, though somewhat diluted, are held by a majority of present-day Americans, and its style is manifested in such diverse contexts as suburban architecture, television advertising, and popular music. In short, the definition being proposed here suggests that Modernism deserves to be treated as a full-fledged historical culture much like Victorianism or the Enlightenment, and that it supplies nothing less than the basic contours of our current mode of thought.

[handwritten margin note: DOES THAT MEAN IT'S OVER?]

ह▪

To locate the inner dynamics of Modernism and to see how it came into being, it is necessary to return briefly to the culture against which the early Modernists rebelled. Victorianism, whose reign in America ran roughly from the 1830s to the early twentieth century, was closely associated with the rapidly expanding urban bourgeois class of that era. Its guiding ethos was centered upon the classic bourgeois values of thrift, diligence, and persistence, so important for success in a burgeoning capitalist economy, along with an immense optimism about the progress that industrialization seemed sure to bring. At the same time, Victorian culture, with its ideal vision of a stable, peaceful society free from sin and discord, proved immensely helpful in enabling the members of this new middle class to keep their balance in a world that was changing very fast, in ways they did not always expect or understand.[4]

At the core of this new culture stood a distinctive set of bedrock assumptions. These included a belief in a predictable universe presided over by a benevolent God and governed by immutable natural laws, a corresponding conviction that humankind was capable of arriving at a unified and fixed set of truths about all aspects of life, and an insistence on preserving absolute standards based on a radical dichotomy between that which was deemed "human" and that regarded as "animal." It was this moral dichotomy above all that constituted the deepest guiding principle of the Victorian outlook. On the "human" or "civilized" side of the dividing line fell everything that served to lift man above the beasts—education, refinement, manners, the arts, religion, and such domesticated emotions as loyalty and family love. The "animal" or "savage" realm, by contrast, contained those instincts and passions that constantly threatened self-control, and that therefore had to be repressed at all costs. Foremost among those threats was, of course, sexuality, which proper Victorians conceived of as a hidden geyser of animality existing within everyone and capable of erupting with little or no warning at the slightest stimulus. All erotic temptations were accordingly supposed to be rooted out, sexual pleasure even within marriage was to be kept to a minimum, and, as Nancy F. Cott has shown, the standard of respectable conduct, especially for women, shifted decisively "from modesty to passionlessness." A glorious future of material abundance and technological advance was possible, Victorians were convinced, but only if the animal component in human nature was effectively suppressed.[5]

Equally important was the way this moral dichotomy fostered a tendency to view the world in polar terms. "There is a value in possibilities," Masao Miyoshi observes, ". . . but the Victorians too often saw them in rigid pairs—all or nothing, white or black." Sharp distinctions were made in every aspect of existence: Victorians characterized societies as either civilized or savage, drew a firm line between what they considered superior and inferior classes, and divided races unambiguously into black and white. They likewise insisted on placing the sexes in "separate spheres," based on what Rosalind Rosenberg describes as "the Victorian faith in sexual polarity," which deemed women as "by nature emotional and passive," while men were "rational and assertive." Such dichotomies, it was believed, were permanently rooted in biology and in the general laws of nature. The "right" way, the moral way, was to keep these various categories distinct and segregated.[6]

Put in slightly different terms, what the Victorians aspired to was a radical standard of innocence. They were engaged in an attempt to wall themselves off as completely as possible from what they regarded as evil and corruption, and to create on their side of the barrier a brave new world suffused, in Matthew Arnold's words, with "harmonious perfection." Nineteenth-century thinkers, writes Donald H. Meyer, "longed for a universe that was not just intelligible, reassuring, and morally challenging, but symphonic as well." To be sure, actual behavior at times seemed to undercut this pursuit of innocence, but the point is that for the Victorian middle class innocence remained a powerful and almost universal cultural ideal. Even when behavior diverged from it, as doubtless happened quite often, the ideal continued to be venerated. Nor was the Victorian ethos regarded as especially oppressive by the great majority of its nineteenth-century middle-class adherents. Rather, in the context of their experience it was both comforting and distinctly uplifting—a set of values that offered moral certainty, spiritual balm, and the hope that civilization might at last rid itself of the barbaric baggage remaining from humankind's dark, preindustrial past.[7]

Nevertheless, by the end of the century various individuals in Europe and the United States were beginning to chafe under the burden of Victorian repression and to challenge their inherited culture in different ways. A belief developed that modern bourgeois existence had become perilously artificial and "over-civilized," and that the degree of self-control that Victorian morality required of each individual was stultifying the personality. "Many yearned to smash the glass and breathe freely," writes T. J. Jackson Lears, "to experience 'real life' in all its intensity." In most instances, though, these early rebels should be seen as post-Victorians rather than incipient Modernists, for they did not at heart desire to overthrow nineteenth-century moralism, but rather to temper or emend it in ways that would make it more bearable. Lears skillfully documents the various exotic devices they resorted to in their futile attempts to break with their conventional existence and regain contact with "reality." But, as he also shows, identifying with medieval knights or taking up Oriental religion were no more than safe substitutes for actual liberation and could not resolve the cultural crisis these people were caught up in. The overwhelming majority of post-Victorians were accordingly fated to dwell in a kind of no-man's land. "Wandering between two worlds," Lears reports, these victims of cultural transition typically "remained outsiders in both." [8]

The first true signs of Modernism appeared in Europe during the latter half of the nineteenth century in the form of a succession of small movements, each making its unique contribution to the new culture that was gradually coming into being. Most conspicuous at the outset were the French Symbolist poets, beginning with Charles Baudelaire in the 1850s, who overturned the traditional mimetic conventions of art by writing as much about what was transpiring within their own minds as about events or objects in the "real" world. "Paint not the thing, but the effect it produces," ran Stephane Mallarmé's dictum. To that end, Symbolist verse employed highly allusive language and imagery that described the subject of the poem only indirectly, but conveyed as fully as possible the poet's emotional response to that subject. The Symbolists were soon joined by the Impressionist painters, who in similar fashion devalued the ostensible subject matter and resolved to capture on canvas their own subjective reactions. Both movements, in other words, moved beyond the stable, rational, and seemingly objective world decreed by nineteenth-century positivism in order to explore the far murkier and less predictable operations of human perception and consciousness. In Symbolism, Impressionism, and other, allied movements, then, one sees emerging one of the foremost tendencies of Modernism—the desire to heighten, savor, and share all varieties of experience.[9]

At the same time, developments taking place in more organized fields of thought were providing a philosophical underpinning for this urge to seek out experience. Writers as diverse as Henri Bergson, Friedrich Nietzsche, and William James agreed in rejecting the prevailing theory that divided the mind into separate compartments or "faculties," and in depicting experience as a continuous flux of sensations and recollections—what James would term "the stream of consciousness." That raw sensory flux, they concurred, was as close as human beings could come to knowing reality. Abstract concepts, along with all the other products of rationality that the Victorians had gloried in as the highest achievements of civilization, were seen as inherently faulty and misleading precisely because they represented an attempt to stop the experiential flow and remove knowledge from its proper dynamic context. A perception imprisoned in an abstraction was as lifeless and imperfect a model of reality as a butterfly impaled in a specimen box. As James insisted: "When we conceptualize we cut and fix, and exclude anything but what we have fixed, whereas in the real concrete sensible flux of life experiences compenetrate each other." To be sure, most of these early Modernist thinkers regarded rational concepts, especially the truths of science, as useful fictions that helped to get the world's work done, so long as those concepts were not confused with permanent truths. Yet the main thrust of their writings involved the obligation to loosen formal and rational restraints, expand one's consciousness, open oneself to the world, and perfect one's ability to experience experience—exactly what the Victorians had most feared.[10]

Further momentum for this cultural sea-change came from new findings in the physical sciences. "In the twenty years between 1895 and 1915," notes Alan Bullock, "the whole picture of the physical universe, which had appeared not only the most impressive but also the most secure achievement of scientific thought, was brought into question." The certainties of Newtonian mechanics, and the Euclidian geometry on which it was based, gave way to a new physics in which everything depended on the relative position and motion of the observer and the object being observed. Non-Euclidian versions of geometry abounded, all equally verifiable, until Henri Poincaré was led to suggest in 1902 that "one geometry cannot be more true than another; it can only be more convenient." Radical theoretical shifts that served to demolish a host of familiar and distinct concepts were taking place at both the cosmic and microscopic levels: space, far from being a void, was now seen as filled by fields of energy, while the atom, far from being solid, was itself made up of tiny particles that orbited one another at a distance. The discovery of radium, demonstrating that seemingly solid matter could turn into energy, was shocking enough, but it was soon followed by Albert Einstein's proof early in the century that space and time could no longer be construed as separate and distinct entities, but must be placed on a continuum. Clearly, the new science had little use for the rigid, dichotomous categories that the Victorians had relied upon to organize their world; it was as enamored of dynamic process and relativism as the new philosophy and art.[11]

By the early twentieth century the profusion of artistic and intellectual movements was striking, especially in Paris, which was fast becoming the international center of Modernist activity. Most important during the first two decades of the century were Post-Impressionism, Cubism, Imagism, Vorticism, and the Italian variant, Futurism, to be followed after the war by Expressionism (mainly based in the Germanic countries), Dadaism, Surrealism, and Russian Constructivism—and eventually by Existentialism and Structuralism. Modernist masters came to dominate in all the arts, from Picasso, Cézanne, Braque, and Klee in painting, to Joyce, Pound, Eliot, and Malraux in literature, Stravinsky and Webern in music, along with Mies van der Rohe and Frank Lloyd Wright in architecture. Moreover, the new theories and values being fashioned by the intellectual elite were increasingly paralleled by similar developments at the level of popular attitudes and behavior, becoming unmistakable in the rampant consumerism and youth culture of the 1920s. In both cases the motor source was the same: a response to the cultural malaise brought about by late Victorian repression.

What all these various manifestations of Modernism had in common was a passion not only for opening the self to new levels of experience, but also for fusing together disparate elements of that experience into new and original "wholes," to the point where one can speak of an "integrative mode" as the basis of the new culture. Put simply, the quintessential aim of Modernists has been to reconnect all that the Victorian moral dichotomy tore asunder—to integrate once more the human and the animal, the civilized and the savage, and to heal the sharp divisions established in the nineteenth century in areas such as class, race, and gender. Only in this way, they have believed, would it be possible to combat the fundamentally dishonest conception of existence that the Victorians had propagated, liberate the natural human instincts and emotions that the nineteenth century had bottled up, and so restore vitality to modern life. In the blunt words of William Carlos Williams, "Man is an animal, and if he forgets that, denies that, he is living a big lie, and soon enough other lies get going." In short, Modernists were intent on nothing less than recovering an entire aspect of being that their predecessors had tried to banish.[12]

Again and again, from art to social policy, Modernists have attempted to bring together that which the previous culture tried to keep separate. Far from being "the mere rehabilitation of the irrational," Malcolm Bradbury and James McFarlane write, Modernism involves "the interpretation, the reconciliation, the coalescence, the fusion—of reason and unreason, intellect and emotion, subjective and objective." McFarlane identifies three stages in the development of the culture: a first stage of early rebellion (in other words, the bohemian stage that is often mistaken for the culture as a whole) during which "the emphasis is on fragmentation, on the breaking up and the progressive disintegration of those meticulously constructed 'systems' and 'types' and 'absolutes'" that the Victorians had assiduously created; a second stage marked by "a restructuring of parts, a re-relating of the fragmented concepts"; and a final, mature stage characterized by "a dissolving, a blending, a merging of things previously held to be forever mutually exclusive." Thus, he concludes, "the defining thing in the Modernist mode is not so much that things fall *apart* but that they fall *together*"; the true end result of Modernism "is not disintegration but (as it were) superintegration."[13]

The most graphic manifestation of this integrative mode was certainly Cubism, a movement that deliberately sought to revitalize the experience of perception by challenging artistic conventions that had stood since the Renaissance. Since there was no such thing as fixed reality or truth, Picasso and his colleagues maintained, all objects would have to be seen in shifting relation to one another. The painter's task was thus to break up forms into component parts and have those parts continuously overlap, conveying not so much a sense of fragmentation as of wholeness. Sharp outlines were always to be avoided; rather, colors and textures were to bleed from one object into another, with subdued colors usually employed to enhance the sense of unity. Whenever possible, both the interior and exterior of a form were to be rendered alongside each other; likewise, the background was to have the same value and prominence as the main subject of the painting, and the two were to interpenetrate. Finally, in Cubist collage "found" objects from the "real" world, such as scraps of metal or pieces of newspaper, were to be incorporated into the work to juxtapose the spheres of aesthetic creation and everyday life, emphasizing how the painting was simultaneously both a collection of pleasing shapes and colors on a flat surface *and* a statement about perceived reality. In this manner, as Eugene Lunn tells us, the Cubists mounted their "revolutionary assault on the seeming stability of objects, which are taken apart, brought into collision, and reassembled on the picture surface" into a series of "contingent syntheses by which human activity and perception remake the world."[14]

This ever-present drive for integration explains so much about the history of Modernism. It allows one to make sense, for example, of the predilection of twentieth-century thinkers and writers for such devices as paradox (which joins seeming opposites) and ambivalence (which fuses contradictory emotions, such as love and hate), and for their tendency to place concepts and empirical observations along a continuum or spectrum rather than in tightly demarcated categories. It also helps account for the practice of cinematic montage, with its juxtaposition of events and experiences; the attempt to break down boundaries between stage and audience in twentieth-century theater; the use of multiple overlapping harmonies and rhythms in contemporary music, especially jazz (which also blends the primitivism of its African origins with modern sophistication); and the concern for maximizing the simultaneity of experience in literature—perhaps most fully achieved in Joyce's *Ulysses*, a novel structured, as Stephen Kern points out, so that "traditional dividers of sequence and distance collapse into a unified whole which the reader must envision after several readings." In the realm of social action, it was this emphasis on breaking down barriers that created the necessary cultural preconditions for the twentieth century's concerted campaigns to eliminate a "separate sphere" for women, and to overthrow that most noxious by-product of Victorian dichotomizing, racial segregation.[15]

Underlying all these efforts at integration has been the Modernist reconstruction of human nature. If the Victorians sought to
place a firm barrier between the "higher" mental functions, such
as rational thought and spirituality, and those "lower" instincts and
passions that Freud would in time ascribe to the "id," Modernists
strove to unite these two levels of the psyche. Thus, where the Victorians held "sincerity," with its injunction that a person's conscious
self remain honest and consistent, to be their most prized character
trait, Modernists have demanded nothing less than "authenticity,"
which requires a blending of the conscious and unconscious strata
of the mind so that the self presented to the world is the "true" self
in every respect. This, as Trilling observes, represents a far "more
strenuous" standard than did the code of sincerity, and necessitates
precisely the sort of intense self-knowledge that the Victorians
sought to avoid. Hence the resort to stream-of-consciousness technique in Modernist novels in order to capture what D. H. Lawrence
called the "real, vital, potential self" as opposed to "the old stable
ego" of nineteenth-century character.[16]

Yet it is just at this point that a massive paradox arises within the
culture, for with the universe characterized by incessant flux, and
human beings unable to know its workings with anything approaching certainty, the goal of perfect integration must always remain unattainable, at least within the natural world. Thus, although
the Modernist seeks integration and authenticity, he or she must
also be aware that they will never fully arrive. Nor would complete
integration really be desirable, for that would mean stasis. The coa-
lescing of the varied fragments of our contemporary existence can
never be consummated, but must constantly be sought. The sole
exceptions to this rule are found in self-contained intellectual systems such as mathematics, language, and logic, as the logical positivists affirmed, or in imaginary settings conjured up for the purposes of art (though Modernist practice typically demands that
artifice of this sort be clearly identified as such). Otherwise, all that
pertains to nature and life must be construed dynamically, as continuous process; the only lasting closure, in Modernist terms, comes
with death.

Herein lies the reason why personal identity has often become
problematic and tension-ridden for those living in the twentieth
century. The Victorian expectation that a person be consistent and

sincere rested on the assumption that character was defined largely by social role, which in turn was normally fixed by heredity, upbringing, and vocation. Accordingly, once an individual matured, any shift in his or her character was viewed with suspicion. By contrast, the Modernists, as Ronald Bush puts it, view human nature "in a state of continuous becoming." Neither the self, nor any work of art designed to portray the self, Bush explains, can achieve "completeness or closure"; such closure would automatically violate the criterion of authenticity. As a result, one must constantly create and re-create an identity based upon one's ongoing experience in the world. Difficult though this effort may be at times, nothing less will meet the Modernist standard.[17]

Finally, this paradoxical quest for and avoidance of integration accounts for the special role of the arts within Modernist culture. Precisely because they represent a realm where that quest can be pursued with relative safety through surrogate experience, the arts have become a medium for radical experimentation in new ways of amplifying perception, organizing the psyche, and extending culture. As Susan Sontag points out, art in this century "has come to be invested with an unprecedented stature" because of its mission of "making forays into and taking up positions on the frontiers of consciousness (often very dangerous to the artist as a person) and reporting back what's there." Art is aided in this task by its ready access to the devices of symbolism, metaphor, and myth, all of which, in Jerome Bruner's words, serve to connect "things that were previously separate in experience" and that cannot be joined through logic. Art in this way "bridges rationality and impulse" by fusing metaphorically the objective and the subjective, the empirical and the introspective—breaking apart conventional beliefs and re-joining the resulting fragments in a manner that creates relationships and meanings not previously suspected. In short, where the Victorians saw art as didactic in purpose—as a vehicle for communicating and illustrating preordained moral truths—to Modernists it has become the principal means of creating whatever provisional order human beings can attain.[18]

Thus the Modernist world-view has taken shape. It begins with the premise of an unpredictable universe where nothing is ever stable, and where, accordingly, human beings must be satisfied with knowledge that is partial and transient at best. Nor is it possible in this situation to devise a fixed and absolute system of morality; moral values must remain in flux, adapting continuously to changing historical circumstances. To create those values and garner whatever knowledge is available, individuals must repeatedly subject themselves—both directly, and vicariously through art—to the trials of experience. Above all, they must not attempt to shield themselves behind illusions or gentility, as so many did during the nineteenth century. To be sure, with passing time the Modernist world-view has, especially at the hands of the mass media, undergone the same tendencies toward corruption and routinization that have beset other major historical cultures. But in its ideal form at least, Modernism—in stark contrast to Victorianism—eschews innocence and demands instead to know "reality" in all its depth and complexity, no matter how incomplete and paradoxical that knowledge might be, and no matter how painful. It offers a demanding, and at times even heroic, vision of life that most of its adherents may in fact have fallen short of, but by which they have been guided nonetheless.

≈a

Although it has become common practice to identify the New York Armory Show of 1913, with its exhibition of Cubist and Postimpressionist painting, as the first shot fired in the battle to establish Modernism on this side of the Atlantic, significant skirmishes had in fact taken place over the previous several decades. By the time the show opened, Gertrude Stein and Ezra Pound, the two principal intermediaries between the United States and European Modernism, were already firmly entrenched at their posts overseas, Greenwich Village was filling up with cultural and artistic rebels, and proponents of the major intellectual breakthroughs in fields such as physics, biology, philosophy, psychology, and the social sciences had long since established beachheads at American universities. Both the Armory Show and the opening of Alfred Stieglitz's famous gallery were important vehicles for communication with headquarters overseas, but in America the war had long since been started, and by the period just before the First World War its effects could be seen everywhere, from muckraking journalism to the

irreverent history of Charles A. Beard to the calls for personal and
political liberation in *The Masses*. There were of course some differences from Europe in John Higham's neat formulation, "Americans
rebelled by extending the breadth of experience, Europeans by
plumbing its depths"—but the essential values and dynamics of the
culture were the same. "What was happening," Richard Hofstadter
sums up, ". . . was that a modern critical intelligentsia was emerging
in the United States. Modernism, in thought as in art, was dawning
upon the American mind." [19]

Surely the two key figures in the process of importing the new
culture to this country and giving it American roots were William
James and John Dewey. James, as conversant with the latest European thought as any American of his day, was won over early in his
career to the Darwinian premise that human beings existed on a
continuum with other animals, and that the human brain was no
more or less than a biological organ designed to select from the
environment those perceptions useful for survival. For James that
meant that the Victorian practice of radically separating the
"higher" rational faculties from the "lower" instinctual ones made
no sense. Rather, the mind must be conceived of as functionally
integrated: "Pretend what we may, the whole man within us is at
work when we form our philosophical opinions. Intellect, will, taste,
and passion co-operate just as they do in practical affairs. . . ." Once
the mind, guided by its passions, had chosen which perceptions to
bring to consciousness, it might proceed to formulate abstract concepts based on them, but in doing so, James insisted, it necessarily
introduced further distortions. The initial raw sensory experience,
he believed, was the closest we could come to knowing reality; each
application of the intellect, however valuable it might be for practical purposes, took us further from the "truth." [20]

For this reason, James concluded, human beings were doomed
forever to epistemological uncertainty. To the great majority of his
contemporaries this was a horrible revelation, but to James it was
infinitely exciting, precisely because it banished the closed, deterministic universe of nineteenth-century positivism in favor of an
"open" universe governed by change and chance where the process
of discovery would be continuous. Embracing pluralism as a positive
good, and grounding his own system of thought on the experiential

basis of "radical empiricism," James became the first important American Modernist intellectual.[21]

Dewey, although heavily influenced by James, was a more systematic thinker inclined to give greater recognition to the virtues of rationality and science. More explicitly, the central purpose of all of Dewey's thought was eradicating the dichotomy between intellect and experience, thought and action, that he and James had inherited. Sensory perceptions, he contended, must be filtered through intelligence to become meaningful, while at the same time scientific theorizing must always be controlled by testing in the real world. One might even say that Dewey, in keeping with the "integrative mode" of Modernist culture, devoted his career to combating dualisms of all kinds—including those dividing mind from body, science from art, the city from the countryside, and the elite from the common people—all the while, of course, resisting final closure. Everywhere one looks in his writings one finds this sensibility at work, as in his discussion of how the basic task of both art and science is to blend elements of perception into integrated "relationships" in such a way that the process can "recur" indefinitely:

> A well-conducted scientific inquiry discovers as it tests, and proves as it explores; it does so in virtue of a method which combines both functions. And conversation, drama, [the] novel, and architectural construction, if there is an ordered experience, reach a stage that at once records and sums up the value of what precedes, and evokes and prophesies what is to come. Every closure is an awakening, and every awakening settles something.

One can likewise see the Modernist ethos at work in Dewey's plan for "progressive education," with its effort to connect the classroom with "real life" experience, its pluralistic stress on breaking down social barriers by encouraging interaction among students from diverse class and ethnic backgrounds, and its imperative that teachers not deliver fixed truths, but rather impress upon children at the earliest age the tentative, pragmatic character of knowledge.[22]

Indeed, one might rightfully speak of two predominant "streams" of American Modernist culture, issuing from James and Dewey, respectively. The Jamesian stream centers its interest on the individual consciousness, celebrates spontaneity, authenticity, and the probing of new realms of personal experience, and flows mainly through the arts and humanities. The Deweyan stream, by contrast, tends to focus on society as a whole, emphasizes the elimination of social barriers (geographic, economic, ethnic, racial, and gender), and tries to weld together reason and emotion in the service of programmatic social aims. With each passing decade of the twentieth century these two streams have increasingly diverged, ultimately creating an important internal tension within American Modernism, but that fact should not obscure their many close resemblances, particularly at the beginning. James, after all, considered himself a professional scientist, while Dewey's educational program was always centered on the individual and designed to tap the child's natural spontaneity. Both streams, moreover, have reflected the frequent preoccupation of American Modernists with pragmatic empiricism and democratic pluralism, as opposed to the tendency of Modernists in war-ravaged Europe to focus on apocalyptic experience and a concomitant cult of the irrational.

By the latter part of the Progressive Era, as Henry May has shown, the cultural revolution that James and Dewey had helped to initiate in America was spreading everywhere. Muckraking journalists were setting aside Victorian codes of gentility and exposing corruption at the highest levels of American life, naming specific names when necessary. Scholars like Charles Beard and Thorstein Veblen were taking a new critical look at their society and its history, determined to shed their nineteenth-century innocence and ferret out "reality" no matter how sordid it might be. Social workers like Jane Addams were praising the earthy vitality of immigrant cultures and insisting that such Old World heritages be blended with rather than overwhelmed by the dominant national culture. In New York, the Young Intellectuals, including Max Eastman, John Reed, Floyd Dell, Margaret Sanger, Eugene O'Neill, Randolph Bourne, and Walter Lippmann, were meeting at Mabel Dodge Luhan's salon, discussing the latest European Modernist authors and calling noisily for sexual, artistic, and political liberation in their own country. At the same time, Frank Lloyd Wright was busy reshaping American architecture along Modernist lines, stripping away "false" ornamentation and facades, employing "authentic" materials such as untreated wood, glass, and stone, and using an abundance of windows and doors to erase the demarcation between interior and exterior. "Wright's first objective," one historian notes, "was to reduce the number of . . . separate parts and make a unified space so that light, air, and vistas permeated the whole." His designs, though attenuated in quality as they were popularized, supplied the basic patterns for the mass suburban housing boom following the Second World War, ensuring that a majority of middle-class Americans in the second half of the century would live in Modernist-styled homes.[23]

Yet perhaps the most influential stirrings of the new culture in America could be found in the work of the anthropologist Franz Boas and the extraordinary group of disciples he trained at Columbia University. In *The Mind of Primitive Man*, published in 1911, Boas took direct aim at the bedrock Victorian dichotomy between civilization and savagery, contending that so-called savage peoples were fully capable of logic, abstraction, aesthetic discrimination, and the inhibition of biological impulses, while Europeans practiced any number of customs, taboos, and rituals that could only be construed as irrational. For Boas such attributes as "human" or "animalistic" were all a matter of cultural perspective, and there was no scientific reason for granting the European perspective superiority over another—the only permissible criterion for normative judgment was the Darwinian one of how successfully a culture allowed a particular society to adapt to its environment. These insights, spreading first within the ranks of social scientists and then through the general population, would in time transform American attitudes concerning race by undermining the reigning stereotype of black people, whom the old moral dichotomy had consigned to "savagery." Indeed, by knocking away the cultural and scientific props of racism and replacing them with a new cultural modality that favored pluralistic integration, this attitudinal change in turn provided the essential foundation upon which the various movements to secure black rights were able to build. As Marshall Hyatt concludes, "Boas's critical contribution . . . lay in providing a new way of thinking, without which America could not have traveled the long road from *Plessy v. Ferguson* to *Brown v. Board of Education*." [24]

Finally, one should take note of how the Modernist sensibility invaded popular culture during the Progressive Era. That process is clearly visible in Lewis Erenberg's study of New York City nightlife, which charts the way members of the more prosperous classes overcame post-Victorian malaise by gradually throwing aside the restraints of gentility and seeking out more sensuous forms of entertainment. In the nineteenth century, he observes, each "sex, class, and race . . . was expected to occupy its exclusive sphere. Public life was increasingly divided, and the private realm of the home diverged from the values of public life." But the cabaret, the focal institution of the new nightlife, was notable precisely because it "relaxed boundaries between the sexes, between audiences and performers, between ethnic groups and Protestants, between black culture and whites." For example, traditional "barriers between the entertainer and his audience" fell with the elimination of the raised stage, curtains, and footlights; performers even went out into the audience during their acts. Moreover, the majority of the leading entertainers and songwriters came from immigrant backgrounds that fell outside the orbit of Victorian respectability and hence were valued in large measure for their ability to put well-to-do patrons in touch with the vitality and experiences of lower-class life—an attribute that became even more prized during the 1920s when cabaret-goers went "slumming" in Harlem in search of black performers thought to be especially "natural, uncivilized, [and] uninhibited." To be sure, patrons demanded an atmosphere of sumptuous elegance to provide a sense of order and to guarantee that they would not be declassed themselves. But the basic thrust of this newly created and rapidly expanding popular culture remained the effort to erase the Victorian dividing line between human and animal and thus "to liberate some of the repressed wilder elements, the more natural elements, that had been contained by gentility." [25]

The most unmistakable evidence of this transformation in public sensibility was surely the dancing craze that swept the nation between 1912 and 1916, foreshadowing the youth rebellion of the 1920s. Victorian-era dances such as the waltz, Erenberg observes, had emphasized "control, regularity and patterned movement," along with "a look but do not touch approach to one's partner." The scores of dances introduced after 1912, most of which had originated in black culture, featured "heightened bodily expression" and far more "intimacy" between partners. The very names of the dances—bunny hug, monkey glide, grizzly bear, and lame duck—suggested a delectable surrender to animality and "rebellion against the older sexual mores." Most notorious was the shimmy, "a black torso-shaking dance" that became the rage just after the war. It was accompanied by a new form of music called jazz, also of black origins, which featured still wilder rhythms, frequent improvisation, and recurrent attempts by early bands to make their instruments "duplicate animal sounds." Moral reformers, ministers, and members of the older generation were predictably aghast at this outbreak of impulse. "Jazz and modern dancing" in their eyes, writes Paula Fass, seemed to herald "the collapse of civilized life." It is clear in retrospect that, viewed from a Victorian perspective, such forebodings were not without justification, for the behavior of middle-class youth during the 1920s demonstrated just how widely Modernist values had spread within the nation and how quickly they were approaching dominance.[26]

To trace the course of Modernist culture in America in full detail would require far more space than is available here. Such a narrative would necessarily include 1920s novelists like Fitzgerald, Hemingway, Dos Passos, and Faulkner, who chronicled the disintegration of modern society and culture, but whose primary concern, Bradbury rightly observes, was somehow "to make the world recohere." It would also encompass the documentary-style writers of the 1930s who sought to immerse themselves in the consciousness of socially marginal groups like southern sharecroppers—most notably James Agee and Walker Evans, in their *Let Us Now Praise Famous Men*, with its impassioned effort to pare away the separation between the authors' consciousness and that of their impoverished, illiterate subjects (along with Agee's pained realization of the impossibility of breaking down those barriers). Other illustrations of the mature American Modernist sensibility would run the gamut of cultural and intellectual activity from the interwar period onward including the "humanist existentialism" of postwar literature, the neo-orthodox theology of Reinhold Niebuhr and Paul Tillich, the pluralism of social science–oriented writers such as Richard Hofstadter and Daniel Bell, the pragmatic social reform initiatives of the New Deal and the Great Society, the "International Style" in urban architecture, and the rise of modern advertising, where, as

Bruce Robbins puts it, the "techniques of the modernist classics have been incorporated into modernist commercials." Finally, a complete account of the new culture's fortunes in America could not leave out the various countervailing movements that arose to challenge Modernist values, either seeking, like the Fundamentalists, Ku Klux Klan and "New Right," to restore nineteenth-century certainties; to proffer some new form of absolutism in the manner of scientism, orthodox Marxism, and the behaviorism of B. F. Skinner; or to provide refuge from the tensions accompanying Modernism through an emphasis on bureaucratic process, as have some varieties of corporate culture.[27]

It would appear that the culminating moment for American Modernism—and perhaps also the beginning of its end—came in the 1960s. The celebration of the animal component of human nature, the quest for spontaneity and authenticity, the desire to raze all dualisms and distinctions, the breaking down of social and cultural barriers, the quest for "wholeness," and the effort to expand consciousness and discover new modes of experience—all were given heightened realization. A new generation of rebels, ironically spoken of as a "counterculture" when they were in fact riding the crest of a cultural tidal wave, carried the Modernist embrace of natural instinct and primitivism to its seemingly inevitable conclusion by letting hair grow wild, experimenting with mind-altering drugs, overthrowing the last vestiges of conventional sexual mores, and creating in acid rock a music of pounding sensuality. The same forces could be found at work among the intellectual elite, where writers like Susan Sontag condemned a supposed "hypertrophy of the intellect at the expense of energy and sensual capability" in contemporary life and demanded that critics forgo all attempts at describing or interpreting art. Contending that "our world" is "impoverished enough," she insisted that we abandon "all duplicates of it, until we again experience more immediately what we have." Numerous performing groups took this philosophy to heart, endeavoring to achieve authenticity by bridging life and art—most notably the Living Theater whose *Paradise Now* invited members of the audience to disrobe on stage and join the troupe in sexual high jinks. In retrospect, what seems most striking about such excesses is the way matters once vested with deep emotion and commitment by those engaged in the initial battle against Victorianism were now often reduced to a pointless game. One senses that the pendulum

PROBLEM WITH MODERNISM WAS ELITISM: WHO CAN READ FINNEGANS WAKE? MADE FOR TWO CLASSES IN CULTURE.

was starting to swing back, that Modernism, much like the late Victorian culture of the 1890s, was at last becoming overripe and starting to caricature itself. If so, then the 1960s, instead of marking the dawn of an Aquarian age, might be more accurately viewed as the death-rattle of a fast-aging culture.[28]   POSTMODERN FUNDAMENTALS—

Since that decade, and partly in reaction to it, there has been increasing discussion of the possible arrival of "postmodernism." As one might expect, those attempting to describe this new sensibility have often disagreed with one another, but they do seem to concur that its presence first became noticeable during the 1960s. It has manifested itself, according to most accounts, in the form of Pop and minimalist art, in an architecture that intentionally draws on cliches from popular culture ("learning from Las Vegas," as Robert Venturi puts it), and in the literary productions of Tom Wolfe, Donald Barthelme, and Joseph Heller, among others. What these various tendencies appear to have in common is what Richard Wolin calls "the valorization of mass culture" by the intellectual elite, "a pseudo-populist ethos which suggests that the gap between (high) art and life has been definitely bridged." To put this in slightly different terms, one might say that the democratic urge within Modernism to break down all division between the elite and the popular has at last overcome the long-standing practice of Modernist thinkers to dismiss mass culture on the grounds of inauthenticity. The result, Wolin argues, is a sensibility that is impatient with "complexity" and "wants instead works of literature . . . as absolute as the sun, as unarguable as orgasm, as delicious as a lollipop." [29]

Fredric Jameson likewise speaks of an "aesthetic populism" as the essence of postmodernism, and complains of a new superficiality, a "waning of content," in which "depth is replaced by surface, or multiple surfaces." "The postmoderns," he claims, "have in fact been fascinated precisely by this whole 'degraded' landscape of schlock and kitsch, of TV series and Readers' Digest culture, of advertising and motels . . . materials they no longer simply 'quote,' as a Joyce or Mahler might have done, but incorporate into their very substance." As he sees it, this new "cultural dominant" has resolved the Modernist crisis of personal identity by the simple expedient of eliminating the self as a subject of art or intellectual speculation. With no ego, there is conveniently no emotion, no troublesome conflict—just problems of "style," to the point where art becomes little more than a matter of "codes" and "pastiche," a "virtual grab-bag" of "random raw materials and impulses" reflecting the peculiar commodity fetishism of "late capitalism." What postmodernism seems to lack, in short, is the creative tension—the refusal to achieve closure—that had characterized Modernist art and thought at their best and provided their special resonance.[30]

If Jameson and Wolin are correct in their descriptions of postmodernism, what its advent may signal is a growing inability to tolerate the formidable demands made by Modernist culture, especially its abiding lack of resolution and certainty—just as post-Victorianism in the 1890s represented an effort to escape nine-teenth-century moral constraints. Where Americans once sought an antidote to excessive repression, they may now be searching out a remedy for excessive liberation. The real force underlying our present cultural activity may thus be the desire to find a stable point of reference, some firm rock upon which to rest our perceptions and values—though preferably without giving up the lessons about the relative nature of truth that Modernism itself provided. Thus, we even find Jameson himself at the end of his critique calling al-most plaintively for a new kind of cultural sextant and compass to fashion what he calls an "aesthetic of cognitive mapping." [31]

Some, including Jameson, seem to believe that the surest path to such regenerative intellectual cartography can be found in French poststructuralist theory, including the work of Derrida, Lacan, Foucault, and Althusser. One suspects, however, that, useful as some of its specific insights and techniques may be, poststructuralism in the long run will be viewed more as part of the post-modernist malady than as a cure. The prime characteristic of its grand systems, as Frederick Crews recently pointed out, has been "a growing apriorism—a willingness to settle issues by theoretical decree, without even a pretense of evidential appeal." In eschewing empiricism this way, he continues, the poststructuralists and their disciples have been proceeding from "an unarticulated feeling that one at least deserves the haven of an all-explanatory theory, a way of making the crazy world cohere." But in the midst of the cultural dilemma posed by late Modernism it does not seem likely that the world will agree to cohere that easily; the expedient of intellectual game-playing, for all its temptations, will not solve the problem.[32]

Moreover, it seems clear that the postmodernist initiative to date has taken place within an essentially Modernist framework. The democratic urge to close the gap between the intellectuals and the "people," the stipulation (in Pop Art and architecture, for example) that all artifacts be clearly identified as artificial and inauthentic while at the same time being seen paradoxically as authentic artifacts, the poststructuralist resort to semiotic analysis—these and other postmodernist traits surely represent extrapolations from the basic Modernist ethos. "Postmodernist anti-art was inherent in the logic of the modernist aesthetic," Gerald Graff observes astutely in support of his contention that a major cultural "breakthrough" has yet to occur in our time. Robert Martin Adams similarly finds that "where modernism has simply pushed ahead, it has exaggerated tendencies which were in it from the very beginning, by making symptomatic jokes out of them." In short, as was the case earlier with post-Victorianism, it would appear that those attempting to free themselves from inherited beliefs and values have thus far been unable to do so. Long-standing internal contradictions have surfaced, the old culture is wobbling, but its successor is still not here.[33]

Where then are we headed? If there is a lesson to be gleaned from the study of history, it is the necessity of expecting the unexpected. Few people at the turn of the twentieth century were able to discern the shape of the cultural era they were entering, and those few saw that shape only in its vaguest outline. There is no reason to think that prognostication will fare better this time. In the meanwhile, now that we are gaining a modicum of critical distance from it, perhaps the wisest course of action would be to occupy ourselves with improving our understanding of Modernism, as well as the more general process of cultural change in America, in order to gain as much perspective as possible on our recent historical experience. That seems the best answer available, though doubtless some will object that, with its relativism and contingency, it is indelibly a Modernist one.

Notes

1. Virginia Woolf, *Mr. Bennett and Mrs. Brown* (London, 1924), 4; Malcolm Bradbury and James McFarlane, "The Name and Nature of Modernism," in Bradbury and McFarlane, eds., *Modernism, 1890–1930* (New York, 1976), 20, 28, 34–35; Peter Gay, *Freud, Jews, and Other Germans: Masters and Victims in Modernist Culture* (New York, 1978), 21–22; Bruce Robbins, "Modernism in History, Modernism in Power," in Robert Kiely, ed., *Modernism Reconsidered* (Cambridge, Mass., 1983), 231–32, 234–39; Daniel Joseph Singal, *The War*

Within: From Victorian to Modernist Thought in the South 1919–1945 (Chapel Hill, 1982), 3–4.

2. On modernization theory, see especially Cyril E. Black, *The Dynamics of Modernization: A Study in Comparative History* (New York, 1966), 7, 9–26, 46–49, and Alex Inkeles and David H. Smith, *Becoming Modern: Individual Change in Six Developing Countries* (Cambridge, Mass., 1974), 15–25; for its applicability within the context of American history, see Richard D. Brown, *Modernization: The Transformation of American Life, 1600–1865* (New York, 1976), especially 3–22. The dialectical linkage between Modernism and modernization is explored in Peter Berger et al., *The Homeless Mind: Modernization and Consciousness* (New York, 1973), though the authors use the term "demodernizing consciousness" in place of "Modernism." See also Eugene Lunn, *Marxism and Modernism: An Historical Study of Lukacs, Brecht, Benjamin and Adorno* (Berkeley, 1982), 40–42. For one among many examples of works that badly confuse Modernism and modernization, see Richard Wolin, "Modernism vs. Postmodernism," *Telos* 62 (Winter 1984–85): 9–11.

3. Gay, *Freud, Jews, and Other Germans*, 22–26; Lionel Trilling, *Beyond Culture: Essays on Literature and Learning* (New York, 1968), xiii, 3, 30; Irving Howe, *The Decline of the New* (New York, 1968), 3–5, 9–10, 21–25; Mark Krupnick, *Lionel Trilling and the Fate of Cultural Criticism* (Evanston, 1986), 135–36, 143–45; Daniel Bell, *The Cultural Contradictions of Capitalism* (New York, 1976), 46–48.

4. Daniel Walker Howe, "American Victorianism as a Culture," *American Quarterly* 27 (December 1975): 508, 511–14, 521.

5. Walter E. Houghton, *The Victorian Frame of Mind 1830–1870* (New Haven, 1957), 14, 144–45, 420; John S. Haller and Robin M. Haller, *The Physician and Sexuality in Victorian America* (New York, 1977), 126–28, 109; Nancy F. Cott, "Passionlessness: An Interpretation of Victorian Sexual Ideology 1790–1850," in Nancy F. Cott and Elizabeth H. Pleck, eds., *A Heritage of Her Own: Toward a New Social History of American Women* (New York, 1979), 166–68.

6. Houghton, *Victorian Frame of Mind*, 162, 171, 144–45; Masao Miyoshi, *The Divided Self: A Perspective on the Literature of the Victorians* (New York, 1969), xv; Rosalind Rosenberg, *Beyond Separate Spheres: Intellectual Roots of Modern Feminism* (New York, 1982), xiv.

7. Houghton, *Victorian Frame of Mind*, 266, 297–300, 356; Matthew Arnold, *Culture and Anarchy*, ed. J. Dover Wilson (Cambridge, Eng., 1971), 11; Donald H. Meyer, "American Intellectuals and the Crisis of Faith," *American Quarterly* 27 (December 1975): 601; W. L. Burn, *The Age of Equipoise: A Study of the Mid-Victorian Generation* (New York, 1964), 41, 106.

8. T. J. Jackson Lears, *No Place of Grace: Antimodernism and the Transformation of American Culture, 1880–1920* (New York, 1981), 5–6, 13, 37, 48, 53, 57, 105–6, 166, 174; John Higham, "The Reorientation of American Culture in the 1890's," in Higham, *Writing American History: Essays on Modern Scholarship* (Bloomington, Ind., 1970), 78–79, 99.

9. Bradbury and McFarlane, "Name and Nature of Modernism," 31; Lunn, *Marxism and Modernism*, 42–43, 45; Stephane Mallarmé, quoted in Stephen

Kern, *The Culture of Time and Space, 1880–1918* (Cambridge, Mass., 1983), 172; Clive Scott, "Symbolism, Decadence and Impressionism," in Bradbury and McFarlane, *Modernism*, 219; Gay, *Freud, Jews, and Other Germans*, 275. For a detailed account of the transition to Modernism in an American setting, see Singal, *The War Within*.

10. Kern, *Culture of Time and Space*, 204; James, quoted in ibid., 204; Sanford Schwartz, *The Matrix of Modernism: Pound, Eliot, and Early Twentieth Century Thought* (Princeton, 1985), 5–6, 12, 17–19.

11. Alan Bullock, "The Double Image," in Bradbury and McFarlane, *Modernism*, 66–67; Robert W. Wald, *Space, Time, and Gravity: The Theory of the Big Bang and Black Holes* (Chicago, 1977), 10–11; Schwartz, *Matrix of Modernism*, 15–17; Henri Poincaré, quoted in ibid., 16; Kern, *Culture of Time and Space*, 18–19, 132–36, 183–85, 153, 206; Albert Einstein, *Relativity: The Special and General Theory* (New York, 1961), 56–57, 94–96, 141–44; George Gamow, "The Declassification of Physics," in John Weiss, ed., *The Origins of Modern Consciousness* (Detroit, 1965), 167, 176–77, 188.

12. Singal, *The War Within*, 7–8; Peter Faulkner, *Modernism* (London, 1977), 19; Richard Hofstadter, *The Progressive Historians: Turner, Beard, Parrington* (New York, 1968), 185; William Carlos Williams, quoted in Robert Coles, "Instances of Modernist Anti-Intellectualism," in Kiely, *Modernism Reconsidered*, 217.

13. Bradbury and McFarlane, "Name and Nature of Modernism," 46, 48–49; James McFarlane, "The Mind of Modernism," in Bradbury and McFarlane, *Modernism*, 80–81, 83–84, 92.

14. Panthea Reid Broughton, "The Cubist Novel: Toward Defining a Genre," in Ann J. Abadie and Doreen Fowler, eds., *A Cosmos of My Own: Faulkner and Yoknapatawpha, 1980* (Jackson, Miss., 1981), 48–52; Eric Cahm, "Revolt, Conservatism and Reaction in Paris, 1905–25," in Bradbury and McFarlane, *Modernism*, 169; Kern, *Culture of Time and Space*, 143–45, 195, 7, 161–62; Lunn, *Marxism and Modernism*, 48–51.

15. McFarlane, "Mind of Modernism," 84–85; Kern, *Culture of Time and Space*, 219–20, 199–201, 75–79; Lunn, *Marxism and Modernism*, 35.

16. Singal, *The War Within*, 7–8; Lionel Trilling, *Sincerity and Authenticity* (Cambridge, Mass., 1972), 6, 11, 143–47; Gay, *Freud, Jews, and Other Germans*, 72; Karen Halttunen, *Confidence Men and Painted Women: A Study of Middle Class Culture in America, 1830–1870* (New Haven, 1982), xvi–xvii, 51–54; D. H. Lawrence, quoted in Ronald Bush, "Modern/Postmodern: Eliot, Perse, Mallarmé, and the Future of the Barbarians," in Kiely, *Modernism Reconsidered*, 197.

17. Jerome H. Buckley, "Towards Early-Modern Autobiography: The Role of Oscar Wilde, George Moore, Edmund Gosse, and Henry Adams," in Kiely, *Modernism Reconsidered*, 1–3; Bush, "Modern/Postmodern," 214, 196–201; McFarlane, "Mind of Modernism," 81; Singal, *The War Within*, 370; Trilling, *Sincerity and Authenticity*, 11; Erik H. Erikson, "The Problem of Ego Identity," in Erikson, *Identity and the Life Cycle* (New York, 1959), 118.

26　　　　　　　*Modernist Culture in America*

18. Bradbury and McFarlane, "Name and Nature of Modernism," 50; McFarlane, "Mind of Modernism," 82–89; Susan Sontag, "The Pornographic Imagination," in *The Susan Sontag Reader* (New York, 1982), 212; Jerome S. Bruner, *On Knowing: Essays for the Left Hand* (Cambridge, Mass., 1962), 62–63. McFarlane, in his otherwise excellent essay, makes the error of describing the "logic" of the dream as the guiding sensibility of Modernism. He notes, for example, how "a great many of the artists and writers of the first two decades of the twentieth century" found in the dream a "paradigm of the whole *Weltbild* in which reality and unreality, logic and fantasy, the banal and the sublime form an indissoluble and inexplicable unity." But surely this is an early and more extreme version of Modernism, and not necessarily a characteristic of the more mature culture. The latter involved not simply an attempt to assimilate the fiery processes of the unconscious, but also an effort to integrate them with those of rational thought. That is why metaphor provides a more accurate representation of the "logic" of Modernism than does dreamwork. See McFarlane, "Mind of Modernism," 86.

19. Higham, "Reorientation of American Culture," 101; Hofstadter, *Progressive Historians*, 184–85.

20. William James, "The Sentiment of Rationality," in James, *The Will to Believe and Other Essays* (New York, 1956), 92, 65–70; Elizabeth Flower and Murray G. Murphey, *A History of Philosophy in America*, 2 vols. (New York, 1977), 2: 643–44, 649–50, 669.

21. William James, *A Pluralistic Universe* (New York, 1909), 318–19; Flower and Murphey, *History of Philosophy*, 2: 683 .

22. John Dewey, *Art as Experience* (1934; New York, 1958), 169; idem, *The School and Society* (1900; Chicago, 1943), 11–14, 26–27. Dewey, with his Modernist animus against dichotomies of any sort, could even wax eloquent about integrating the various levels of education: "We want to bring all things educational together; to break down the barriers that divide the education of the little child from the instruction of the maturing youth; to identify the lower and the higher education, so that it shall be demonstrated to the eye that there is no lower and higher, but simply education." Ibid., 92.

23. Henry F. May, *The End of American Innocence: A Study of the First Years of Our Own Time* (New York, 1959), 220, 280–84; Hofstadter, *Progressive Historians*, 184; John Higham, *Strangers in the Land Patterns of American Nativism, 1860–1925* (New York, 1963), 251, 121; Kern, *Culture of Time and Space*, 186–87, 179; Frank Lloyd Wright, *The Natural House* (New York, 1954), 14–20, 38–40, 51–54, 62–65. The best treatment of the Greenwich Village movement is Leslie Fishbein, *Rebels in Bohemia: The Radicals of The Masses, 1911–1917* (Chapel Hill, 1982).

24. Franz Boas, *The Mind of Primitive Man* (1911; New York, 1965), 17, 29, 160–61, 154, 201, 205–10; Lewis Perry, *Intellectual Life in America: A History* (New York, 1984), 320–23; George W. Stocking, Jr., *Race, Culture and Evolution: Essays in the History of Anthropology* (New York, 1968), 217–22, 226, 190–91; Marshall Hyatt, "Franz Boas and the Struggle for Black Equality: The Dynamics of Ethnicity," *Perspectives in American History* 2 (1985): 295, 269.

25. Lewis A. Erenberg, *Steppin' Out: New York Nightlife and the Transformation of American Culture, 1890–1930* (Westport, Conn., 1981), 5, 23, xii–xiv, 113, 125–26, 131, 187, 195, 255–56, 240–41, 154.

26. Ibid., 148, 150–51, 153–54, 249–51; Paula S. Fass, *The Damned and the Beautiful: American Youth in the 1920's* (New York, 1977), 301–3, 22.

27. Malcolm Bradbury, *The Modern American Novel* (New York, 1983), 61–62; James Agee and Walker Evans, *Let Us Now Praise Famous Men* (1941; New York, 1966), esp. 121, 129, 376–77; William Stott, *Documentary Expression and Thirties America* (New York, 1973), 302, 305–7, 310–11; Daniel Joseph Singal, "Beyond Consensus: Richard Hofstadter and American Historiography," *American Historical Review* 89 (October 1984): 978, 996; Howard Brick, *Daniel Bell and the Decline of Intellectual Radicalism: Social Theory and Political Reconciliation in the 1940s* (Madison, 1986), 20–21, 38–39,165, 191–92, 208; Robbins, "Modernism in History," 234–35.

28. William L. O'Neill, *Coming Apart: An Informal History of America in the 1960s* (New York, 1971), 200–202, 204–8; Susan Sontag, "Against Interpretation," in *Sontag Reader*, 98–99, 104.

29. Fredric Jameson, "Postmodernism, or the Cultural Logic of Late Capitalism," *New Left Review* 146 (July–August 1984), 53–54; Wolin, "Modernism vs. Postmodernism," 18–20, 25, 26; Gerald Graff, "The Myth of the Postmodernist Breakthrough," *Triquarterly* 26 (Winter 1973): 392; Bradbury, *Modern American Novel*, 160–64; Robert Venturi et al., *Learning from Las Vegas: The Forgotten Symbolism of Architectural Form* (Cambridge, Mass., 1977), 6–9 and passim; Dell Upton and John Michael Vlach, eds., *Common Places: Readings in American Vernacular Architecture* (Athens, Ga., 1986). For an early view of literary postmodernism that now seems somewhat dated, see Ihab Hassan, "POSTmodernISM: A Paracritical Bibliography," *New Literary History* 3 (Autumn 1971): 5–30.

30. Jameson, "Postmodernism," 54–55, 59–62, 65, 72–73, 75.

31. Ibid., 87, 89–90.

32. Ibid., 71–72, 91–92; Frederick Crews, "In the Big House of Theory," *New York Review of Books*, 33 (May 29, 1986), 37, 39–42. On this debate, see also Jean Lyotard, *The Postmodern Condition*, trans. Geoff Bennington and Brian Masumi (Minneapolis, 1984).

33. Graff, "Myth of the Postmodernist Breakthrough," 387; Robert Martin Adams, "What Was Modernism?" *Hudson Review* 31 (Spring 1978): 29–30.

ზა

The Nonhomemade World: European and American Modernism

Malcolm Bradbury
University of East Anglia

At the beginning of *A Homemade World: The American Modernist Writers* (1975), Hugh Kenner performs an elegant act of metaphorical magic by yoking violently together two items in the history of modernity separately much celebrated, but not usually associated. One is the flight of the Wright brothers at Kitty Hawk in 1903, the first serious proof of powered flight, and a clear triumph of American technological inventiveness. The other is a work of fiction started the next year in which the image of the artist as modern flyer has a striking place. That fiction, of course, is Joyce's *A Portrait of the Artist as a Young Man,* where Stephen Dedalus's flight into the unknown arts provides us with a figure for the rising spirit of artistic modernism. Metaphorically juxtaposing the one with the other, Kenner can now link two powers, those of American modernity and those of European modernism. As he says of the Wrights: "Their Dedalian deed on the North Carolina shore

This paper was first presented in lecture form to the 1986 meeting of the International Association of University Professors of English.

may be accounted the first American input into the great imaginative enterprise on which artists were to collaborate for half a century." The cunning connection gives him his book. American flyers came to the First World War, and also to the not much less embattled bohemias of Paris and London, where the new arts were being forged. At this stage American technological dominance and European forms were separate. To most Americans, Modernism was foreign; but since it was modern they wanted it, but made in a homemade way. Poets like William Carlos Williams and Wallace Stevens, and many American novelists, musicians, and painters obliged, becoming Modernist without even going to Europe, exploring the new preoccupations as an aspect of the problems of the American language, the needs of American perception and American consciousness, American plenitude and American emptiness. This Kenner explains: "That doctrine of perception, like general semantics, seems peculiarly adapted to the American weather, which fact helps explain why, from Pound's early days until now, modern poetry in whatever country has borne so unmistakably American an impress." [1]

I have done little justice to Kenner's cunning book; but I start with it because it serves as an example of a familiar historiographical process, providing as it does both a narrative of an American act of artistic appropriation and a skillful critical mechanism for reinforcing it. It is a way of telling Modernism's story largely by dislodging the venturesome modern spirit in the arts from a European soil, in which it appears unrooted, to modern American soil, where it prospers and fertilizes, grows with the American grain, and then, an abundant crop, returns to the world market, rather like Frank Norris's nirvanic wheat. Modernism bears the American impress, even outside America, it and American modernity being natural kin. Such narratives are, of course, not new, but they have flourished powerfully since the 1940s when, with F. O. Matthiessen's *American Renaissance* (1941), the modern history of American literature began to be seriously written, and the idea of the native grain, of an encompassing and modern American tradition based on American vision and American mythology, enlarged. Matthiessen's brilliant book, the first truly convincing exploration of the way the American writers of the Transcendentalist pre–Civil War period constructed a new art that seemed to pass beyond inherited forms,

AMERICA CCUNL TO RSSCLISM,
VI2 DEVELOPMENT OR
HARTLEY 45 USE CAUSE
Claims.

constructing itself anew, released a fresh idea of the relation between the American imagination and American culture. In the same
year, Alfred Kazin, in *On Native Grounds*, made a similar case for
American Naturalism, which might well have been thought to owe
much to European ventures of the same kind; after all, Frank Norris
had studied art in Paris and was seen around the Berkeley campus
with a volume of Zola in his hand, and the European Naturalists
were much in vogue among the young American writers. But Kazin
seeks to establish a difference: where in Europe Naturalism had the
force of a literary doctrine, in America it "just came, . . . grew out of
the bewilderment, and fed on the simple grimness of a generation
brought face to face with the pervasive materialism of American
capitalism"—and it "had no center, no unifying principle, no philosophy, no joy in its coming, no climate of experiment." It was the
art of an American process, of industrialization and modernization,
and all done on native grounds.

This sense of the power of native soil, the guiding texture of the
American grain, stimulated a splendid new generation of critical
studies that have shaped all our thinking. In Richard Chase's fine
The American Novel and Its Tradition (1957) the novel-form comes to
the United States in rather the same way, countermanding the European tradition of the social and moral novel and generating its
own neo-mythic form, the romance. This was a season for nativizing
literature, valuably giving the modern American arts a tradition, a
sense of a usable past. American mythographies arising from
American beliefs and motifs, ideologies and theologies, American
institutions and landscapes, American notions of election, mission,
and destiny, powerfully illuminated a literature that, while it might
run curiously parallel to the arts of Europe, and assimilate much
from them, had self-creating powers in the homemade world. And
this notion was reinforced by another—that the American arts had
from the beginning a special relation to the modern itself. That
view owed as much to the European Enlightenment as America
itself, and its notions of the course of empire—according to which,
as Bishop Berkeley reminded Americans, history moved ever west-
ward, and brought the new arts in its train. When the Revolution
brought into being the First New Nation, itself a startling appropriation of modern history, the motif intensified, supplementing
the Calvinist sense of mission that came with settlement with the

diachronic notion of rising modernity that came with continental spread and intensive development of industry and resources. As Hegel famously said, America was "the land of the future where, in the ages that lie before us, the burden of the world's history shall reveal itself" (we sometimes forget that Hegel saw that revelation taking the form of a conflict between North and South America). Such ideas had a natural appeal to Americans, and applied alike to society and the arts. As Melville declared in *Pierre*, the Americans were history's own *avant-garde*, a people advancing into the wilderness of untried things. In Whitman the message grew clearer, modernity in society and experience leading to modernity of form in the arts. "One main contrast of the ideas behind every page of my verses, compared with establish'd poems, is their different relative attitude towards God, towards the objective universe, and still more (by reflection, confessional, assumption, &c.), the quite changed attitude of the ego, the one chanting or talking towards himself and towards his fellow-humanity," he wrote in *A Backward Glance*, going on to add that the material, inventive, and war-produced revolutions of the times, but above all the *moral* one, had produced what he called a change of army-front through the whole civilized world. And this meant modern form: "For all these new and evolutionary facts, meanings, purposes, new poetic forms and expressions, are inevitable."

This sense of alliance—between America's modern history and modernity of form—Gertrude Stein took with her when, with the twentieth century in her blood (she meant, she said, to be historical, from almost a baby on, and was there "to kill what was not dead, the nineteenth century which was so sure of evolution and prayers"), she went in 1903 to settle in bohemian Paris, where among the *refusés* the spirit of twentieth-century modernism was in process of birth. "So the twentieth century had come it began with 1901," she wrote in *Paris France*.[2] The new century was widely hailed in the United States as "the American century," and Stein shared the view, saying that the twentieth century came in America even though it had to go to France to happen. England was consciously refusing the new era, "knowing full well that they had gloriously created the nineteenth century and perhaps the twentieth was going to be one too many for them," while France took it all in its stride, since "what is was and what was is, was their point of view of which they were not very conscious." They were soon made conscious, in part by the Americans who came to Montparnasse, collecting, hunting the new, purchasing modern art on an extraordinary scale that can best be tested by inspecting the collections of the major American galleries and their dates of purchase, and stirring modernity into action. It had to be admitted that the novelties had a European source, and that the United States was puritanical and unartistic—"a half-savage country, out of date," said Ezra Pound, who played a somewhat similar role in motivating and stimulating London with American energies at around the same time—and so, argued Stein, Americans needed Paris because they could not be artists, they could be dentists at home. But she carried with her the familiar American conviction, that the United States was a nation with a special disposition toward progress, and with its technological advance, democratic social order, and distinctive space-time continuum, it required the "new composition." By this interpretation Modernism was a progressive movement of the arts aptly suited to a progressive nation, and we can see how powerful this kind of account of Modernist evolution has been in the development of the new arts in America.

It needs hardly be said that these ideas have been held in Europe also, both by those seeking to fund the modernity of Modernism and by those attempting to expel it and all its works. Al Alvarez said that for English-language writing, Modernism "has been a predominantly American concern"; Philip Larkin was happy to hand over to Americans "the two principal themes of modernism, mystification and outrage," and stay near the line of Hardy, and sanity. European Modernists often acknowledged their connection with the American spirit, Picasso observing that if Modernism was born in France it was the product of Spaniards and Americans. The images of rapidity and synchronicity that came from American culture, the beat of American popular music, the rhythms of jazz and the American dances, had great appeal to those artists in Paris who were moving toward both spontaneous primitivism and a new abstraction. The American motif was widespread, in Picabia, Duchamp, Cocteau, and many more. Mondrian explained that "True Boogie-Woogie I conceive as homogenous in intention with mine in painting." Mayakovsky saw the skyscraper American city as the heart of the modern, and read the implications of the Brook-

lyn Bridge with the same radical intensity as Hart Crane. The motif
has lasted, in Sartre, Butor, Robbe-Grillet, and has much to do with
the engagement of many European critics with American literature
and culture. The "modern" image of America that so strongly affected Russian and Italian Futurism, and German Expressionism,
even made its mark in Britain. Indeed, D. H. Lawrence's *Studies in
Classic American Literature* (1923) recovered, in a remarkable and
visionary way, from the little-read classic American tradition the
same sense of modernity: "Two bodies of modern literature seem
to me to come to the real verge: the Russian and the American. . . .
The furtherest frenzies of French modernism or futurism have not
yet reached the pitch of extreme consciousness that Poe, Melville,
Hawthorne, Whitman reached. The Europeans were all trying to be
extreme. The great Americans I mention just were it. Which is why
the world has funked them, and funks them today."

&

Yet if Modernism was to become, as Alvarez said, "a predominantly
American concern," it hardly started as such. It began in Europe,
and took a long time to cross the Atlantic; indeed, the American
writers from the 1890s to the First World War were largely preoccupied with a Zola-esque Naturalism that in Europe was mostly
considered exhausted. Indeed the full impact of the Modernist
tendency came in America at least a generation later than it did in
Europe; we normally date it from the ferments around 1912, when
Freud and Cubism, the abstract art of the Armory Show, and the
new poetry that Pound sought to press upon *Poetry*, Harriet
Monroe's magazine, begin to implant in American soil. This is not
the place to expatiate at length on what we mean by Modernism, a
contentious matter now as it always was, in part because on detailed
inspection it dissolves into a plurality of different, often substantially
conflicting, movements or tendencies, with many different sources,
philosophies, and culture-readings, many different versions of the
modern and the deliverances required of the modern arts. The
complex problems of definition James McFarlane and I sought to
address are discussed at length in the introduction to *Modernism:
1890–1930*, where we note the heterodoxy of ideas that have gone

into most of the attempted definitions.[3] But let me here suggest that for many Western writers and thinkers a nineteenth-century synthesis seems to dissolve or come to crisis in the 1880s and 1890s—when positivism struggles with intuitionalism, sociology with psychology, Naturalism with aestheticism, when there is a deep sense of perceptual crisis that throws attention onto consciousness, when world-views pluralize, and dusks and dawns in both the arts and civilization are much thought of. The result in ideas and forms is a period of remarkable intellectual and aesthetic innovation, a general upheaval manifest also in science and philosophy; this all has some prophetic or precursory relation to both the dislocation of the Great War and the postwar synthesis. These changes and disorientations are strongly manifested in the arts, displacing the role of artists, privatizing and specializing them, in some sense dislocating them from the familiar or the homemade. All this has social roots in the processes of late nineteenth-century change, the political upheavals of growing democratization and radical if not revolutionary feeling. It was an international affair, and if any one thing distinguishes modernism it is surely its international interfusion—which is to say that, whether through simultaneous generation or traceable flows of ideas and influence, related artistic phenomena occur right across the Western nations, from Oslo to Rome, Moscow to Chicago. One then should add that they do not occur at quite the same time, in the same order, with the same aims or underlying philosophies, with the same degrees of hope or despair, or with the same historical expectations.

And since the familiar perspective in much English language–centered theory sees Modernism largely as an affair of Paris, London, and New York, let us consider how wide a movement it was, and how enormous was the thought-flow passing through the European cities, being felt in various capitals and provinces at different times. Ibsenite Naturalism started in Scandinavia, went to Germany to happen, and turned with late Ibsen and Strindberg toward Expressionism. In France Zola-esque Naturalism turned toward aestheticism, symbolism, and the art of the soul and the senses; both of these traditions seemed to cross over in German Expressionism in the immediately prewar years. Paris gave London much of its 1890s Naturalism and its aestheticism, but Germany won some attention, especially via Nietzsche and Ibsen, and D. H. Lawrence of course was drawn by Frieda toward Expressionism. In Russia another version of Symbolism moved toward Futurism; in Vienna another compound evolved that linked modern music, psychology, and new linguistic theory. In Paris, Marinetti was inventing and disseminating Italian futurism, though there were many other crucial movements, including Unanimisme, to the point where Pound, constantly visiting, felt that movements were just what London needed to stir the pot. Imagism in London derived in part from French Symbolism, in part from the German art historian Wilhelm Worringer, and to some not very great degree from Whitman, with whom Pound contracted a painfully slow pact. It did have a significant American constituent, though Pound denied America as the main source of its ideas, and credited, amongst others, Selwyn Image, T. E. Hulme, and F. S. Flint, as well as the Chinese ideogram. Vorticism, on the other hand, was both borrowed from Worringer and the Futurists and was in revolt against them; fittingly, one of its founding figures, Wyndham Lewis, was born on a ship at sea. Dada *TRAVESTIS* came to a wartime Zurich that, as Tom Stoppard shows, contained the odd synthesis of Tristan Tzara, Lenin, and Joyce. The war over, it took off in two directions—to Berlin and to Paris, where it interacted with French Surrealism, which inherited from earlier Symbolism the impact of Cubism and generated the Revolution of the ? Word, which brought together, or broke apart, contingents from France, Germany, England, Ireland, Romania, and the United States, to name but a few.

What we can say is that Modernism was an affair of many movements, of a common *avant-gardizing* tendency, with international origins, a massive and constant change of personnel, and considerable capacity for transit. It was also an affair centered in certain cosmopolitanizing cities capable of concentrating the flow of artnews and sustaining a large bohemian population of polyglot character. And one of the marks of Modernism was that it seemed to have no home. That flight Stephen takes in *Portrait of the Artist* into the unknown arts is a voyage of broken ties, fracturing the bonds of kinship, religion, and country as he goes off to Paris, certainly to forge the uncreated conscience of his race, but to do so from an anxious expatriate distance, which set over Joyce's tales of Dublin, the paralyzed city, a modern pluralism and polyglotism. Homelessness was part of the story. As George Steiner says, it was largely an

art unhoused, an art of "extra-territoriality," and it was no accident
that multilinguists have been the major artists of our age. Indeed,
he says of Nabokov, so clearly a part of this tradition, "It seems
proper that those who create art in a civilization of quasi-barbarism
in which so many are made homeless, which has torn up tongues
and peoples by the root, should themselves be poets unhoused
and wanderers across language." That wandering of language, that
separation of the signifier from the signified which Saussure was
intuiting in the immediate prewar climate, that "defamiliarization"
of which the Russian formalist critics began to speak at much the
same time, indeed seems near to the heart of Modernism. Thus,
what Kenner domesticates, and makes friendly with modern society
and modern change, Steiner deracinates, and associates with modern anxiety and historical suffering. There are indeed many versions of Modernism.

In this Americans, essentially the expatriate ones, played their
part from the early stages, a part that intensified in quantity and
influence as time went on: James, Henry Harland, Pound, Eliot,
Robert Frost, and John Gould Fletcher in London; Gertrude and
Leo Stein in Paris, to be followed by the expatriate wave of the
1920s; and so on. But support funds at home were not great, as
Pound discovered when he tried to transmit European news back
to Harriet Monroe. When Pound explained that American bards
had to study Remy de Gourmont, Henri de Regnier, Francis
Jammes, and Tristan Corbiere, her magazine waved its homemade
banner in behalf of its version of Modernism: "Mr [Vachel] Lindsay
did not go to France for *The Congo* or *General William Booth Enters
Into Heaven*. He did not even stay on the eastern side of the
Alleghanies. . . ." It was the midwestern "moderns" like Lindsay,
Masters, and Sandburg that the magazine took pride in, while the
great modern epic Monroe was looking for was not "Prufrock,"
which Pound sent her and which she tried to edit down, but a
nativist epic celebrating the Panama Canal. Much of what Pound
was saying was in fact an embarrassment. Nonetheless a "homemade" school did evolve with Williams, Wallace Stevens, Marianne
Moore, and others, who may not have headed for Europe but who
took much of their funding from Pound, Imagism, and French
Symbolism. Williams may have felt that *The Waste Land* set back poetry by twenty years, but his Imagist debts are clear. Stevens for

some time impersonated a French Symbolist poet, and submitted poems under the dandy-name of "Peter Parasol," taking many of his titles from French poetry and paintings. American writing itself bred many modernisms, from the cultural despair of Eliot and Pound to the contrary affirmation and surer nativism of Stein and Williams. Indeed, an assimilation took place, so that we see the American arts as modern not simply because they explore the cultural experience of an advanced or futuristic society, but because they have incorporated into that culture the lore of the modern art forms.

Not all saw the elegant equation of American modernity and European modernism as virtue. Stein's tactics of takeover, representing Cubism as an art that, though invented by Frenchmen and Spaniards, was really American, fitting prairie space, skyscraper cities, and filmic speed, were not universally accepted. Braque, in the famous "transition" testimony against Gertrude Stein, said: "Miss Stein obviously saw everything from the outside and never the real struggle we were engaged in. For one who poses as an authority on the epoch it is safe to say that she never went beyond the stage of a tourist." Certainly she perceived in terms of abstract, detachable styles justified by broad reference to twentieth-century needs, and never touched the deeper historical and perceptual anguish behind much modernism. Yet in her way she was right. Americans had a taste for stylistic radicalism, for forms that suggested a modern version of life, for new structures. American modern style did assimilate much from modernist style, in architecture and art. Indeed modernism seemed to pull together the apparently lonely and eccentric history of American artistic endeavor right through the nineteenth century. By the mid-1920s Americans seemed in one fashion or another major participants, and a modernism of sorts settled as an acceptable American style, along with Freud and Jung, Picabia and Picasso, the skyscraper and the futurist lines of the motor car, the radical spontaneity of jazz. And when in the 1930s the rise of Hitler and Mussolini reversed the tide of intellectual and artistic migrations, the alliance between Modernism and modern America seemed secured. Mann and Brecht, Auden and Isherwood, along with many of the intellectual supporters and major figures of theater and architecture, found themselves on American soil, and in the American grain. In 1939, the year of new war, Joyce published *Finnegan's Wake*, that summative and polyglot myth; a year later he died, displaced back to Zurich, and around the same time so did Virginia Woolf, a clear casualty of war. Of the two great American expatriate figures who had so much to do with the transaction, Pound, staying in Italy, was threatened with charges of treason, and Stein, remaining in France, just survived the war, still asserting that America was her country and Paris was her home town. In America modernism seemed settled, and Bauhaus became not so much our house as the American corporate office building. Stein's prophecy for the century seemed fulfilled. Modernism had become the twentieth-century American style, the language of its progressivism, pluralism, cultural convergence; its commerce, its aesthetic drive, its modernity.

Thus, we seem to agree now, Modernism both endured and ended, fractured by the war but leaving its overwhelming trace on the Modern. Its demise left us with a problem, at least of nomenclature, for what comes after the modern, what follows the future, what happens when now turns suddenly into then, is not easy to define. But after the war there came, as Sartre said, a "third generation" of writers, called by the historical fracture and the collapse of entire social orders to new responsibilities. Modernism was now historicized, something came after, and we have come to talk of Postmodernism. No one has been more helpful and thoughtful than Ihab Hassan in trying to interpret the transition and gloss the term, and I quote him in paracritical flight: "If we can arbitrarily state that literary Modernism includes certain work between Jarry's *Ubu Roi* (1896) and Joyce's *Finnegan's Wake* (1939), where will we arbitrarily state that Postmodernism begins? A year earlier than the Wake? With Sartre's *La Nausée* (1938) or Beckett's *Murphy* (1938)? In any case, Postmodernism includes works by writers as different as *B*arth, arthelme, ecker, eckett, ense, lanchot, orges, urroughs, utor. . . ." The list, you will notice, is provisional, capacious and international, with a large European contingent. So is that in another fine and undernoticed book on the same topic, Christopher Butler's *After the Wake: An Essay on the Contemporary Avant Garde* (1980), which also takes the wake as a break, the break as a wake, but sees a distinctive new phase of style developing after Existentialism, during the 1950s, with the *nouveau roman*, the *nouvelle vague* in cinema, a new music and a new painting. "For better or worse," he says, identifying this postmodern time, "this is the age of Beckett and Robbe-Grillet, of Cage, Messiaen, Boulez, of Pollock, Rothko, Stella, and Rauschenberg." Butler not only emphasizes the internationality of the matter but draws less than usual on contemporary literary theory, concentrating on the statements of artists themselves. And I suppose that most Europeans (and even the British now call themselves European, or certainly when it is in their interest to do so) would recognize some such history, seeing the aftermodern or postmodern tendency or aesthetic equation as owing much to the postwar evolution of Existentialism, with its struggle between the humanistic and the absurd, and to the subsequent challenges to it in successor arts and philosophies, the reassimilation of some aspects of Modernism, the rejection of others, the pervasive sense of the "imaginary museum" of plenitude and emptiness that passed through so many Western arts, the spirit of what Nathalie Sarraute calls "the ear of suspicion," when, as Robbe-Grillet puts it, in an era beyond humanism and tragedy art lives with "the smooth, meaningless, amoral surface of the world."

What is clear is that Postmodernism does have a larger American constituent, reflecting in part the fortunes of Modernism, and the dominance of America as modern art patron, high stylistic consumer, and *emigré* haven. It is surely equally clear that its great marking figures include Beckett, an Irishman writing in Paris in French; Nabokov, a Russian refugee writing in his native language, German, French, and eventually English; and Borges, an Argentinian writing in Spanish and with a Latin American, Iberian, French, and Anglophile background. Thus it draws on a tradition that had moved through Modernism and the Absurd toward a new minimalism, a tradition based in a latter-day adaptation of early Russian Symbolism, and a South American tradition that relates the fantastic to historical realism. Its present centers certainly include South America, Paris, Italy, Germany, to some degree Britain, and to some further degree the Indian subcontinent, Australasia, and Canada. Its intellectual sources appear to be, among other things, Russian formalism, Saussurian linguistics, later Surrealism, Existentialist philosophy, and what has followed it, that Deconstructionist revolution that spread throughout the entire Gallic World (as I believe Yale University is sometimes called). It includes, I would say virtually by definition, an eclectic principle of multiple quotation, stylistic pluralism, creative misprision. There has indeed been a strong American contingent, which Saul Bellow, who has made clear his resistance to the tendency, has distinguished from the *nouveaux romanciers* and European writers "whose novels and plays are derived from definite theories which make a historical reckoning of the human condition and are particularly responsive to new physical, psychological, and philosophical theories." In this matter, he says, American writers are again the modern primitives, writing in the same spirit but "seldom encumbered by such intellectual baggage, and this fact pleases their European contemporaries, who find in them a natural, that is, a brutal or violent acceptance of the new universal truth by minds free from intellectual preconceptions." If this is not entirely true, some part of American Postmodernism having a clear intellectual face related to those European philosophies, it does seem that there is a Postmodernism of the homemade world.

Today the tendency indeed seems to have been domesticated within the cultural heterodoxy of American culture, and become a convention. As Alan Wilde says with some irony in *Horizons of Assent: Modernism, Postmodernism, and the Ironic Imagination* (1980), "postmodernism is an essentially American affair." The term has been generalized to apply to the broad eclecticism of forms and referents in contemporary American writing, architecture and art, a way of speaking of an art that appears "self-creating" *and* "in the American grain." Indeed this is the form of modern writing that has grown particularly exemplary, so literary that Postmodernism often seems to mean innovative American fiction read—or rather misread—with the methods and slippages of French Deconstructionist criticism. It is, in effect, the art of the "homemade world," a consequence of American stylistic abundance, provisional form, intermedia arts, futurism and, often, optimism. So, says one American critic, James Rother, "to be American is, quite simply, to be postmodern, and to be postmodern entails nothing more than knowing (in the full light of a communally held fiction) that one is."

I have suggested here that for a sufficient account of Modernism we need many Modernisms, and a far more challenging and international perception of the relation between American and broader international culture. By necessary logic the same would apply to

Postmodernism, which has inherited, certainly, the plurality and multiple signification of Modernism and a good part of its philosophical, linguistic, and formal skepticism. If the term means anything, it surely means an art of stylistic plurality and cultural synchronicity, rebarbative plenitude and decultured emptiness, formal enquiry and parodic self-reference, random signification and infinite quotation, that marks much of world-culture in our multimedia, high-noise, wide-traveling internationalist age. To attend to it we need a capacious attention, if we are to construct not only a sufficient historiography of the immediate past of our arts but of their present. For we live, after all, in the age of Marquez, Calvino, Handke, Eco, Fowles, Pinter, Stoppard, Wittig, Coetzee, and many more, and there is a major international literature of extraordinary power that needs drawing into any cogent mapping of the late twentieth-century arts that both succeed to and react to the overwhelming Modernist inheritance. The arts of Postmodernism, like those of Modernism, are of no single and unidirectional kind; they are a contention, a quarrel, seeded in many places, often floating free of them in a large extraterritoriality, and funded by polyglot and multistylistic sources. It is almost forty years after the wake, as indeed the wake was just around forty years after *Ubu Roi*. The task of charting this is immense, and hardly begun in terms of a conceptual historiography. But as we begin to assimilate theoretically the arts of our own long time, we will find almost certainly that in our age of cultural melting-pot and extraordinary global interfusion they are hardly the arts of a homemade world.

Notes

1. Hugh Kenner, *A Homemade World: The American Modernist Writers* (New York, 1975), xii, xviii.
2. Gertrude Stein, *Paris France* (New York, 1940).
3. Malcolm Bradbury and James McFarlane, eds., *Modernism 1890–1930* (Harmondsworth, Eng., 1976), 19–55.

ॐ

The Knower and the Artificer

David A. Hollinger
University of Michigan

Iᴛ ɪs ᴇᴀsɪᴇʀ ᴛᴏ ᴛᴀʟᴋ ᴀʙᴏᴜᴛ sᴏᴍᴇᴛʜɪɴɢ ɪғ ʏᴏᴜ ʜᴀᴠᴇ ᴡᴏʀᴅs ғᴏʀ ɪᴛ. A ʟᴀᴄᴋ of good terms for talking about "the modern" has rendered the study of much recent intellectual history a walk through a multi-sided room of mirrors. Each wall is said to be "modernist," yet each reflects light differently, and makes it difficult to get a clear view of any object in the room, including the walls themselves. It has long been suspected that this effect derives in large part from the limited language we use to discuss our recent past. One savant after an-other has called for a richer vocabulary,[1] but no one seems willing to give up on "modernism," which, for all its vagueness, continues to confer a unique, almost spiritual authority. To demonstrate that a previously neglected or underappreciated author is actually a modernist remains, after several decades of this literary game, the most effective means of bringing such an author to the critical

For critical reactions to a draft of this essay I wish to thank Thomas Bender, Thomas Haskell, John Higham, and Daniel Singal. I wish also to acknowledge the support of the Center for Advanced Study in the Behavioral Sciences.

42

attention of the cognoscenti.[2] One can talk about versions of modernism, or variations on modern themes, but the notion of a single, overarching "Modernist impulse" continues to reign amid admissions that its essence eludes definition. Scholars seem reluctant to remove anything they really care about from the formidable company of the "modern." Where else is there to go with any aspect of recent intellectual history that isn't (shudder) "Victorian"?

Certain American political scientists, we are told, have accepted a philosophy of "modernism." This philosophy is based on the reality and social efficacy of "scientific knowledge": once such knowledge "is accumulated and gained," modernism holds, "conflicts thought to be endemic to modern society could be rationally controlled, mediated and contained justly, equitably and democratically."[3] Could anything be farther from the family of perspectives on modern life normally attributed to Kafka, Eliot, Lawrence, or Heidegger? This modernism of a major American academic tradition would remain alien from the canonical literary modernists even if deprived of the complacency here attributed to it, and endowed with a greater sense of contradiction and irony. What defines this peculiar modernism is its faith in science, its sense that what our civilization requires in order to be rescued from itself is more likely to come from communities of knowers than from a succession of artist-heroes. If Joyce's Stephen Dedalus expected to forge the uncreated conscience of a race in the smithy of his soul, Joyce had plenty of contemporaries, fictional and real, who expected instead to constitute culture through a more cognitive, public, cooperative enterprise: the steady accumulation of scientific knowledge. Their numbers included John Dewey, Charles Beard, H. G. Wells, Karl Popper, Sinclair Lewis's Martin Arrowsmith, most of the characters in Jacob Bronowski's *The Ascent of Man*, campuses full of social scientists, many proponents of "realism" in the arts, and some of the most illustrious theorists of social democracy and progressivism.

There is a sense in which some of these science-admiring intellectuals can be called "modernist" with a minimum of confusion. Some of them did share with Joyce, and other artists to whom this label is conventionally applied, at least a few of the recognitions thought to be hidden from men and women who lived on the other side of the great spiritual divide identified by Virginia Woolf when she quipped that "on or about December, 1910, human

character changed." This is to say that scientific intellectuals, as
well as Bloomsbury aesthetes, sometimes recognized that knowledge
of the external world was not so easy to come by, that contradictions persisted in human experience, that a real price was paid for
the benefits of bureaucratic rationality, that a large measure of uncertainty was an enduring condition of life, that human beings had
a propensity to act irrationally, that it was difficult to find an un-
changing standard for moral judgments, that God might be dead,
and that many sensitive individuals felt alienated from industrial
society. Such recognitions are the stuff out of which most formulations of "the modern predicament" are made. While it is possible
to insist that all are essentially modernists who have seen through
an innocent Victorian world to confront by one strategy or another
the more complicated and recalcitrant world we call "modern,"[4] it
is at the level of strategies that confusion and contention concerning modernism most frequently arise.

There may be a modernist diagnosis of the human condition,
but is there a distinctly modernist family of strategies for dealing
with it? Much of our critical and historiographical literature says
that there is: *strategies of artifice.* Given "the modern predicament,"
our best course of cultural action is to make meanings anew, out of
the resources of the self. This approach draws upon the romantic
heritage of the artist as creative genius. Yet "the modern predicament" has also been met by *strategies of reference:* just because knowledge turned out to be more contingent, more fragmentary, and
harder to obtain than Condorcet and Comte supposed, one need
not give up on the effort to organize culture around science. Objects of knowledge, critically apprehended, might still provide a
basis of meaning. This approach draws upon the admiration for
scientists that, like the romantic notion of creative genius, predated
"the modern predicament."

Are strategies of reference part of modernism? If the edifice of
modernism were truly as commodious as its hall-of-mirrors effect
implies, the answer would be an easy and perhaps meaningless
"yes." Yet scholarly discourse about modernism is haunted by a
vague but powerful sense that certain of the ideas sometimes said
to be modern are decidedly more modern than others. A "dominant reading" of modernism, complains Peter Gay, has concentrated our attention on "anti-rationalism, experimentalism, and
alienation."[5] In a similar spirit, the late Paul de Man protested the

"bias against analytical modes" he detected in *The Modern Tradition*, a 953-page anthology edited by Richard Ellman and Charles Feidelson, Jr.[6] Commentators on the most logically coherent, epistemologically confident, socially conscious, and politically liberal or "progressive" themes in twentieth-century thought have found themselves speaking about their subjects in a "me, too" voice: our subjects are just as modernistic as yours!

The strain derives, of course, from the fact that modernism has come to be so intimately associated with literature and the arts, and especially with the preoccupations of such leading canonical modernists as Dostoevsky, Joyce, Kafka, Yeats, and Pound. It is by this literary touchstone, for example, that Anthony Quinton answers the question, "Which Philosophy is Modernistic?" The philosophers who emerge from Quinton's survey as the most akin to Mallarmé, Eliot, Joyce, et al., are of course existentialists rather than analysts; Kierkegaard, Nietzsche, and Sartre rather than Russell, Carnap, and Popper.[7] And it is against this same literary touchstone that Daniel Singal struggles when seeking to construct modernism broadly enough to include the "critical realism" of American social science.[8] Elusive and multitudinous as the edifice of modernism may appear, it turns out to have an implicit structure.

One response to this structure is to challenge it in the interests of a wider, deeper, and presumably more adequate account of modernism. Gay, for example, calls for "enlarging the territory of modernism" in order to address in its name "a pervasive cultural revolution, a second Renaissance." There are risks in this movement to debohemianize modernism. One might make modernism "a synonym for everything he likes, or dislikes," Gay concedes, or dilute the term by calling modernist "every idea, every artifact, made since 1850."[9] Yet the advantages are manifest: one retains a claim to the most commanding, most talismanic word in the critical study of twentieth-century intellectual life.

Another, contrasting response is to accept, to sharpen, and to make more explicit the specific sense of "modernism" that has been the most persistently developed around the modernist literary canon. This entails yielding to the strongest of our linguistic conventions, and saving our more strenuous exertions for a very different task: the developing of new terms for addressing the aspects of twentieth-century intellectual history that do not fit comfortably within the conventionally modernist framework.

The choice between these two responses to the implicit structure of the modernist edifice—stick around and reform the place, or move out and let the old residents keep it all the more to themselves—is perhaps the central issue in the current historiography of modernism. Although this essay is written more in the second, let-them-keep-it mode than in the first, make-room-for-my-topic mode, its point is not to argue for any definition of modernism. I want instead to single out one cultural ideal consistently identified with the modernist literary canon, artifice, and to address this ideal in juxtaposition to a historically contemporary, logically contrasting ideal whose relation to modernism is far from clear in our scholarly literature: the ideal of cognition. Whether the rivalry between these two ideals amounts to a tension within a single modernist culture or illuminates the divide between modernism and something else is less important, surely, than the clarification of these two ideals in relation to each other in the intellectual history of the twentieth century.

Knowing is frequently understood to entail an element of artifice, and vice versa, but I want for the moment to be willfully simple, to set forth in the most sweeping of terms two ideal types embodying strategies of reference and of artifice. The one purports to assign meanings cognitively, by finding out what is the case, while the other purports to perform this service through the creation of myths. Hence we may speak of two figures—two clusters of ideal characteristics—as the Knower and the Artificer. Their defining modes are as follows:

THE KNOWER	THE ARTIFICER
finding	making
referential	generative
demystifying	myth-constructing
authenticating	contriving
interdependent	self-sufficient
intersubjective	intrasubjective
suspicious of moral commitments	makes its own morality
uniformitarian	discontinuity-affirming

These two personae represent typical constructions of the modern scientist and the modern artist on the part of intellectuals who have seen one or the other as a cultural hero. Hence the Knower and the Artificer are not merely parallel presumptions concerning the values embodied in modern scientific and artistic practice; these constructions are also rival prescriptions for the foundations of culture. Although they may often surface within movements *in* literature, the arts, the sciences, and philosophy, these cultural ideals are essentially ideas *about* art and science and about the roles art and science should play in constituting culture. If one were to place these ideals in the framework of the science-art-morality division of spheres proposed by Immanuel Kant and powerfully reinforced by Max Weber, one could say that the Knower and the Artificer are agents of the spheres of science and art, straining against their prescribed limits, encroaching on the sphere of morality.

Historically, these two cultural ideals have been developed in a dialectical relation: men and women who see the self-sufficient artist as the hope of our culture have often been convinced that science produces only meaningless facts, while men and women willing to look at culture in cognitive terms have often doubted that the arts could do more than express emotions. This dialectic is a durable one in the West; revolts and counterrevolts of this kind helped to define the Enlightenment, the Romantic movement, and the varieties of nineteenth-century positivism. Indeed, part of the appeal of the Knower in the twentieth century has still been based on suspicions of romantic art popularized by Victorian positivists, and much of this century's celebration of modernism in the arts has been predicated on neo-romantic notions of the cultural bankruptcy of science. Especially during the middle decades of this century, American literary intellectuals celebrated the self-sufficient, infinitely resourceful artist as one who, faced with the spiritual wasteland attendant upon science, technology, and industry, would eschew mimesis, and create out of the self a distinctly modern culture.[10] If the Knower is a shallow, naively optimistic ideal according to many men and women attracted in the context of "the modern predicament" to strategies of artifice, the Artificer is in the same context— according to many defenders of strategies of reference— an ideal of capitulation, of acquiescence in demonic and authoritarian tendencies. At its most polemical, discourse about the Knower and the Artificer emerges in the form of invidious characterizations of the problem of the "two cultures": blithely innocent proponents of the sciences are mocked by humanists who claim a more profound measure of the human dilemma (the "scientistic" Bertrand Russell can be dismissed; he was so narrowly and naively logical, the last Victorian), while decadent and parochial literati are condemned by scientific intellectuals who claim a more promising basis for human community (the "subjectivist" Martin Heidegger can be dismissed; he made his peace with the Nazis, and then began to holler for God's help).

The Artificer is a familiar character within the modernist literary canon. "Old father, old artificer, stand by me now and ever in good stead," concludes *The Portrait of the Artist as a Young Man.* "Make it new," cried Pound. Yeats called upon the soul to become "its own betrayer, its own deliverer, the mirror turn lamp." According to Wilde, "The first duty in life is to be as artificial as possible." [11] Wilde's "assertion that life imitates art may be seen as the key to modernist spirit," Phyllis Rose has assured us,[12] and one scholar or another has said the same with reference to each of these kindred, legendary pronouncements. Hugh Kenner's study of the American modernist poets and novelists, *A Homemade World, is* organized around the concept of artifice.[13] The Knower, on the other hand, is less honored within the modernist literary canon. The canonical authors and their sympathetic commentators have often been suspicious of strategies of reference. That "paradigmatic modernist," [14] Nietzsche, set forth a century ago the terms on which partisans of artifice have been inclined to feel spiritually superior to men of science:

> . . . the *ideal* scholar . . . is only an instrument; let us say, he is a *mirror* he is accustomed to submit before whatever wants to be known, without any other pleasure than that found in knowing and "mirroring" . . . his mirror soul, eternally smoothing itself out, no longer knows how to affirm or negate; he does not command, neither does he destroy. . . . The objective man is . . . still less a beginning, a begetting and first cause, nothing tough, powerful, self-reliant that wants to be master—rather only a delicate, carefully dusted, fine, mobile pot for forms that still has to wait for some content and substance in order to "shape" itself accordingly—for the most part, a man without substance and content, a "selfless" man. Consequently, also nothing for women. . . . [15]

Many science-admiring intellectuals have been too sophisticated epistemologically to accept the passive image of the mirror, and

Nietzsche's words would be libelous if applied even to the great Victorian savant, William Whewell,[16] to say nothing of Nietzsche's near-contemporary Weber, nor of the falsificationist Popper, nor of the pragmatist Dewey. But it is exactly such science-admiring intellectuals as these who have developed and popularized knowing as a cultural ideal. It is to them, rather than to the modernist literary canon, that one must look in order to confront the Knower most directly. Yet when we do look to them, we cannot easily do so through a recognized, standard category of intellectual history.

The diverse efforts of nineteenth- and twentieth-century intellectuals to create a culture on the basis of the human ability to know might well be treated as a single movement, yet we tend to divide up this cognitive enthusiasm with the same intensity that we insist on referring in the singular to modernism. We divide it into a host of little "isms," including various kinds of empiricism, progressivism, positivism, Naturalism, and realism. These discriminations are indispensable, but they can lead us to miss a larger enthusiasm that has as much specificity as do these familiar persuasions. The object of this larger enthusiasm was not simply knowledge, but the *cognitive capability of human beings*. Celebrants of knowledge have sometimes implied that knowledge grows by its own mystical powers, but the presumption has remained that the crucial dynamism in its wondrous advance was human energy, distinctly organized. Whatever might be the ontological status of truth itself, knowledge of it was inseparable from the human activity of truth-seeking. Believers in a solid, largely discovered world and a "certain" science shared with their more epistemologically sophisticated comrades a reverence for the human ability to know. A distinctive culture uniquely appropriate for modern society was to be based on the knowledge achieved by men and women, and on the method and ethic believed to be the human source of discovery.

The aspiration to organize culture around the cognitive capacities of human beings took shape in the context of the nineteenth-century's sharpening of what it meant to "know." Early in that century it was still possible to use the terms "knowledge" and "science" to describe inquiries and bodies of ideas that, if so described late in the century, invited puzzlement if not contention. That a stricter sense of "scientific knowledge" became current in the Victorian era is a commonplace of intellectual history: building on the heritage of the Scientific Revolution and the Enlightenment, mid-nineteenth-century thinkers gradually put into wider and wider practice a portentous distinction between the knowledge one got from science and the insights—still called "knowledge" by some—one got from poetry, religion, and those parts of philosophy that remained when "natural philosophy" departed to become "science" in the new, restricted sense of the term. In response to this sharpened division of intellectual labor, some moralists became concerned about the relation of "science" to "culture," and began to dispute over the possibility that this relatively new, and apparently prodigious, enterprise of science—as most influentially described and celebrated in the Anglophone world by Mill's *Logic*—might itself reconstitute culture and perform services previously left to religion, literature, political authority, and social custom.

There were of course national and linguistic variations on this sharpening of the distinction between scientific knowing and the remainder of the intellectual life. While the German notion of *Wissenschaft* advanced an ideal of rigorous, specialized study that applied to scholarship as well as to what came to be called the physical and biological sciences, the latter were what French and English speakers generally meant by "science." Yet it was the broader, German sense of science—embracing humanistic and social scientific scholarship—that informed most efforts to address the promise of a scientific culture, whether in America, in Britain, or on the continent of Europe. Even this broader vision of science connoted a very distinctive human activity. The truths sought by *Wissenschaft* were exact and secular, and were "empirical" in the general, modern sense of this English word. They were discovered, not divined. Excluded were truths one might claim on the basis of religious experience, poetic insight, speculation, common sense, or practical but undisciplined experience in the workaday world.

What it meant to "know" even in this relatively limited, *wissenschaftliche* sense has remained uncertain enough to inspire epistemological controversies the intensity and range of which are themselves indicators of the culturally strategic position of knowledge in modern times. Yet people sensitive to these uncertainties have generally shared with the larger ranks of epistemologically untroubled commentators on *wissenschaftliche* knowledge a recognition that knowing is something special—a peculiarly referential enterprise—and that a culture organized around it is bound to differ from one organized around warfare, around business activities, or around fine arts. To look to man or woman as "knower" for cultural leadership is to expect relatively less from man or woman as soldier, as manager, as entrepreneur, as priest, as parent, as artificer, or as clown. This faith in the cultural capacities of man or woman as "knower" I propose to call "cognitivism." [17]

It is reasonable to protest that the last thing we need in the study of modern intellectual history is another "ism." We must already keep track of romanticism, Victorianism, socialism, historicism, and of course, modernism, to say nothing of all of the varieties of realism and idealism, and then of liberalism and conservatism. Where science and culture are discussed, one must pay due attention also to Naturalism, empiricism, positivism, and agnosticism. Yet none of these terms captures with appropriate specificity a faith in the cultural capacities of the *wissenschaftliche* knower. Those that come the closest serve also to entangle this faith with other, extraneous ideas. The various meanings of "naturalism" converge in the idea that a given phenomenon is to be explained in terms of the order of nature, rather than in terms of spiritual efficacy, cultural traditions, or some other nonnatural agency. Many cognitivists are also naturalists, but Naturalism takes its sense from nature, not from any distinctive human enterprise. Naturalism, moreover, is often taken to refer to a specific, distinctly biocentric conception of "man's place in nature," downplaying the qualities that distinguish the human species from the rest of the animal kingdom. "Positivism" does more directly address human knowledge as a foundation for culture, but prominent among the many variations of positivism are tendencies to restrict radically the sphere of knowledge, to separate knowledge very sharply from any authentic object of cognition, and to associate faith in science with the specific program advanced by Auguste Comte. Moreover, "positivism" has sometimes been taken to imply a belief in the absolute certainty of truly verified knowledge; cognitivism, while by definition generous in its assessment of the validity of what scientists at any given time choose to count as knowledge, is limited by no such extravagance.

The word "scientism" is sometimes taken to cover a range of ideas broader than either naturalism or positivism, but the common denominator of its many definitions is a highly censorious tone.

Although some scholars have sought to make it a neutral term for the support and admiration of science,[18] "scientism" is normally an opprobrious epithet directed at what the speaker regards as an arrogant or naive effort to extend the methods or authority of science into a field of experience where it does not belong.[19] Many expressions of cognitivism were arrogant or naive, or both, but to presume that all aspirations toward a scientific culture were thus "scientistic" is to confine our view of the movement to its most easily ridiculed manifestations.

This cognitive enthusiasm has reformulated and brought into the nineteenth and twentieth centuries some of the great idealistic and optimistic currents of the Baconian movement and of the Enlightenment. Knowledge has traditionally been felt to be a good thing, but cognitivism developed a sharper definition of knowledge and at the same time placed on the shoulders of knowledge as heavy a burden as it had ever been asked to carry. Men and women as knowers were to perpetuate what was most worthy in the Western tradition while placing under critical scrutiny what was least worthy; they were to create a culture congruent with and ultimately in control of the machines, the bureaucracies, and the system of capital accumulation and use we have come to associate with the term "modernization." Some cognitivists were more critical of classically modern institutions than were others. Critical as well as technocratic outlooks were elaborated extensively within the frame of cognitivism.[20] Cognitivism was a way of insisting that human beings and their knowledge defined modern civilization, or were capable of defining it. One might imagine that so "pro-modern" a cultural program might end up being called "modernism," [21] but the ironic confiscation of this term on behalf of the rather different movement culminating in the modernist literary canon may be a blessing in disguise. "Cognitivism" is a potentially more powerful concept, as it has a clearer, more particular referent: the Knower.

If the cultural hero most consistently identified with the modernist literary canon has been the self-sufficient artist, and if the cultural hero of the socialist movement has been the industrial worker, the cultural hero of cognitivism has been another major character in the drama of modern history: the professional scientist, in whom is most fully embodied our belief in our ability to *know*. All three of these "characters" reflect authentic collectivities of practicing human beings, but each is also a mystification developed in the interest of a program. The mystification of "the worker" by socialist intellectuals has been widely commented upon, and professional humanists are becoming increasingly aware of their own mystification of creative artists in the interests of advancing a culture at once responsive to the decline in authority of biblical religion and resistant to the hegemony of science. Such hegemony, in turn, has been promoted by the mystification of the professional scientist as first carried out on a large scale in the middle decades of the nineteenth century by T. H. Huxley and other ideologues of what was then a new professional role.[22] Hence it might make sense to speak in the present context of the Scientist, instead of the Knower. Indeed, this would seem all the more appropriate in view of the fact that the word "scientist" entered the English language only in the 1840s, exactly when the new "professional" inquirers appeared and their mystification began.[23] Yet the word "scientist" has come to be so extensively associated with the specific subject matter of the physical and biological sciences that its use here promises to obscure more than it clarifies. While some proponents of the physical and biological sciences have been willing to limit the realm of genuine "meanings" to the findings of these sciences (standing "agnostic," not "knowing" about anything else), cognitivism embraced many intellectuals who took knowledge to have a much wider scope.

The promise of thus identifying the Knower and the Artificer would be needlessly diminished were it construed only as an invitation to divide up individual intellectuals into columns purporting to list adherents of one cultural program or the other. Although both programs have had their pure exemplars (Charles Darwin and William Butler Yeats?) and true-believing ideological champions (Charles Peirce and Jean-Paul Sartre?), many of the careers we normally take to be major episodes in the intellectual history of the last century were responsive to both. Even Nietzsche, while providing the Artificer with an arsenal of nasty aphorisms to throw at the Knower, was unmistakably attracted to the latter.[24] William James's representation of the knowing enterprise as akin to the sculpting of a figure out of stone bespeaks an effort to bring the Artificer to bear on a theory of science.[25] American pragmatism as led by Dewey was profoundly under the sway of the ideal of the

Knower, but few thinkers of any time or place have insisted more indefatigably than Dewey that "finding" was a form of "making," that science entailed acting upon and reshaping the world rather than merely mirroring it. Proponents of a "realist" aesthetic from William Dean Howells to Georg Lukacs have resisted turning art into science while reaffirming the mission of the arts to tell truths closer to a sociologist's than to those of Blake or Proust. The chief significance of the Knower and Artificer is not that so many intellectuals were willing to choose one absolutely over the other, but that so many were willing to define the dilemmas and opportunities of modern culture so extensively in the terms of these two personae. This is illustrated by the construction of these dilemmas and opportunities found in three texts often taken as classics of the articulation of "modernism" in the United States: Joseph Wood Krutch's *The Modern Temper* (1929), Edmund Wilson's *Axel's Castle* (1931), and F. Scott Fitzgerald's *The Great Gatsby* (1925).

Knowing and artifice dominate *The Modern Temper* from its opening epigraph— lines of Mark Van Doren's contrasting the strivings of actors in the "game" of life with the ultimate judgments about these strivings made by "knowledge"—to Krutch's final, stoic resolution "to know rather than to be," to die cognizant rather than to sustain life by hiding from the facts. What we *know* about life is what renders impossible an option to which Krutch is strongly attracted: the treating of life "as an art" to be "lived by each person in accordance with the rules of his own being." Down this road of artifice are found not only nihilism, but anarchy. The world as it is has too many unmalleable realities to enable one to live in the mode of art. To do so would be to ignore all outside influences, material and moral, and to be fully autonomous and artificial. The artist creates out of the self, but the "scientist," on the other hand, "must submit to the judgment of others." Krutch's artist is the modern, self-sufficient Artificer and is thus not at all in the business of mimesis. Krutch's scientist is equally specific: not the individual "philosophical" inquirer, the generic savant, but the modern, intersubjective, empirical, professional Knower:

> The scientist . . . is in search of truths which owe their name to the fact that they correspond to something in the world outside himself, while the artist is in search of those which need to be true only in the sense that they seem true to him and that they hold good within the artificial universe which is inclosed within the frame of the work of art he is creating.

Krutch does not unambiguously endorse the Knower, for Krutch is dismayed at the unresponsive, thoroughly materialist universe he believes is the ultimate legacy of science. Yet the values Krutch prescribes for coping with a disenchanted world are exactly those of the Knower: we are to eschew imaginary certainties and comforting illusions in order to face relentlessly the truth, developing precisely those capacities for skepticism, disinterestedness, and rigorous analysis that alienate us from inherited values and diminish our chances for survival in a world dominated by physical appetites. The great choice for Krutch is between fiction and fact; the supreme satisfaction left to modern men and women is to be able to say that "whatever else we may be we are no longer dupes." Here, the Knower is no great liberator, as for Mill, for T. H. Huxley, or for many of Krutch's contemporaries among social scientists and liberal intellectuals.[26] The Knower for Krutch, as for Weber, lives in a field of contradictions, and embodies something of a tragic destiny; it represents what is simply the best available option in a world of diminished possibilities.[27]

Axel's Castle takes its name from an apotheosis of artifice, the extraordinary aesthete, Count Axel, created by Villiers de l'Isle-Adam in a story of 1890. The Count prefers the isolation of his Black Forest castle to social interaction, and insists that fantasy is more fulfilling than even the most heroic or sensually satisfying of worldly adventures. When presented with incalculable wealth and a beautiful woman with whom to spend it in the capitals of Europe and the Orient, Axel instead chooses death on the grounds that his imaginary version of this experience had been so intense as to render the reality of it unbearably banal. Wilson's sardonic account expresses his fascination with, as well as his revulsion at, the Symbolists' characteristic admiration for heroes who "would rather drop out of the common life than struggle to make themselves a place in it."

> He proposes that they [Axel and his prospective mate, who have just toured the world by imagination] shall kill themselves at once. Sara demurs: she suggests one night of love. But Axel begs her not to be trivial. "Oh, my beloved," he tries to explain to her, "tomorrow I should be the prisoner of thy wondrous body! Its delights would have enchained the chaste energy which animates me now!" . . . She pleads still: "But remember the human race!" "The example I leave it," he answers, "is well worth those it has given me." . . . And finally he succeeds in persuading her: they drink a goblet of poison together and perish in a rapture.

Wilson contrasts Axel to a second version of artifice, as represented by the fin-de-siècle quest of Arthur Rimbaud for a life of pure action. Wilson details Rimbaud's restless adventures in Africa and the Near East, culminating in his career as a desert trader in the Ogaden, surrounded by a harem of women from many tribes. In the extremity of Rimbaud's rejection of the conventions of all European culture, Wilson finds the specter of life considered "as if it were a great play." The "violence," the "moral interest," and "tragic completeness" of Rimbaud's performance leaves Wilson with the feeling of having "watched the human spirit, strained to its most resolute sincerity and in possession of its highest faculties, breaking itself" in an effort to escape the humiliations of compromise and chaos. While Wilson prefers Rimbaud's dynamism to the "leaden acquiescence in defeat" he finds even in Yeats—the greatest, in Wilson's view, of those to have followed the path of Axel— the chief significance for Wilson of the Rimbaud-Axel contrast is what both versions of artifice eschew: the challenge of social reality. Even when the symbolists turn in the direction of social criticism, Wilson complains, this criticism aims at nothing: "it is an exercise—Proust is the great example—of the pure intelligence playing luminously," driven by no social vision. Wilson admires the technical lessons in language taught by the Symbolists, but he wants to make social use of such lessons. Wilson notes that worthy tasks await to be performed with these new skills: writers may wish to connect with society "by studying it scientifically, by attempting to reform it, or by satirizing it." [28]

Wilson's hope is not to replace the Artificer with the Knower, but to "make art and science one." Following Alfred North Whitehead, Wilson viewed the intellectual history of the previous three centuries as a series of oscillations between objectivist and subjectivist enthusiasms. If the nineteenth-century naturalists "believed that composing a novel was like performing a laboratory experiment," their symbolist successors had gone to the other extreme, rendering poetry "even more a matter of the sensations and emotions of the individual than had been the case with Romanticism." That "this oscillation may finally cease," Wilson asks his literary comrades to update their understandings of science in keeping with the antimechanistic views of Whitehead and other contemporary commentators on science and philosophy: "the researches of science" do not, after all, yield so mechanical a universe as to drive the sensitive soul to create artificial worlds, nor are these researches, as carried out in the era of Einstein and Eddington, so methodologically alien to creativity in the arts as is presumed by the neo-romantic champions of artifice. Hence the key stroke in Wilson's critique of the Artificer is to confront its adherents with a more sophisticated construction of the Knower.[29]

If Wilson was something of a reconciler, determined to harvest the benefits of both major cultural ideals of his milieu, Fitzgerald left a more subtle and divided monument to the attractions of the Artificer and to the authority of the Knower. *The Great Gatsby* is about many things, but at its center is the supreme American artificer, James Gatz, the North Dakota nobody who made himself into the Long Island millionaire Jay Gatsby. Gatsby represents the effort to use as a guide to life a structure of meanings that is wholly fictional. Commentators on this novel have long emphasized a tension between its celebration of the human "capacity for wonder" and its "realistic" assessment of what the American social order had become by the 1920s. One can view this tension as the product of two stories that Fitzgerald managed to tell simultaneously. The first story is a myth-appreciating, artifice-respecting, idealist narrative: the figure created out of a "Platonic conception of himself" overcomes one material obstacle after another, and converts to his side the earthly and moralistic Nick Carraway, Fitzgerald's vehicle for the reader's emotions. After Gatsby's physical defeat and death, Carraway "becomes," as Frederick J. Hoffman has succinctly put it, "the guardian of Gatsby's illusion." Against the grain of this story cuts a second, demystifying-realist narrative based on what the reader is to accept as knowledge of the facts of life. The objects of this second story are the realities—the actual referents—to which Gatsby and other "American dreamers" are oblivious. Chief among these realities is the power of wealth and social standing, which crushes all pretenders, from the lowly Myrtle Wilson to Gatsby himself, whose dream is worth no more than the "obscene word" scrawled on the white steps of Gatsby's mansion by "some boy with a piece of brick."[30]

Shortly before writing *The Great Gatsby* Fitzgerald read with some appreciation one of the most purely cognitivist narratives ever written, James Harvey Robinson's *The Mind in the Making*. Yet the second story in *Gatsby* is not quite the fictional counterpart of Robinson's history of the triumph of the scientific intellect in Western civilization.[31] The knowledge Gatsby ignores is of the practical, commonsensical rather than the *wissenschaftliche* sort. Hence the second story in *Gatsby* has more in common with something else Fitzgerald read prior to writing *Gatsby*: the muckraking realism of Upton Sinclair. But if Fitzgerald's second story partakes of a "progressive" affirmation of socially validated truth, the affirmation is muted and ultimately suppressed by the rival, mystifying narrative. Carraway will not allow the obscene word to stand as Gatsby's benediction; he "erased it," drawing his shoe "raspingly along the stone." At the end of the novel we are unsure what Nick Carraway will do with the rest of his life, but we do know that bearing witness to Gatsby's "heightened sensitivity to the promises of life" (a point of the first narrative) is for Nick a more compelling mission than exposing in the public interest the illusory character of the American dream of upward social mobility (a point of the second). Fitzgerald's effect is thus to protect against what Krutch fears—that we shall be "dupes"—while at the same time enabling us to value creative imagination above all else, above even the close scrutiny of our actual condition.[32]

Whatever may be the sense in which these three literary works partake of a modernist impulse, each contains an element of cognitivism. Krutch and Wilson explicitly advance strategies of reference associated with contemporary science. All three books display in an adamantly post-Victorian, self-consciously modern context an engagement with strategies of both artifice and reference. These books also display a suspicion, if not a conviction, that the Knower and the Artificer are genuine rivals, potentially in contradiction to each other.

It need not follow from this vital sense of rivalry that we must regard cognitivism as mutually exclusive with the movement culminating in the consolidation of the modernist literary canon. Perhaps in the long run we shall come to speak routinely of "modernism" as a persuasion embracing both, rent by a tension between the Knower and the Artificer, yet defined by something else. Nothing of the sort is likely to happen until the cognitive tradition as such is recognized to an extent not remotely approached by the existing scholarship addressed to "modernism." Whatever the future of our analytic language for talking about the intellectual history of the twentieth century—whether the edifice of modernism is left in the hands of its old residents, or refashioned to accommodate cognitivism—we can at least distinguish cognitivism from the "canonical modernism" that has invested so much more in strategies of artifice than in strategies of reference. We can also identify some features common to both strategies that help to explain their simultaneous appeal.

One such common feature is sociopolitical: canonical modernism and cognitivism are both bourgeois in social base and offer means by which bourgeois society can be simultaneously criticized and perpetuated. This is simply to say that both have been most aggressively developed with Western, middle-class elites too dependent upon capitalism to take revolutionary steps against it yet possessed of enough misgivings about it to desire a culture at least independent of capitalism, and perhaps capable of giving instruction to it. The preoccupation with bourgeois society on the part of Mann, Proust, and other canonical modernists has been discussed with varying degrees of sympathy by a number of commentators.[33] Cognitivism's less volatile relationship with the prosperous, dominant middle classes of the Western democracies has been noted primarily in studies of liberal reformers hoping to install "science" as a basis for public policy.[34] To be sure, the Knower was sometimes invoked in relation to the decidedly nonbourgeois politics of Lenin, Trotsky, and Bukharin; and some servants of the Artificer—especially Ezra Pound—believed for a time that fascism was the political coordinate of their cultural ideal. Still, the sociopolitical histories of cognitivism and canonical modernism have consisted predominantly of various modes of accommodation with bourgeois society, especially the social democratic reform of it and the apolitical flight from it.

Cognitivism and canonical modernism also share acute self-consciousness. Scholars willing to define modernism very broadly have sometimes designated this self-consciousness as the "truly central insight of modernity." Paul de Man makes exactly this claim while criticizing colleagues for confining their picture of modernism to variations on "the Death of Reason." Modern thought "at its best," argues de Man, has featured "the persistent attempt of a consciousness to reach an understanding of itself." De Man has in mind

Rousseau, Hegel, and William and Henry James as well as
Nietzsche, Proust, and Dostoevsky; to these varied exemplars of his
modernism de Man contrasts both the "positivists" and the "primi-
tivists" who have surrendered the conscious mind to the "unques-
tioned hegemony of the physical world." [35] Certainly the ranks of
"positivists" (although "naturalists" might here be the more apt
term) include thinkers who have made this surrender, but a virtue
of the concept of "cognitivism" is its ability to capture and direct
our attention to the genuine element of self-consciousness we can
find in the writings of many of the greatest and most sympathetic
of commentators on the scientific enterprise: Herschel, Whewell,
Mill, Huxley, Helmholtz, Bernard, Peirce, Dewey, Weber,
Whitehead, Russell, Carnap, Popper, Kuhn, and Habermas. And in
what did Kant's "Copernican revolution in philosophy" consist? The
turning from an uncritical pursuit of the objects of the world to
the knowing process itself, the shift "inwards," as Ernest Gellner
has put it, "to our cognitive equipment, to our criteria of sound
knowledge." [36] None but Huxley of the names I have just invoked,
running chronologically from Kant to Kuhn and Habermas, are
even remotely guilty of the unquestioning "surrender" to physicality
against which de Man wants to define modernism. These scientists
and philosophers are the people who have constructed the Knower
as it has been taken up (often by others, and by some of these
thinkers themselves) as a cultural ideal. This is not to insist that
acute self-consciousness is equally significant to the Knower and to
the Artificer; on the contrary, the referential-generative dichotomy
essential to these two cultural ideals implies for the Artificer a
greater dependence upon, and consciousness of, the self.
Cognitivism and canonical modernism partake in different degrees
of the self-consciousness that so dominates nineteenth- and twentieth-century intellectual life.

A third common feature is perhaps the most important.
Cognitivism and canonical modernism are resoundingly postbiblical
and invoke humanist principles of authority. Both share a common
religious ancestry, and both entail serious, enduring revolts against
that ancestry. It is in the rejection of inherited religious authority
by the Knower and the Artificer that the acknowledged secularity
of modern intellectual life most obviously consists. The truth of
this in regard to canonical modernism was recently underscored by

Denis Donoghue. Searching for an appropriate starting point for clarifying the nature of modernism in literature and the arts, Donoghue identified a historical moment in the relations of science and religion: a moment Donoghue flags with the names Darwin, Renan, and First Vatican Council. Just then was "the force of a distinctively modern biblical scholarship" provocatively brought to bear on "the Old and New Testaments." Now, this moment happens also to mark a unique effusion of something Donoghue does not explicitly discuss: confidence in the cultural contributions of science. Donoghue is correct to characterize this historical moment as displaying "interrogative" relations with institutionalized authority and "a corresponding scruple, often regarded as fateful, in defense of one's own personal and spiritual integrity," but he develops these qualities only in regard to the standard literary modernism of Eliot, Joyce, Kafka, et al., and not at all in regard to the direct moral and professional descendants of the iconoclastic biblical scholars with whom he began. Who are these direct lineal descendants? The *wissenschaftliche* knowers who worked next door to the authors of the modern canon! Some of these scholars and scientists do attract Donoghue's attention—he mentions Simmel and Weber—but not as themselves the exemplars of any sensibility, only as helpful analysts of the material conditions that foster the socially alienated, subjectivist sensibility expressed by the great modern poets and novelists.[37] The point is not to insist that Donoghue should have assimilated cognitivism into modernism, but to call attention to a continuity between these two movements. Both partook of a struggle to ground spiritual authority in one set or another of distinctly human capabilities. The canonical modernists of interest to Donoghue looked for this authority inside individual selves, while the cognitivists looked to the intersubjective discipline of science.

Some adherents of both persuasions retained religious connections, but this fact does not alter the case. At issue is the matrix out of which the meanings that constitute culture are understood to be developed. Although some individuals and groups can be found to insist that, for them, this matrix is singly biblical-ecclesiastical, scientific, artistic, or something else, most constructions of this matrix are implicitly or explicitly plural and eclectic. Hence the matter is relative, and what makes so much of our culture secular is the weakened authority of the Bible in this matrix, relative especially to knowing and artifice. There is room for quarreling, moreover, about the significance of the religious affirmations announced by some of the canonical modernists: was the Christianity of the later Eliot justified by an essentially aesthetic principle, and thus controlled by Eliot's loyalty to the ideal of the Artificer? Even if this quarrel were resolved in the negative by attributing to the later Eliot a pristine and unaffected biblicism, Eliot's reputation as a modernist was already made by his earlier, profoundly secular poems and essays.

The word "modernism" achieved its initial currency within a distinctly theological discourse, but neither does this fact diminish the postbiblical character of the movement this word later came to denote. During the last third of the nineteenth century and the first third of the twentieth, "modernists" were theological liberals inclined to reformulate the Christian gospel in terms compatible with the general outlook and specific findings of "modern science." [38] Although "modernism" was sometimes a pejorative term in this context, the label came to be widely accepted, especially in the United States, where one of its most prominent spokesmen declared it in 1924 to consist in *"the use of the methods of modern science to find, state and use the permanent and central values of inherited orthodoxy in meeting the needs of a modern world."* [39] The tradition of religious modernism, then, presents in relation to knowing the same question presented in relation to artifice by the putative orthodoxy of the likes of Eliot: were the liberal enthusiasts for a more scientific religion not themselves postbiblical, for all their protests to the contrary? Even were this query resolved in the negative, and no aspersions cast on the claims of the liberals to an authentically biblical faith, religious modernism was—by virtue of its confidence in a benevolent deity and in a potentially harmonious relation between the individual soul and modern social institutions—so distant from the preoccupations of the canonical poets, novelists, and philosophers of secular modernism as to render all the more ironic the transferral of the same name from one modernism to the other. [40]

If cognitivism and canonical modernism shared some qualities that help us to understand their simultaneous appeal to intellectuals of the last century or more, the fact remains that canonical modernism is a more distinctly twentieth-century phenomenon.

Cognitivism crossed Virginia Woolf's great divide. Dewey and Popper remained closer to Mill and Whewell than Yeats and Kafka were to Tennyson and Arnold. Yet there is a danger in regarding cognitivism as merely a lingering, nineteenth-century enthusiasm. The Knower not only survived the emergence of the Artificer and long coexisted with it, but, after being blown about by various winds of epistemological doctrine, has remained on hand to observe canonical modernism's recent, much-ballyhooed decline.[41]

Canonical modernism's decline is now measured chiefly in relation to "postmodernism," but two remarkable, apparent features of this new sensibility are its receptivity to strategies of artifice and its hostility to strategies of reference. One treatise after another on the transition from modernism to postmodernism informs us that postmodernism is radically nonreferential. We also learn that postmodernism treats history as a repository of images and insights to be rearranged in any synchronic order that an individual may will into being: it is discontinuity-affirming. Canonical modernism, it would seem, did not go far enough in exactly the directions that most distinguished that modernism from the cognitivist tradition.[42] "The new age of postmodernity," explains one observer, will be free from the "metaphysical and homocentric illusions" of modernism. Rather, that new age, continues Richard Wolin,

> will in a Nietzschean vein become *an age of sheer illusion*, since the inhibiting, hypocritical metaphysical dualisms of 'truth' and 'falsehood,' 'good' and 'evil,' 'reality' and 'illusion' will have been vanquished and the pure play of 'difference' will come into its own. We must be liberated from history and historical thinking in general, since history, as the pernicious realm of 'referentiality,' represents an insupportable condition or limitation placed on the present. Historical thinking, thinking in terms of continuity, contains overt identitarian biases which prove inimical to the proliferation of difference. The new ideal is that of the reign of 'free-floating signifiers,' signifiers fully emancipated from the tyranny of the 'referent,' signifiers that are unconditioned.[43]

To suggest that postmodernism might just as well be called "postcognitivism" would be too much, of course, but the parts of modernism against which postmodernism is the most sharply defined would seem to have less to do with the Artificer than with the Knower.[44] Could there be a more striking index of the extent to which the term "modernism" dominates our discussion of the intellectual history of the early and middle decades of this century? There is nothing else *against* which to define cultural novelty.

The Knower and the Artificer are historically specific concentrations of ideas: they combine, intensify, and reformulate certain elements of a cultural inventory inherited by the intellectuals who made and used them. Although constructs of such generality invite oversimplification, our need for basic tools to work with the strivings of bourgeois, postbiblical, self-conscious American and European intellectuals during the last century is manifest; and the concept of "modernism" has proven to be a crude instrument. It would be a scholastic conceit to imagine that a little fussing with words can cause the field to fall into coherent order, but it may help to at least connect some of our words to historically specific cultural ideals.

The fate of the Knower and of the Artificer is now uncertain. One result of calling them out into the open is surely to confront the potential confinements of each, and to feed a healthy suspicion toward any culture designed by one without the criticism of the other. Some may also find the old conflict between the Knower and the Artificer a bit stale, and wish for an altogether new, or at least different, set of strategic exemplars. But it may be too early to consign either or both of these figures exclusively to the past. Should our coming fin-de-siècle yield a new sensibility to challenge postmodernism for the loyalties of the most methodologically self-conscious of our postbiblical, bourgeois intellectuals, it would be no surprise to find the Knower enlisted in the cause.

Notes

1. E.g., Frank Kermode, "The Modern," an essay of 1965 reprinted in Kermode's collection, *Modern Essays* (London, 1971), 66, and Robert Martin Adams, "What Was Modernism?" *Hudson Review* (1978): 32–33.

2. For an unusually self-conscious example of the genre, see Phyllis Rose, "Modernism: The Case of Willa Cather," in Robert Kiely, ed., assisted by John Hildebidle, *Modernism Reconsidered* (Cambridge, Mass., 1983), 122–45, esp. 123–24 and 142–45.

3. Raymond Seidelman, with the assistance of Edward J. Harpham, *Disenchanted Realists: Political Science and the American Crisis, 1884–1984* (Albany, N.Y., 1985), 9–10. Apart from its utility as an example of a certain use of "modernism," this is a thoughtful, fresh study of its subject.

4. The best recent work of this orientation addressed to an episode in American history is Daniel J. Singal, *The War Within: From Victorian to Modernist Thought in the South, 1919–1945* (Chapel Hill, 1982).

5. Peter Gay, *Freud, Jews, and Other Germans: Masters and Victims in Modern Culture* (New York, 1978), 23.

6. Paul de Man,"What Is Modern?" *New York Review of Books* (26 August 1965): 10–13; Richard Ellmann and Charles Feidelson, Jr., eds., *The Modern Tradition: Backgrounds of Modern Literature* (New York, 1965). De Man's characterization is not unfair, although the editors did manage to include brief selections from Immanuel Kant, Karl Marx, John Dewey, and Matthew Arnold.

7. Anthony Quinton, "Which Philosophy Is Modernistic?" in Quinton, *Thoughts and Thinkers* (London, 1982), 39–50. See also the interpretation of modernism and postmodernism in Allan Megill, *Prophets of Extremity: Nietzsche, Heidegger, Foucault, Derrida* (Berkeley, 1985). Megill's work is highly pertinent, but I did not see it until this essay had been completed. Megill's discussion of his subject-philosophers in terms of an overarching aestheticist impulse is fully consistent with the way of talking about modernism for which I argue here.

8. Singal, *The War Within*, e.g., 4, 314. Cf. the interpretation of "postprogressive social theory" in terms of the sensibility of literary modernism in Howard Brick, *Daniel Bell and the Decline of Intellectual Radicalism: Social Theory and Political Reconciliation in the 1940s* (Madison, 1986), esp. 38–39.

9. Gay, *Freud, Jews, and Other Germans*, 21, 26–27.

10. I have sought to interpret this episode in "The Canon and Its Keepers: Modernism and Mid-Twentieth-Century American Intellectuals," in my *In the American Province: Studies in the History and Historiography of Ideas* (Bloomington, Ind., 1985), 74–91.

11. James Joyce, *The Portrait of the Artist as a Young Man* (New York, 1916), 253; Oscar Wilde, "Phrases and Philosophies for the Use of the Young," in Richard Ellmann, ed., *The Artist as Critic: Critical Writings of Oscar Wilde* (London, 1970), 433.

12. Rose, "Modernism," 142.

13. Hugh Kenner, *A Homemade World: The American Modernist Writers* (New York, 1975). My sense of the Artificer, and of its role in modernist literature, owes much to this work. I am also much indebted to the many articles in Malcom Bradbury and James McFarlane, eds., *Modernism, 1890–1930* (London, 1976).

14. Robert B. Pippin, "Nietzsche and the Origin of the Idea of Modernism," *Inquiry* 26 (1983): 151.

15. Friedrich Nietzsche, *Beyond Good and Evil*, trans. Walter Kaufmann (New York, 1966), 126, 128 (emphasis in original).

16. A selection of Whewell's work has recently been made easily available; see William Whewell, *Selected Writing on the History of Science*, ed. Yehuda Elkana (Chicago, 1984).

17. Outside the perimeter of cognitivism there has always remained a more restricted sense of science's value: science could provide us with facts, laws, and various material benefits, but it could not be expected to serve as a primary source of meanings, as a foundation for culture. In this view, the scientist is not a cultural hero, but merely the provider of technical information useful to a society that derives from other sources the meanings it assigns to important human experiences.

18. E.g, Joseph Ben-David, *The Scientist's Role in Society: A Comparative Study* (Englewood Cliffs, N.J., 1971), 78.

19. For a discussion of this fact about usage, see Fritz Machlup, *Knowledge and Production of Knowledge* (Princeton, 1980), 77. Gerald Holton uses the word "scientism" to denote "addiction to science": Gerald Holton, "Modern Science and the Intellectual Tradition," in Paul C. Obler and Herman A. Estrin, eds., *The New Scientist: Essays on the Methods and Values of Modern Science* (New York, 1962), 31. Roland N. Stromberg defines it as a highly utopian and sectarian persuasion: "the view that scientific knowledge is the only valid kind, and can solve all human problems": Roland N. Stromberg, in his editorial introduction to *Realism, Naturalism, and Symbolism: Modes of Thought and Expression in Europe, 1848–1914* (New York, 1968), x–xi.

20. Dewey, for example, found much fault with these institutions, while his sanguine contemporary, Robert A. Millikan, regarded them as the natural and unproblematic benefits of "science." An especially strong example of Dewey's combination of confidence in "knowing" and his critical attitude toward the political status quo of his era is his *The Public and Its Problems* (New York, 1927); Millikan's notorious Babbitry in the name of science is manifest, for example, in his *Science and the New Civilization* (New York, 1930).

21. The disjunction between the literature on modernization and modernism has been often noticed recently; one book largely inspired by this disjunction is Marshall Berman, *All That Is Solid Melts into Air: The Experience of Modernity* (New York, 1981). In a perspicacious review of this book, Leo Bersani calls attention to Berman's effort to defend a "good," humanistic, largely nineteenth-century modernism— embracing Marx and Goethe, even—against a "bad," dehumanized, twentieth-century modernism; see Bersani, "Who Are the True Modernists?" *New York Times Book Review* (14 February 1982): 9, 29.

22. I have addressed this mystification in my "Inquiry and Uplift: Late Nineteenth Century American Academics and the Moral Efficacy of Scientific Practice," in Thomas L. Haskell, ed., *The Authority of Experts Studies in History and Theory* (Bloomington, Ind., 1984), 141–56, and in my "Justification by Verification: The Scientific Challenge to the Moral Authority of Christianity in Modern America," in Michael Lacey, ed., untitled volume on religion and American intellectual history, forthcoming.

23. Sidney Ross, "Scientist: The Story of a Word," *Annals of Science* 18 (1962): 65–85.

24. See Nietzsche's various meditations on "the will to truth," e.g., in *The Genealogy of Morals*, trans. Francis Golffing (1956), 289, 297, and in *The Gay Science*,

trans. Walter Kaufmann (New York, 1974), 280–83. See also Mary Warnock, "Nietzsche's Conception of Truth," in Malcolm Pasley, ed., *Nietzsche: Imagery and Thought* (Berkeley, 1978), 33–63, esp. 58–62, and John T. Wilcox, *Truth and Value in Nietzsche* (Ann Arbor, 1974), 98, 171.

25. James's reference to the sculptor is in William James, *The Will to Believe* (Cambridge, Mass., 1979), 103. See also my "William James and the Culture of Inquiry" in my *Province*, 3–22.

26. Joseph Wood Krutch, *The Modern Temper: A Study and a Confession* (New York, 1929), vii, 103, 107, 114, 124, 169. For an excellent study of this text, see Peter Gregg Slater, "The Negative Secularism of *The Modern Temper:* Joseph Wood Krutch," *American Quarterly* 33 (Summer 1981): 185–205. Although Slater is primarily concerned to illuminate Krutch's religious sensibility, I believe my analysis is consistent with his.

27. Krutch's despair can be compared with the less deterministic construction Robert Penn Warren attributes to Jack Burden when hesitating to open a telegram Burden soon realizes he must confront. "The end of man is knowledge, but there is one thing he can't know . . . whether knowledge will save him or kill him. He will be killed, all right, but he can't know whether he is killed because of the knowledge which he has got or because of the knowledge which he hasn't got and which if he had it, would save him. . . you have to open the envelope, for the end of man is to know." When Warren leaves his protagonist at the end of his novel, Burden is indeed engaged in a project of *wissenschaftliche* knowing, which Warren requires him to complete before "going out of history into history and the awful responsibility of time": he is writing a work of historical scholarship. Robert Penn Warren, *All the King's Men* (New York, 1946; Bantam Edition, 1951), 9, 438.

28. Edmund Wilson, *Axel's Castle: A Study in the Imaginative Literature of 1870–1930* (New York, 1931), 263–64, 266, 282–83, 287, 290.

29. Ibid., 3, 5–6, 20, 294–98. Alfred North Whitehead's *Science and the Modern World* (New York, 1925) is a resoundingly cognitivist interpretation of Western thought since the seventeenth century. The frequency with which it is quoted by Wilson and many others is a mark of the authority of cognitivism among literary intellectuals of the era.

30. F. Scott Fitzgerald, *The Great Gatsby* (New York, 1925), 2, 99, 181–82; Frederick J. Hoffman, *The 20's: American Writing in the Postwar Decade*, rev. ed. (New York, 1962), 140.

31. Such a fictional counterpart did exist at the same moment: another literary landmark of 1925, Sinclair Lewis's *Arrowsmith*, in which the laboratory scientist was explicitly celebrated as a moral exemplar.

32. Fitzgerald, *Gatsby*, 2, 181; Fitzgerald's reactions to James Harvey Robinson and Upton Sinclair are discussed in Robert Sklar, *F. Scott Fitzgerald: The Last Laocoon* (New York, 1967), 148–49.

33. E.g., Lionel Trilling, *Beyond Culture Essays on Literature and Learning* (New York, 1965), esp. 30, and Georg Lukacs, "The Ideology of Modernism," in

Lukacs, *The Meaning of Contemporary Realism*, trans. John and Necke Mander (London, 1962), 17–46.

34. The freshest and most discerning treatment of this episode in social thought is found within a recent work of wider scope, James T. Kloppenberg, *Uncertain Victory: Social Democracy and Progressivism in European and American Thought, 1870–1920* (New York, 1986).

35. De Man, "What Is Modern?" 12–13.

36. Ernest Gellner, *Legitimation of Belief* (Cambridge, Eng., 1974), 28.

37. Denis Donoghue, "The Promiscuous Cool of Postmodernism," *New York Times Book Review* (22 June 1986): 36.

38. The ranks of the theological liberals conventionally called "modernist" also included some who moved in a noncognitive direction, following Schlieiermacher in an emphasis on "religious feelings." Yet this mystical strain was not denoted as "modernist" until its adherents made common cause against orthodoxy with the more scientifically oriented thinkers to which the notion of modernism became more firmly attached. For the history of both the mystical and the cognitive strains of religious liberalism, see William R. Hutchinson, *The Modernist Impulse in American Protestantism* (Cambridge, Mass., 1976).

39. Shailer Mathews, *The Faith of Modernism* (New York, 1924), 23 (emphasis in original).

40. The centrality of religious liberalism to the concept of modernism was apparent as late as the early 1930s. See, for example, Horace Kallen's article, "Modernism," in *The Encyclopedia of the Social Sciences* 10: 564–68. This article is an important episode in the history of the concept of modernism. Kallen defines all forms of modernism as accommodations to the advance of science; see esp. 565.

41. As Eugene Lunn puts it with appropriate weariness: "For approximately three decades now, we have been hearing of the end of the avant-garde; the absorption of modernist techniques into advertising in a consumer society; the rejection of the difficult aesthetic forms of the early twentieth century by many recent writers and artists; or, in general, the exhaustion of the modernist creative impulse." Eugene Lunn, *Marxism and Modernism: An Historical Study of Lukacs, Brecht, Benjamin and Adorno* (Berkeley, 1982), 282.

42. The argument that postmodernism consists in the intensification of the sensibilities and strategies of canonical modernism has been made compellingly by Gerald Graff, "The Myth of the Postmodernist Breakthrough, *TriQuarterly* 26 (1973): 383–417.

43. Richard Wolin, "Modernism vs. Postmodernism," *Telos* 62 (Winter 1984–85): 26 (emphasis in original). It should be pointed out that Wolin offers this characterization of postmodernism without endorsing what he describes. See also Donoghue, "Promiscuous Cool," 37.

44. This suspicion is reinforced by Richard Rorty's recent adoption of the term "postmodernist" to describe his campaign to liberate modern liberal thought from rationalism, especially of the Kantian variety. See Rorty, "Postmodernist Bourgeois Liberalism," *Journal of Philosophy* 80 (1983): 583–89, and Rorty, "Habermas and Lyotard on Postmodernity," in Richard Bernstein, ed., *Habermas and Modernity* (Cambridge, Mass., 1985), 161–75.

æ

What Have Modernists
Looked At?
Experiential Roots of
Twentieth-Century
American Painting

George H. Roeder, Jr.
The School of the Art Institute of Chicago

One cannot live on a visual diet of skyscrapers and produce the
same sort of art as one who fed visually on the Acropolis.
—Jacques Lipchitz[1]

If this acknowledgment is poorly written it is because this is the only part of the
article that has not benefited from one or more careful readings from Daniel
Joseph Singal, who proved equally adept at everything from helping me to clarify
the article's organizing concepts to getting commas in the right place. James
McManus, Douglas W. Nelson, and Janice Radway each read one or more drafts
of the article, and made visible to me flaws that otherwise would have gone
uncorrected and the possibilities that might not have been developed. I also am
grateful for the assistance I received from Emile de Antonio, Thomas Briggs,
Roger Gilmore, Roland Hansen, Anthony Jones, Donna Linden, Robert Loescher,
Garnett McCoy, Virginia Ormsby Roeder, Robert Skaggs, Thomas Sloan, Shirley
Wajda, Sandi Wisenberg, Colin Westerbeck, and my colleagues and students at
the School of the Art Institute of Chicago and at Northwestern University. The
School of the Art Institute provided travel money, which allowed me to do the
type of research that mattered most in writing this article: looking at paintings.

AT THE BEGINNING OF EMILE DE ANTONIO'S BRILLIANT FILM ON POST–
World War II American painting, *Painters Painting*, the screen fills
with what seems to be a familiar type of modern art: bold, precise
horizontal and vertical black lines on a white background with a
carefully placed dash of red. As the camera pulls back viewers discover that what they had been reading as a painting was instead a
shot of a fire door (the dash of red) high up on the grid-like
facade of an international-style New York building. In the spirit of
de Antonio's opening sequence, this article studies the meaning of
modernism as manifested in American painting by relating what
artists have made to what they have seen, by asking "what have
modernists looked at?" Because the way in which one looks at the
world shapes what one sees, implicit in the first question is a second: "how have modernists looked at what they have looked at?"

The "modernists" whose habits of looking I examine are
American artists of the past seventy-five to eighty years who, finding that the early twentieth-century academic traditions of painting that prevailed in this country (and that have continued to
influence public expectations as to what art should be) did not
allow them to express the experiential reality of contemporary life,
broke sharply with these traditions in order to narrow the gap
between experience and expression. This emphasis on the relation between seeing and making does not deny the importance of
other major thrusts of modernism, such as the expression of the
artist's inner experience and self-conscious exploration of painting as a medium. As will be seen, the way artists conceived of and
translated into paint these introspective and formal/conceptual
concerns often was influenced by and had an influence on their
visual experience. Because the conditions that made modernism
possible affected almost all twentieth-century American artists, and
because this chapter pays equal attention to these conditions and
to the art they engendered, some of the artists discussed do not
fit neatly into the "broke sharply" definition of "modernist," a
definition clarified by the examples and explanations that follow.
However, it is these artists who do fit the definition clearly that I
have most in mind when I suggest a three-part answer to the
question "what have modernists looked at?"—new things, parts of
things, everything.

New Things

Americans, at first especially those in urban areas, have had abundant inducement and opportunity to look at new things during the past century and a half. Train, automobile, and airplane, illustrated magazine, photograph, motion picture, and television, visual aids to education, scientific exploration, and the concept and practice of planned obsolescence—all have given innumerable producers, retailers, financiers, promotional agents, media people, designers, educators, performers, and public officials, as well as artists, reasons to excite and satisfy a desire among the citizenry for new things to look at. Modernist painters have played only a small role in this vast transformation of American visual experience. Despite that fact, their art, ever since the 1913 Armory Show alerted millions of Americans to its existence, has been an emblem of the rapidity and perplexing nature of visual change in contemporary life.

Among the new things scrutinized most carefully by the first American modernists were recent European paintings. The first large American show of advanced European painting came in an 1886 New York "Impressionist" exhibition that included paintings by Monet, Degas, Manet, Seurat, and other artists whose works, in retrospect, hovered near the vague chronological and conceptual boundary between traditional and modern art. For the next two decades, artists who wished to see what was happening in Europe after Impressionism had to go to the source. Ambitious American artists had been crossing the Atlantic since the colonial period for inspiration and training, but to an extent reminiscent of explorer/artist John White's trip in the other direction in 1585, some early-twentieth-century travelers encountered a visual new world that changed their lives. Often the transforming experience came at 27, rue de Fleurus, in Paris, the quarters of Gertrude and Leo Stein. Here soon-to-be or recently become modernists such as Max Weber, Alfred Maurer, Arthur B. Frost, Jr., H. Lyman Saÿen, Patrick Henry Bruce, Morgan Russell, Marsden Hartley, Manierre Dawson, Arthur Dove, and Charles Demuth came for conversation and the chance to look at works by Cézanne, Picasso, Matisse, and other, mostly French, modernists. Americans also had occasional opportunities to view non-French works: Joseph Stella saw Italian Futurist painting and sculpture at a 1912 Paris exhibition, and

Marsden Hartley encountered German Expressionism in Berlin around the time World War I began.

Until World War II almost all American artists with a serious interest in the new art found ways of visiting Europe, but increasingly they also had opportunities to see this work in the United States. Initially the only place for modernist-watching was New York, where modern paintings joined all the other new things in a city establishing a claim as the world center for visual novelty. In 1907 Alfred Stieglitz, a master of one recent addition to the realm of visual experience, photography, began showing modern paintings at his small "291" gallery on Fifth Avenue. In the five years prior to the Armory Show he had exhibited works by Europeans such as Matisse and Picasso, and by a majority of America's earliest modernists, including Maurer, Weber, Hartley, Dove, Abraham Walkowitz, and John Marin. Many artists and critics found their way to "291," but since Stieglitz's two rooms could accommodate only about a dozen viewers at a time and he refused to be a publicist, his audience remained limited.[2]

Few limits of any sort applied to the Armory Show, which established modern art as a visual fact of American life.[3] Organized by a group of artists whose own work ranged from the moderate side of modernism to the progressive side of traditionalism, the show gave several hundred thousand people in New York, Chicago, and Boston their first encounter with the revolution in painting and sculpture, and achieved on a grand scale the organizers' desire to create a sensation. The show included, among many others, works by Van Gogh, Gauguin, Cézanne, Matisse, Derain, Braque, and Picasso, and by about one-half of the dozen or so American artists who had already developed modernist styles. Among the artists whose work was radicalized by this visual assault/feast were Stuart Davis, Charles Sheeler, Andrew Dasburg, Henry Fitch Taylor, Tom Benrimo, and Glenn Coleman.[4]

Partly due to the success of the show, there were approximately 250 exhibitions of modern art in the next five years, most taking place at dealer galleries in New York. During the 1920s museums in Chicago, Philadelphia, Dallas, Cleveland, Boston, and other cities mounted exhibitions of modernist works. By 1929 the opening in New York of the Museum of Modern Art (MOMA) and other institutions committed to modernism, and the addition of modern

Alfred Stieglitz, *From the Shelton Hotel,* n.d. The Metropolitan Museum of Art, The Alfred Stieglitz Collection, 1949 (49.55.45). Stieglitz challenged artists to create paintings as visually compelling as the urban landscapes outside of their studios. The city's visual dynamism provided not a model to be copied, but a standard to be matched.

paintings to the permanent collections of museums in at least twenty-five other cities, assured continuous, if selective, showing of modern works even during the 1930s, when hard times and international conflict led to sharp questioning of modernism's inaccessibility to the larger public. As American art achieved preeminence after World War II, modern paintings became so common in urban areas that virtually all aspiring artists had at least some visual experience of modernist work.

At first most European modern paintings on view in this country were French; notable exceptions included single paintings by Ernst Kirchner and Wassily Kandinsky at the Armory Show. Further insight into forms taken elsewhere by modernism was provided by travelers such as Hartley and Stella, and by immigrant artists. According to the report of disgruntled Princeton art historian Frank Jewett Mather, most work at the 1921 Independent Show was of "the Post-Impressionist type," most of the exhibitors seemed to be recent immigrants, and among these "a high proportion [were] Russian and German Jews."[5] Political turmoil and repression in Hitler's Europe greatly increased the transatlantic flow of modernists in the years before and during World War II. Among those who arrived between 1930 and 1945 were Josef Albers, Marc Chagall, Salvador Dali, Max Ernst, Stanley Hayter, Hans Hofmann, Fernand Légèr, Jacques Lipchitz, André Masson, Lazlo Moholy-Nagy, Piet Mondrian, Amedee Ozenfant, and Yves Tanguy. Nor did American modernists restrict their looking to unequivocally modernist work; in the 1930s some were influenced by the expressive, politically charged, representational work of visiting Mexican muralists José Clemente Orozco, Diego Rivera, and David Siqueiros.

The purposeful activities of individuals and organizations also helped determine which paintings artists had been able to look at. Because of New York gallery owner Julien Levy's interest in Surrealism, residents of Hartford, Connecticut, had the chance to see a large show of works by Dali, Masson, Tanguy, and other Surrealists in 1931, before most Europeans had the opportunity.[6] Especially influential were MOMA's controversial collection and exhibition policies, which initially favored formally sophisticated European work, but which provided visitors to the museum or to its widely seen traveling exhibits a visible demonstration of modernism's diversity. For example, numerous paintings by American modernists record the impact of three quite different MOMA shows mounted in 1936: "Cubism and Abstract Art," "Fantastic Art, Dada, and Surrealism," and a traveling Van Gogh exhibition. The opportunity to look carefully and frequently at a particular painting often has been important to artists. The presence of Seurat's *Sunday Afternoon on the Island of the Grand Jatte* (1884–86) in the collection of the Art Institute of Chicago has influenced dozens of modernists in that city.[7] Recently, vigorous promotion of new Italian and German art has assured this work exposure in American art schools and museums.

Such influences, however, result from interaction between what there is to see and what viewers are disposed to look at. European modernist paintings—mostly products of an urban sensibility even when painted in the country or on a South Seas island—captured the imagination of American artists partly because other new things that these artists saw around them created a visual context into which the European works could fit. Visitors to the 1913 exhibition encountered signs of dramatic visual change outside as well as inside of Manhattan's 69th Regiment Armory. Most conspicuous were the new "skyscrapers" thrusting into previously inviolate air space. The Woolworth Building, which opened the month after the Armory Show closed, became, at 792 feet, the tallest in the world until overtaken at the end of the next decade by the Chrysler Building, itself soon surpassed by the Empire State Building. Nearly three times as high as the steeple of Trinity Church (1846), the tallest structure in New York until 1890, the Woolworth was a hard-to-ignore visual reminder of the obsolescence of constraints that had governed previous human activity. The function as well as size of recent buildings testified to change: a few decades earlier there would have been no need for the Grand Central Terminal, which had opened just two weeks before the Armory Show, or the movie theaters, department stores, highly differentiated factories, and public museums that appeared around the same time.

Interest in skyscrapers and other city sights seemed universal, and many different artists incorporated images of them into their works. Sometimes the desire to record the sensations of urban life led artists to challenge traditional conceptions of beauty, technical proficiency, and nobility of purpose honored by art schools, museums, and especially the National Academy of Design (NAD), which, with the European counterparts from which it was derived, had given academic art its name and definition. NAD standards, although not rigidly codified or strictly followed, carried considerable weight because participation in NAD's legitimizing exhibitions was of great importance to artists who wished to sell their works to prestigious institutions and collectors. The NAD encouraged stylistic diversity, innovation, and personal expression in moderate doses but not to the extent of threatening the traditions it defended. These traditions required well-composed and carefully drawn portrayals of dignified subject matter, use of Renaissance conventions of perspective and other techniques that created an illusionary representation of the "real" world into which viewers could peer, and avoidance of excess, whether in the form of flamboyant color or conspicuous display of the artist's emotions. An early challenge to these traditions came in the decade before the Armory Show from John Sloan, George Luks, and other painters inspired by artist/teacher Robert Henri, who was more interested in getting "life" into paintings than in respecting restrictive conventions.[8] These painters offended many academicians when they depicted in their work gritty realities of urban life (leading later writers to refer to them as the "Ash Can School") or when, drawing on the experience some had as newspaper illustrators, they gave their finished paintings the feel of sketches in order to convey the rapid change characteristic of the urban scene.

The difference between the Henri group and those artists who clearly satisfy the definition of "modernist" turns on the interpretation of the phrase "broke sharply with prevailing traditions." The Henri group challenged and stretched, but still worked mainly within those traditions. Modernists did not. Most obviously, they did not restrict themselves, as the Henri group usually did, to paintings that, in the commonly understood meaning of the term, "looked like" the depicted subjects. Max Weber's description of one of the series of paintings he did of New York between 1912 and 1916 suggests why his canvas was covered by a dynamic pattern of form and color, derived in part from his visual encounters with the city, rather than with a traditionally realistic depiction of buildings: "Electrically illumined contours of buildings, rising height

Louis Lozowick, *Cleveland*, 1923. National Museum of American Art, Smithsonian Institution, Gift of Adele Lozowick.

upon height against the blackness of the sky now diffused, now interknotted, now interpierced by occasional shafts of colored light. Altogether—a web of colored geometric shapes, characteristic only of the Grand Canyons of New York at night." [9]

If Weber found established traditions inadequate for portraying the sensations of urban life, Louis Lozowick, in order to reveal the underlying structure obscured by the sensations, stripped his paintings of expected particularizing detail. He wrote, amidst the urban growth of the 1920s, that "the dominant trend in America of today, beneath all the apparent chaos and confusion is towards order and organization which find their outward sign and symbol in the rigid geometry of the American city: in the verticals of its smoke stacks, in the parallels of its car tracks, the squares of its streets, the cubes of its factories, the arc of its bridges, the cylinders of its gas tanks." [10] Neither Weber nor Lozowick had as their primary goal the expression of one particular visual experience; rather, they wished to respond to certain qualities of contemporary visual experience, and could not do so without violating academic conventions.

Throughout the century modernists have continued to suggest new ways of looking at the city, while the look of the city has encouraged further development of modernism. Modernism's wide range, extending often to the point of contradiction, has proved well suited to capturing the dynamic activity and underlying regularities, the excitement and despair, the collective achievement and ingrained violence of urban life. Among the many modern paintings which indicate that their makers looked closely at the urban visual environment are Stuart Davis's heterophonic compositions, which make visible rhythmic links and oppositions that bring together yet keep distinct disparate elements in the seeming visual chaos of urban life; George Tooker's ominous *The Subway* (1950), which shows urban masses channeled into conformity by the bars, cubicles, and corridors of their constructed environment; and Richard Estes' "superrealist" cityscapes, which surpass the limits of traditional art by providing viewers with an overlay of reflected and directly observed images that are more intricate, yet more precisely defined, than any which could be perceived in an actual visit to the site depicted. Paintings by these artists, and by Marin, Georgia O'Keeffe, Roger Brown, and other modernists whose works show the influence of their urban experience, represent records of the impact of the modern city's unique visual presence on some of its keenest observers.

The absence of centuries-old rivals made new buildings more visually dominant in American cities than they were in Europe,

George Tooker, *The Subway*, 1950. Collection of Whitney Museum of American Art, New York, Juliana Force Purchase.

and the same can be said of other objects made possible by new mechanical, chemical, and electronic technologies increasingly found in American life. This was particularly obvious to outsiders such as French painter Francis Picabia, who exclaimed in the midst of a 1915 trip to the United States that his visit had "brought about a complete revolution in my methods of work. . . . Almost immediately upon coming to America it flashed on me that the genius of the modern world is in machinery and that through machinery art ought to find a most vivid expression." [11] According to Mexican-born caricaturist Marius de Zayas, a member of the Stieglitz circle, academic traditions blinded most Americans to the artistic possibilities of the mechanized civilization emerging around them. Yet exposure to attitudes such as Picabia's and to European movements intoxicated with the promise of modern technology helped artists such as Lozowick and Joseph Stella see their surroundings in new ways. When the Ukrainian-born Lozowick came to the United States in 1906 he found skyscrapers "forbidding." By the 1920s, inspired by his encounters with Fernand Légèr's paintings and the works and ideas of the Russian Constructivists, he allied himself with Constructivist efforts to develop "a new esthetic approach to the civilization of today—a new plastic interpretation of the machine age." [12] Similarly, Stella's 1912 exposure to Italian Futurism helped shape the way he looked at and translated into paint such scenes as the lights and rapid movement of Coney Island and the innovatively structured majesty of the Brooklyn Bridge. Upon his return from the 1912 trip, he went on nightly spiritual and sensory adventures, seeking out "the most salient spectacles" of the transformed urban landscape, which made this impression on him: "I was thrilled to find America so rich with so many new motives to be translated in to a new art. Steel and electricity had created a new world. A new drama had surged . . . new poliphony was ringing all around the scintillating, brightly-colored lights. The steel had leaped to hyperbolic altitudes and expanded to vast latitudes." [13]

Numerous early modernists had training in or other special contact with the fields of architecture or engineering, which had encouraged them to ponder closely visual aspects of the newly emerging technical world. Stieglitz had studied mechanical engineering at the Technische Hochschule in Berlin during 1882–83, Marin worked as an architectural draftsman in the early 1890s, and Chicago modernist, civil engineer, and architect Manierre Dawson graduated from the Armour Institute of Technology in 1908 shortly before doing some of the country's first nonrepresentational paintings. Fauvist H. Lyman Saÿen, who designed precision instruments and electrical circuitry, was commissioned to construct and operate the first military X-ray laboratory in the country in 1898, a decade before he began doing modernist paintings.[14] Other early modernists with such contact included Morgan Russell, Man Ray, Willard Nash, Patrick Henry Bruce, Jay Van Everen, Oscar Bluemner, Morton Schamberg, and Tom Benrimo.

The percentage of modernists with architectural or engineering training was never again so high, but the influence of machine-age visual experience on American art was pervasive in the decades between the two world wars.[15] In addition, many later modernists had other types of educational or occupational exposure to the plenitude of new things the century provided. For example, Mark Tobey, Andy Warhol, and James Rosenquist had experience in commercial art. The history of modern painting in America overlaps with the history of multicolored, graphically striking, and large-scale advertising; interactions between these two areas were frequent, if often uneasy. Other modernists were influenced by the habits of looking they developed as photographers and filmmakers (Charles Sheeler, for example), magazine illustrators (Stella), and painters of billboards (Rosenquist) or camouflage (Abraham Rattner).

More important to the history of modernism than the skyscrapers, trains, or photographs themselves was the cumulative sense these and other new objects provided that previous restrictions on visual experience no longer held. The emerging world of human design transformed every aspect of perceptual experience of importance to the artist: space, time, vantage point, distance, size, duration, and, to choose one example for closer analysis, light. With Edison's introduction of an effective incandescent light in 1879, the availability of electric power in large cities soon after, and the subsequent redesigning of work, recreation, and social life encouraged by the new freedom from dependence on sunlight or less versatile alternatives such as gaslight, more and more activities, including, increasingly, the making of art, were carried out under artificial light. The conditions of urban life also greatly modified natural light. In Chicago at the turn of the century, for instance,

Still from *Safety Last*, 1923. Courtesy the Museum of Modern Art/Film Stills Archive. In the process of analysis and synthesis that created the world of human design which nurtured modernism, things were broken into parts, then reassembled in a manner shaped by human choice. This photograph is a captured moment segmented out of the flow of experience; the typical motion picture consisted of over 100,000 distinct segments. Harold Lloyd is dangling from a clock that subjects time to a similar process; application of the process to manufacturing made possible the abundance of automobiles on the street below.

sprouting skyscrapers and the soft coal used to power proliferating locomotives, river and lake boats, industrial boilers and home furnaces, assured that no unmodified sunlight would reach downtown streets. Painter Jerome Blum, soon to become one of Chicago's first modernists, was stunned when, as a visually alert young man, he traveled away from the city and noticed that under unimpeded and undiffused sunlight he had a sharply distinct shadow rather than the hazy, ghostlike image he had assumed to be natural.

All but the most isolated or self-contained painters responded to the new sights and to the sense they provided of a loosening of restraints, for better and for worse, on human choice. Future NAD president Edwin Blashfield, who said in a 1910 speech that "we must be modern and we must be American," [16] was one of many academic painters who depicted in their paintings such new things as telegraph poles, skyscrapers, and electric dynamos. But as they did so they continued to respect the conventions of academic art, which, they believed, embodied insights into fundamental aspects of human and physical nature derived from centuries of artistic effort. As citizens living in an era that proudly labeled itself progressive and in a country with an amendable Constitution, these academicians accepted change in art, but insisted it must take the form of a gradual evolution.

Individually many modernists adhered to one or another of the academic conventions; collectively they questioned all of the givens of art. In the decades before World War II, American modernists usually were not as bold in their views as Europeans such as Russian Constructivist Kasimir Malevich, who declared, "let us seize the world from the hands of nature and build a new world belonging to man himself." [17] Perhaps this is because they had less to build on. Working without the benefit of a strong native tradition of innovation in the visual arts, and relegated to a culturally peripheral role, American modernists in the years between the wars were more likely to be transmitters and interpreters of new artistic ideas than the originators of such ideas, and thus had less of a sense of power. Yet many could share the French Cubist Georges Braque's more modest conclusion that, at least within the boundaries of their canvases, modern painters were creating new worlds rather than re-creating existing ones: "The aim is not to reconstitute an anecdotal fact but to constitute a pictorial fact." [18] Modern paintings took their place alongside other evidence that choice could shape aspects of visual experience previously thought to be determined by the structure of the physical universe, the laws of optics, "human nature," and the indispensable requirements of civilized life.

Parts of Things

The eyeful of new things that demonstrated the expanded range of human choice also gave evidence that this glut of novel experience might not fit into a coherent whole. Even before World War I revealed that a vast landscape transformed with unprecedented thoroughness by human action could be a "no man's land," perceptive observers such as Henry Adams, as well as many less privileged victims of modernization, recognized that new worlds made possible by loosened constraints might not be desirable, manageable, or comprehensible. Adams's account of how New York appeared to him as he returned from Europe in 1904 emphasized its visual unwieldiness. The sight meeting him was

> unlike anything man had ever seen—and like nothing he had ever much cared to see. The outline of the city became frantic in its effort to explain something that defied meaning. Power seemed to have outgrown its servitude and to have asserted its freedom. The cylinder had exploded, and thrown great masses of stone and steam against the sky. . . . Prosperity never before imagined, power never yet wielded by man, speed never reached by anything but a meteor, had made the world irritable, nervous, querulous, unreasonable, and afraid.[19]

The comprehensive Christian faith of Adams's Puritan ancestors had allowed them to give meaning to the visual strangeness they encountered when they arrived in the New World. But they had come to America partly due to multiplying fissures within traditional religion, and by the time of the Armory Show centuries of accelerating scientific discovery, political revolution, and other intellectual, social, and material changes had challenged virtually all traditional ways of ordering the perceived facts of existence, even if many of those ways still prevailed.

In a novel written shortly after World War I, F. Scott Fitzgerald described some of the visual contradictions obstructing a unified view of things. One of his characters had gotten "into that humor

Charles Henry Demuth, *I Saw the Figure Five in Gold,* 1928. The Metropolitan Museum of Art, The Alfred Stieglitz Collection, 1949 (49.59.1). Charles Demuth's 1928 "poster portrait" of William Carlos Williams, keyed to Williams's poem "I Saw the Figure Five in Gold," evokes the kaleidoscopic sight and sound juxtapositions of urban life.

in which men and women were graceless and absurd phantasms, grotesquely curved and rounded in a rectangular world of their own building. They inspired the same sensations in him as did those strange and monstrous fish who inhabit the esoteric world of green in the aquarium." [20] The most striking visual counterpart to this passage is Edward Hopper's *Nighthawks* (1942), although Fitzgerald makes no reference to the quality of light, a concern central to Hopper's painting. Hopper's work defies categorization as either modern or traditional, but this clash between constructed and organic forms is a pervasive by-product of the emerging world of human design and a crucial part of the experience that nurtured modernism.

Although rapid change in the physical environment of American cities meant that the type of visual clash described by Fitzgerald may have been more common in the United States than anywhere else in the world, artists in this country were insulated from some of the disintegrative forces affecting European culture. No American modernist painter saw the carnage of World War I at first hand, nor did any American artists record feeling in its aftermath, as did German artist Kurt Schwitters, that "everything had broken down ... new things had to be made from fragments." [21] But then and later some modernists expressed a sense of loss because they lived in a world without compelling shared values. Responding to assaults on the human spirit delivered by two world wars and a depression, and convinced that artists were valued, if at all, for the wrong reasons in an America enjoying unprecedented material affluence and military might, the Abstract Expressionists in the 1940s and 1950s were especially likely to express such feelings in words, and arguably also in paint. In 1951 Robert Motherwell reported that many artists felt a "sense of being unwedded to the universe," and three years later Adolph Gottlieb described artists as uncomfortably "footloose" in a society lacking shared "fundamental religious, political, or social beliefs" that thoughtful people could embrace. [22]

Not all modernists reported such feelings of apartness, but all made their art in a world inundated by unassimilated visual phenomena and bereft of credible, comprehensive ordering systems. One way to create coherent art in a world of chaotic and contradictory visual experience was through emphasis on each artist's distinctly personal vision. John Marin, for example, in cityscapes first shown at Stieglitz's "291" gallery before the Armory Show, gave New York buildings an animated plasticity that made them compatible with organic forms. This emphasis on individual sensibility (and the related quality of originality), deeply rooted in Western history, had become especially important since the Romantic era and was taken to new extremes with modernism. But it created integrity only within the circumscribed world of a particular work of art. The work of some artists had enough in common with that of other artists to support talk of this or that movement, but the totality of modern art relies on such diverse ways of seeing and making that it provides evidence of the ineluctable discreteness of twentieth-century visual experience, rather than of any unifying force.

In troubled response artists such as Dutch painter Piet Mondrian followed a classical urge to deemphasize the personal in their paintings and to shape a shared "new way of seeing" expressive of life's underlying spiritual and material essence. Mondrian, who did not come to live in this country until 1940, but who influenced many American modernists well before then, systematically eliminated the organic in his work. Around 1907 he began abstracting essential forms as he painted trees; seven years later the abstraction had gone so far that only earthy colors and some irrepressible curves maintained visual contact with the natural world. The earthy colors remained for a few more years, but by the 1920s he had rigorously restricted himself to orthogonal forms, sometimes set off against diamond-shaped canvases, and to synthetic colors refined by human effort. Like many other modernists, he balanced the segmented nature of his visual experience by attending more to relations than to objects. But in the absence of cultural confirmation of his vision of wholeness, his efforts resulted in paintings that seemed to be only one aspect of a multifaceted and elusive reality, an expression of one way of looking at things. His paintings were and are "Mondrians."

The partible quality of contemporary visual experience could be liberating as well as alienating. The camera and other devices that chopped the flow of experience into previously invisible segments, the train and other forms of transportation that parceled out reality in quick glimpses, and the proclivity for breaking tasks into elemental parts, characteristic of contemporary methods of production from meat packing through computerized data processing, all opened up new artistic possibilities. Sometimes the relation was direct and specific. Charles Sheeler derived his 1921 painting *Church Street El* from a single frame of *Manhatta*, a film he made in that year with photographer Paul Strand.[23] More often the relation was of the general type described by Stuart Davis in discussing the impact of motion pictures and radio, which allowed artists "to experience hundreds of diverse scenes, sounds and ideas in a juxtaposition that has never before been possible. Regardless of their significance they force a new sense of reality and this must of course be reflected in art." [24]

Segmented modes of viewing joined with developments internal to painting to foster art that focused on one or a few of the various elements, such as line, color, form, volume, texture, materiality, subject matter, and concept, that were brought together or modulated in a less radical way in traditional paintings. Cubist paintings, in addition to faceting depicted objects, often muted color in order to emphasize form. Synchromist painting, by contrast, constructed all other elements from color. Modernist paintings that have narrative elements usually tell parts of uncompleted stories; if the cross, a part that signifies a known whole, is the most pervasive symbol in earlier Western art, the most pervasive form in modern art is the grid, an unbounded pattern that breaks things into parts.[25] A frequent feature of American modernist painting, from early works such as Alfred Maurer's through recent works such as Robert Rauschenberg's, is visual dissonance, the juxtaposition of jarringly disparate images and formal elements. Even when used to produce imaginatively integrated works that suggest new relations among things, as it was by Maurer and Rauschenberg, dissonance encouraged viewers as well as artists to look at the separate elements interacting within the work.

This modernist focus on parts has extended the choice available to artists by allowing them to exclude, if they wish, elements previously considered mandatory. Kandinsky, perhaps the first modernist to do nonrepresentational paintings, explains how he was led to the choice of excluding subject matter: "I was returning from my sketching, deep in thought, when, on opening the studio door, I was suddenly confronted with a picture of indescribable incandescent loveliness. Bewildered, I stopped, staring at it. The painting lacked all subject, depicted no recognizable object. . . . Finally I . . . recognized it for what it really was—my own painting, standing on its side on the easel." [26] After seeing a part—the interplay of color and form disassociated from subject—by accident, Kandinsky began to create paintings that would allow him (and, later, others) to look at this part by choice. By so doing he not only helped

Philip Pearlstein, *Man and Female Leaning on Chair,* 1970. Courtesy of The Art Institute of Chicago, 20th Century Purchase Fund, 1971.334. The abruptly cut-off figures in this work by Philip Pearlstein are visual reminders that the painting represents one of an infinite number of possible variations of one individual's view of a particular scene. Compositional demands and the artist's sensibility, rather than necessities that flow from some overarching system of meaning, determine which segment of experience is presented to the viewer.

make attention to parts of things a feature of European and American modernism, but he also contributed to a modernist compulsion that brought together attention to new things and parts of things in a comprehensive effort to see everything.

Everything

If modernists shared no common understanding of what larger whole could be formed from the segments of expressed experience that they created, it was not because they had failed to look hard enough. They have looked, with aesthetic intent, everywhere that imagination, inspiration, irreverence, affluence, greed, egotism, technology, and a "think-everything" approach to knowledge made possible. Modernists were not the first painters to have had insatiable visual curiosities. Earlier artists explored undocumented parts of the world, responded pictorially to the latest scientific discoveries, traced the play of light in all its variety, noted ignored aspects of ordinary life, and revealed social conditions kept undercover. But modern paintings indicate that their makers—freed from many of the constraints that limited earlier explorations—have had the motives, as well as the means, to push further than ever before the quest to see everything.

Some of the reasons for this compulsive quest can be found in the history of Western visual experience. Distinct earlier events such as Columbus's return from the New World and Galileo's observations of the moons of Jupiter have in the past 150 years merged into a continuous flow of convincing proof that previous ages had formed their beliefs on the basis of shockingly incomplete visual information. These revelations also have encouraged the habit of looking beneath appearances, the expectation of further visual surprises, and continued visual exploration. Combined with the voracious appetite for experience that engendered and was engendered by modernism, and the breakdown of older hierarchies of knowledge, social order, and artistic production, this visual quest undermined existing distinctions between things considered deserving of an artist's attention and those considered undeserving.

Few modernists have been as visually omnivorous as Robert Rauschenberg, who said he saw no reason why the whole world should not be considered as a painting, and who since the 1950s has included found objects such as stuffed goats, old bedding, tires, and cardboard boxes in his painted collages. Some modernists have focused purposefully on narrow aspects of their visual experience. And certainly there has been no agreement among modernists (who would not all agree that there is even such a thing as modernism) that they were engaged in a cooperative effort to see everything. But such an effort has resulted from the cumulative effect of the individual decisions made by many different artists.

These decisions have led modernists to direct their gaze inward, to look at things that previously were invisible, and to scrutinize art itself. Often the inward gaze was more metaphorical than literal, a meditative exploration of the nature of consciousness that took to the next step the centuries-long movement from ideal depiction of the external world to portrayal of that world as filtered through an individual sensibility. For some modernists, however, the inward gaze actually yielded visible content. Guided by Surrealist precedents, by the writings of Freud, Jung, and their popularizers and sometimes with the help of analysis, American modernists such as Jackson Pollock developed habits of attentiveness and recall that gave them access to images from their own dreams. These artists also incorporated into their experience visual details of other persons' dreams, as recorded in psychological and anthropological writings, or revealed in myths and other works of art.

Important as internal experience has been in modernism, at its best modern painting, even when nonrepresentational, usually has been in constant and probing dialogue with the external world. As shown earlier, among the experiences compelling modernists to break with traditional forms were their encounters with new things such as skyscrapers. Modernists also responded to things made newly visible through technological extensions of sight. In his 1927 painting *Wasp and Pear*, Gerald Murphy graphically represented the multiple levels of reality opened up by modern science by depicting both a wasp and a microscopic segment of the wasp's leg. Many other artists, including Sheeler, Chuck Close, Andy Warhol, and Ed Paschke, have invested their energies in scrutinizing the mediated visual environment created by photography, film, mass-produced graphic images, and television.

The barriers to sight that have fallen in this century have been conceptual as often as physical. The choices made by artists have been an important component of the processes that have helped make visible many things previously "invisible" in the sense intended in Ralph Ellison's *Invisible Man*, in which prejudice blinds whites to the individuality—to the existential and visual distinctiveness—of the black central character. The visual respect that modernists have accorded objects from African and native American

Charles Sheeler, *The Artist Looks at Nature,* 1943. Courtesy of the Art
Institute of Chicago, Gift of Society for American Art, 1944.32. Modern
technology pressed upon artists new ways of looking at things as well as
new things to look at. His work with photography and film helped make
Charles Sheeler aware of the extent to which new technologies—either
directly or through the habits of perception that they encouraged—
mediated all of his visual encounters with the world.

societies has challenged persistent Western assumptions of cultural superiority. In 1909, when Max Weber returned from four years in Paris, he brought along a love for African art that had been aroused in part by his contact with European modernists, who satisfied their voracious appetite for conventionally unsanctioned experience at the Trocadero and other museums stocked with trophies of ongoing imperialist ventures. Five years later, in part due to Weber's influence, Robert Coady displayed African works as well as examples of European modernism in his newly opened Washington Square Gallery; then, several months afterwards, Stieglitz showed wooden African statuary at "291"; other shows followed. Few modernists studied carefully the cultures that produced these admired works, but the deviation from established customs of valuing and seeing represented by early modernist attention to African art was demonstrated by the frequency with which modernists were ridiculed for taking seriously "the Nigger gods of Africa." In a comment that revealed the profundity of the cultural issues involved, the *American Magazine of Art* warned modernists in 1926 that they never would win respect while they gave "the blue ribbon to African sculpture, Indian totem poles, and the like." [27]

As the quotations suggest, the visual menu from which modernists could choose their inspirations was enlarged as much by disregard for established values as by new enthusiasms. Traditionalists appalled by the Armory Show's threat to lines of distinction separating the noble from the common in art and in life might have considered their worst fears confirmed by Stuart Davis's report, thirty years later, that the most important influence on one of his recent paintings had been "the T-Formation as sprung by the Chicago Bears in 1943." Even more distressing would have been sculptor Claes Oldenburg's expressed preference for "art you can sit on. . . . I am for art that is flipped on and off like a switch. Art you can eat or squeeze. . . ." Under the combined influence of discarded inhibitions and novel fascinations, among the things various modernists have looked at intently are comic strips, cartoons, and other products of popular and commercial culture, children's and folk art and the art of the insane (whose "cracked" minds "may let in light which does not enter . . . intact minds"),[28] and the vast and variegated refuse of industrial civilization. Some of these things have been valued by artists in other places and times, but never before

Robert A. Birmelin, *City Crowd—Cop and Ear*, 1980. The Metropolitan Museum of Art, Gift of Mr. and Mrs. Frederico Quadrani, 1981 (1981.510). The title of this painting suggests, and its imagery exploits, the expanded possibilities for content, viewpoint, and aesthetic stance opened up by the modernist commitment to see everything. Robert Birmelin also builds, wittily, with visually striking results, on the modernist attention to parts of things.

Arthur G. Dove, *Portrait of Ralph Dusenberry*, 1924. The Metropolitan
Museum of Art, The Alfred Stieglitz Collection, 1949 (49.70.36). With an
openness to materials from everyday life that became even more
pronounced among American modernists after World War II, Arthur
Dove incorporated folding rulers, pieces of wood, and a scrap of music
into this 1924 painting.

this century have artists had the actual and conceptual opportunity to incorporate into their vision such a wide range of things.

Modernism has also stimulated to a greater extent than earlier art efforts to make visible the structure, presumptions, and methods of art itself. Emphasis on the two-dimensionality ("flatness") and materiality of paintings has been a frequent result. Although always a feature of some modernist works, and consistent with the attention to parts of things, in American modernism explicit references to the processes involved in creating a work have been especially common since the 1960s, when international prominence fostered self-consciousness, and anti-authoritarian currents of the Vietnam era encouraged a "let it all hang out" approach. Jasper Johns's paintings have been particularly revealing. For instance, in *According to What* (1964), he left intact one of the stencils used in making color circles on the painting, and in *Device* (1962) he screwed to the painting two rulers used to create the sweeping semicircles which are among its key compositional features. Other works, such as Josef Albers's paintings that make careful viewers aware of simultaneous contrast, helped viewers see themselves seeing.

Albers's paintings remind us that no matter how much help we get from improved microscopes and enlightened views of previously despised visual phenomena, the attempt to see everything is an infinitely open-ended project because any given object of perception looks different when viewed for different lengths of time. Surely the average length of glance in the car/TV/and supermall culture of late-twentieth-century America must be among the shortest in human history. In response, modernists often have created works that attempt to force, trick, or seduce viewers into seeing some of the "everythings" that would be revealed by prolonged gazing. Few have made such excessive demands as Marcel Duchamps, who titled one of his pieces *To be Looked at . . . with One Eye Closed, For Almost an Hour* (1918), but many works require at least a thirty-second gaze before they become art even by expansive modern definitions.

Paintings that a long look can transform from innocuously ornamental objects or technical exercises into vibrant, multileveled, emotionally and conceptually rich visual phenomena include, for instance, works by Barnett Newman, Mark Rothko, Morris Louis, and Ad Reinhardt. A typical Reinhardt painting demands close

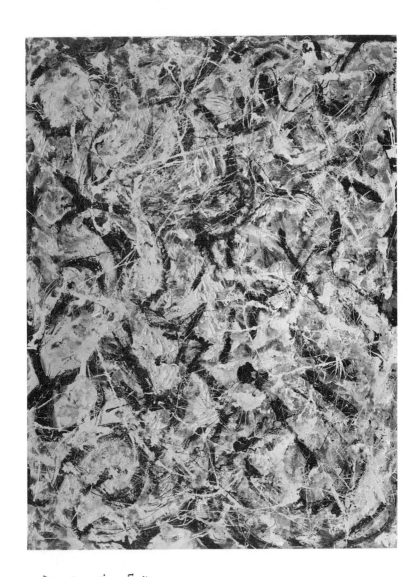

Jackson Pollock, *Grayed Rainbow*, 1953. Courtesy of the Art Institute of Chicago, Gift of Society for Contemporary American Art, 1955.494. The physical movements made by artists in creating their works are vividly conveyed in Abstract Expressionist "action paintings" such as Jackson Pollock's *Grayed Rainbow*.

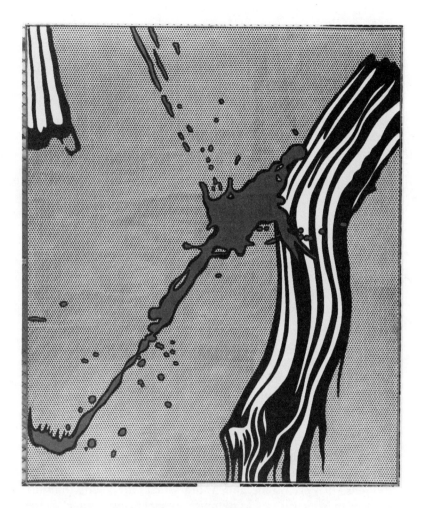

Roy Lichtenstein, *Brushstroke with Splatter*, 1966. Courtesy of The Art
Institute of Chicago, Barbara Neff Smith and Solomon Byron Smith
Purchase Fund, 1966.4. Modernist paintings include an unprecedented
degree of explicit visual commentary on the processes involved in their
own making and in the making of other works. Roy Lichtenstein, who is
able to digest any subject matter by breaking it down into parts, does
both in his brushstroke series.

attention by presenting the viewer with what at first appears to be uniformly black canvas, but turns out on close inspection to consist of pattern-forming areas of slightly different shades of very dark blue. Some honorably devious artists, such as Stuart Davis and James Rosenquist, have captured the attention of viewers with de-signed-to-be-looked-at-quickly images, borrowed from popular cul-ture, that in their painted versions have less obvious qualities that ensnare the glance for longer looking (see for example, Davis's *Lucky Strike,* 1921). Georgia O'Keeffe wrote of her flower paintings, "paint it big and they will be surprised into taking time to see what I see of flowers," [29] and other modernists such as Mondrian have sought to create total ways of looking that would bring to a con-clusion the quest to see everything by providing a new means of vision that redefines which things are worth seeing. Modernism's range has been wide enough to encompass such exclusive visions. And to subvert them.

Conclusion: Modernism as the Condition of Choice

During the past decade and a half many observers have concluded that modernism should be declared a completed historical move-ment, that we have entered the "postmodern" era. If there is an important connection between artists' visual experience and their art, events offer some basis for this declaration. The closeups of the moon's surface provided by the Apollo missions, and more importantly, the views of Earth as seen from the moon, brought to a certain culmination the compulsion to see everything, leading to the sense that even something as dramatic as the Viking transmis-sions from Mars were a sort of interplanetary mannerism, elaborat-ing in a contrived way on what had come before. With the moon-seen Earth, its nakedness tantalizingly glimpsable beneath the encircling clouds, soon serving as a model for ballpoint pen adver-tisements and airline promotions, what was there for artists or the rest of us to do but find entertaining ways to rearrange the known, albeit in ways that allowed us, when successful, to know the known in previously unknown ways?

Thus, perhaps, the label "postmodernism" does help identify a shift in the tenor of our collective visual experience. But like other declarations of the end of modern painting, it is dependent on a definition of modernism as a particular set of choices that have been made and exhausted. At the time of the Armory Show critics of modernism declared that intentionally shocking novelty was its essence; wide exposure would bring a quick end to the novelty and the art. Others argued in the 1920s that modernism defined itself only through opposition to official art, and thus lost its raison d'etre when made official through its acceptance by museums, galleries, collectors, and schools. As viewed from the crisis-shaped perspective of the 1930s, modernism seemed to many to be an extreme example of indulgent individualism and esoteric concerns, unlikely to survive an era committed to collective action and popular art. The vitality of American painting in the aftermath of World War II brought modernism off the obituary page, but also strengthened the conviction of some that it must be killed. On the political right Republican Congressman George Dondero of Michigan denounced it as a communist plot that would so addle the brains of Americans that the Soviets would be able to capture New York without firing a shot, while critics on the left later concluded that government and big money interests promoted it as an alternative to art that carried an easily understood message of social protest and as a way of enhancing America's Cold War image as a cultural as well as military and economic power.[30]

By the 1960s reductionist extremes such as minimalism and conceptual art, along with other movements that brought to some end point aspects of modernism introduced in Europe during its formative period, seemed to prove that the modernist idea had been carried to its destined conclusion of self-annihilation. It was at this point that artists and critics began to detect the emergence of Postmodernism, bolstering their analysis by discovering that modernism had "laws," "rules," "dogma," "norms," "taboos," "faith," and something called "standard modernist taste." [31] According to the narrow view of its history that this analysis provided, modernism could be seen primarily as a working out of the sequence identified in influential critic Clement Greenberg's observation that the dynamic propelling modernism through its various phases was "the use of the characteristic methods of a discipline to criticize the discipline itself . . . to entrench it more firmly in its area of competence." [32]

Such a definition covers more paintings than most single-thrust accounts of modernism, but it assumes implausibly that modern art has developed independently of the century's massive changes in visual experience, except those internal to painting. I would argue instead that, at least as applied to twentieth-century American painting, it does not make good historical sense to attribute to modernism any restrictive set of aesthetic predispositions, formal practices, or philosophical beliefs. Such tightly focused definitions must exclude too many of this century's paintings. One way to accommodate these diverse works is to define modernism as the unprecedented condition of choice that historical circumstances and their own activities have presented to artists in this century. Modernist paintings are those made possible by this clamor of choices; modernists are artists who have broken sharply with earlier conventions in order variously to confront, explore, extend, strip bare, and celebrate this condition of, if not unbounded possibility, then possibility with no discernible boundaries. Many individual modernists have encountered restrictions imposed by economic duress, an intolerant public, a hostile government, or the insistent trends of a particular year or even decade, but thus far each limit accepted by some modernists has become a point of departure for others.

No equally open-ended condition of choice has occurred in the past. Little surprise that the eye's encounters with the interior of the atom, the dark side of the moon and of the mind, the explosive moment when a bullet penetrates an apple or a forehead, the infrared and ultraviolet ranges of the electromagnetic spectrum, and objects from a great variety of times and places, as well as its glimpses through both the most guarded and the most abject keyholes of our own culture, have proved difficult to assimilate into an integrated and comprehensive vision, and have encouraged artists to create new ways of visual exploration, expression, entertainment, and communication.

Modernism persists because the condition of choice persists. We continue to enjoy and endure an unprecedented opportunity to shape our visual destiny, for better and for worse. Modernism will remain the clearest expression of our artistic and social condition until we have collectively formed an agreed-upon coherence out

William Clift, *Reflection of Old St. Louis County Court House,* 1976. The
Metropolitan Museum of Art Purchase, gift of various donors and
matching funds from NEA, 1981 (1981.1044.1). William Clift's bicenten-
nial-year photograph is an expression of, and a record of some experiential roots for, the diverse elements encompassed by modernism. The
traditional is still present, whether in the form of a nineteenth-century
courthouse based on earlier models or a historic river, but the visual and
cultural meaning of these earlier elements is transformed by their
juxtaposition with and reflection in what came after.

of these choices, which would seem likely to take a long time. Or
until we have reconciled ourselves to lasting pluralism, or irrevoca-
bly segmented ourselves because of it. Or until we impose or have
imposed upon us some Orwellian coherence, a possible outcome
but one resisted by, among many other things, the modernist urge
to see, experience, and express everything. Or until we are all
dead, an option always at hand in our world of human design.

Notes

1. Lipchitz quoted in James J. Sweeney, *Vision and Image: A Way of Seeing* (New York, 1968), 62.

2. On Stieglitz and on early American modernism, see Edward Abrahams, *The Lyrical Left: Randolph Bourne, Alfred Stieglitz, and the Origins of Cultural Radicalism in America* (Charlottesville, Va., 1986); *Avant-Garde Painting and Sculpture in America, 1910–1925*, exh. cat., Delaware Art Museum (Wilmington, 1975); Milton W. Brown, *American Painting from the Armory Show to the Depression* (Princeton, 1955); Abraham A. Davidson, *Early American Modernist Painting, 1910–1937* (New York, 1981); and William Innes Homer, *Alfred Stieglitz and the American Avant-Garde* (Boston, 1977). On this and most other topics mentioned in this article, for additional material, including further bibliographical information, see George H. Roeder, Jr., *Forum of Uncertainty: Confrontations with Modern Painting in Twentieth-Century American Thought* (Ann Arbor, 1980).

3. The fullest account of the Armory Show is in Milton W. Brown, *The Story of the Armory Show* (New York, 1963).

4. On the show's impact, see ibid., 209; Davidson, *American Modernist Painting*, 168; and the biographies of individual artists in *The Advent of Modernism: Post-Impressionism and North American Art, 1900–1918*, exh. cat., High Art Museum (Atlanta, 1986).

5. F. J. Mather, "The Academy and the Independents," *The Weekly Review* 4 (23 March 1921): 271.

6. A few Surrealist works had been displayed in the United States during the late 1920s, but Levy arranged the first full American show at Hartford's Wadsworth Athenaeum shortly before showing the same works in his New York gallery in January 1932. See Roeder, *Forum*, 152, and Julien Levy, *Memoir of an Art Gallery* (New York, 1977), 79–82.

7. Mary Gedo demonstrated the Seurat influence in an exhibition she curated for the Roy Boyd Gallery, Chicago, summer 1986.

8. On Henri, see Robert Henri, *The Art Spirit*, comp. Margery Ryerson (New York, 1923), and William Innes Homer, *Robert Henri and His Circle* (Ithaca, N.Y., 1969).

9. Weber quoted in Davidson, *American Modernist Painting*, 33.

10. Louis Lozowick, "The Americanization of Art," in *catalogue* for Machine-Age Exposition, New York, May 5–28, 1927 (available through Archives of American Art, microfilm roll N44, frame 1240).

11. Picabia quoted in Davidson, *American Modernist Painting*, 86.

12. Barbara Zabel, "Louis Lozowick and Technological Optimism of the 1920s," diss. Univ. of Virginia, 1978, 4; idem, "Louis Lozowick and Urban Optimism of the 1920s," *Archives of American Art Journal* 14:2 (1974): 19–21; Davidson, *American Modernist Painting*, 201.

13. Stella quoted in Henry Geldzahler, *American Painting in the Twentieth Century* (New York, 1965), 69. See also Irma B. Jaffe, *Joseph Stella* (Cambridge, Mass., 1970).

14. On Saÿen see Adelyn D. Breeskin, *H. Lyman Saÿen*, exh. cat., National Collection of Fine Arts (Washington, D.C., 1970).

15. An excellent exhibition, organized through the Brooklyn Museum, on "The Machine Age in America, 1918–1941," was accompanied by a catalogue by Richard Guy Wilson, Dianne H. Pilgrim, and Dickran Tashjian (New York, 1986). The catalogue includes discussion of the varying machine motifs most influential on art and design at different times during the 1918–1941 period. See esp. 45, 50–51.

16. Edward Blashfield, "The Actual State of Art Among Us," *North American Review* 191 (March 1910): 322–29.

17. Malevich quoted in T. J. Clark, "On the Social History of Art," in Francis Frascina and Charles Harrison, eds., *Modern Art and Modernism: A Critical Anthology* (New York, 1982), 258.

18. Braque quoted in Max Kozloff, *Cubism/Futurism* (New York, 1973), 11.

19. Henry Adams, *The Education of Henry Adams* (Boston, 1973), 499.

20. F. Scott Fitzgerald, *The Beautiful and the Damned* (New York, 1922), 122.

21. Schwitters quoted in John Ashbery, "Fragments of Celestial Trash," *Newsweek* (1 July 1985): 59. Marsden Hartley was in Germany during the early part of World War I, but as far as I know neither he nor any other recognized American modern painter, in contrast to American writers and European modern artists, actually witnessed battle. Stieglitz's associate Edward J. Steichen, who served in France, had done some modernist paintings before the war, but devoted himself to his primary interest, photography, after his return. Among other artists influenced by modernism, but not clearly identifiable as modernists, who did participate in the European war were George Biddle and Rockwell Kent. A "naive" artist much admired by some modernists, Horace Pippin, recorded his direct wartime experiences in his art, and while in Paris modernist Andrew Dasburg witnessed a brief encounter between French and German aircraft. Failing health prevented H. Lyman Saÿen from carrying out his plan to organize an artist's unit to fight in France.

22. Robert Motherwell contribution to a symposium on "What Abstract Art Means to Me," printed in *Bulletin of the Museum of Modern Art* 18 (Spring 1951): 12; Adolf Gottlieb, "The Artist and the Public," *Art in America* 42 (December 1954): 268. On Abstract Expressionism and what followed, see Irving Sandler, *The Triumph of American Painting: A History of Abstract Expressionism* (New York, 1970); Dore Ashton, *The New York School: A Cultural Reckoning* (New York, 1972); and Lawrence Alloway, *Topics in American Art Since 1945* (New York, 1975).

23. Davidson, *American Modernist Painting*, 190.

24. Stuart Davis, "Self-Interview," *Creative Art* 9 (September 1931): 211.

25. Rosalind E. Krauss points out that as handled by artists such as Ad Reinhardt, grids yield crosses. See the essay on "grids" in *The Originality of the Avant-Garde and Other Modernist Myths* (Cambridge, Mass., 1985), 10.

26. Kandinsky quoted in Alan Bowness, *Modern European Art* (London, 1972), 130.

27. Roeder, *Forum*, 99–101; *The Arts* 6 (December 1924); *American Magazine of Art* 17 (September 1926): 488–90.

28. The "cracked minds" quote is from British psychiatrist R. D. Laing in *Wilson Quarterly* (Summer 1986): 35. The modernist urge to see everything is part of a larger compulsion to experience everything that, as well as calling attention to ways in which insanity can nurture art, blurs the point at which art disintegrates into insanity. Consider conceptual artist Chris Burden's explanation of why for one of his art works he had a friend shoot him in the arm at close range with a .22-caliber rifle: "It's something to experience. How can you know what it feels like to be shot if you don't get shot?"

29. O'Keeffe quoted in Davidson, *American Modernist Painting*, 204.

30. On modernism and the Cold War, see Roeder, *Forum*, 220–24, and sources cited there; Serge Guilbaut, *How New York Stole the Idea of Modern Art: Abstract Expressionism, Freedom, and the Cold War* (Chicago, 1983); and my review of that book in *American Historical Review* 89 (October 1984): 1177–78.

31. All of these terms are used with reference to modernism in Richard Hertz, *Theories of Contemporary Art* (Englewood Cliffs, N.J., 1985).

32. Clement Greenberg, "Modernist Painting," in Frascina, *Modern Art and Modernism*, 5.

Modernism and the Harlem Renaissance

Houston A. Baker, Jr.
University of Pennsylvania

Harlem is vicious
modernism. Bangclash.
Vicious the way its made.
Can you stand such Beauty?
So violent and transforming.
—Amin Baraka, "Return of the Native"

THE TERM *MODERNISM* HAS SOMETHING OF THE CHARACTER OF KEATS'S COLD pastoral. Promising a wealth of meaning, it locks observers into a questing indecision that can end in unctuous chiasmus. Teased out of thought by the term's promise, essayists often conclude with

This essay is, in part, a direct excerpt from a book-length study of the same title issued by the University of Chicago Press in 1987, and, in part, an abbreviated summary of claims argued at some length in that book. The principal aim of both the essay and the book is to suggest a problematic, or an analytical model, that will enable a useful reassessment of the Harlem Renaissance. Such an analysis would escape the pitfalls of a period analysis of Afro-American expressivity and take Harlem as a moment not in a developing and exclusive literary enterprise, but in a general and distinctive Afro-American discursive history comprised of a definable array of strategies. The presentation that follows will, hopefully, give impetus to such a reassessment. Versions of this essay were prepared and delivered as lectures for the English Institute (August 1985) and the Afro-American Studies Department at Yale University (November 1985). At Yale, I had the privilege of delivering the Richard Wright Lecture.

frustratingly vague specifications. Harry Levin's essay "What Was Modernism?" for example, after providing lists, catalogues, and thought problems, concludes with the claim that modernism's distinguishing feature is its attempt to create "a conscience for a scientific age" (630).[1] Modernism's definitive act, according to Levin, traces its ancestry to "Rabelais, at the very dawn of modernity."

Such an analysis can only be characterized as a terribly general claim about scientific mastery and the emergence of the modern. It shifts the burden of definition from "modernism" to "science," without defining either enterprise.

Robert Martin Adams, in an essay bearing the same title as Levin's, offers a key to modernism's teasing semantics.[2] Adams writes:

> Of all the empty and meaningless categories, hardly any is inherently as empty as "the modern." Like "youth," it is a self-destroying concept; unlike "youth," it has a million and one potential meanings. Nothing is so dated as yesterday's modern, and nothing, however dated in itself, fails to qualify as "modern" so long as it enjoys the exquisite privilege of having been created yesterday. (31-32)

Adams implies that bare chronology makes modernists of us all. The latest moment's production—by definition—instantiates "the modern." And unless we arbitrarily terminate modernism's allowable tomorrows, the movement is unending. Moreover, the temporal indeterminacy of the term allows us to select (quite randomly) structural features that we will call distinctively "modern" on the basis of their chronological proximity to us. We can then read these features over past millennia. Like Matthew Arnold in his Oxford inaugural lecture entitled "On the Modern Element in Literature," we can discover what is most distinctively modern in works a thousand years old.

As one reads essay after essay, one becomes convinced that Ihab Hassan's set of provocative questions in a work entitled "POST-modernISM A Paracritical Bibliography" are apt and suggestive for understanding the frustrating persistence of "modernism" as a critical sign. Hassan queries:

> When will the Modern Period end?
>
> Has ever a period waited so long? Renaissance? Baroque? Neo-Classical? Romantic? Victorian?

When will Modernism cease and what comes thereafter?

What will the twenty-first century call us? and will its voice come from the same side of our graves?

Does Modernism stretch merely to stretch out our lives? Or, ductile, does it give a new sense of time? The end of periodization? the slow arrival of simultaneity?

If change changes ever more rapidly, and the future jolts us now, do men, paradoxically, resist both endings and beginnings?[3] (7)

Certainly it is the case that scholars resist consensus on everything—beginnings, dominant trends, and endings—where *modernism* is concerned.

Yet, for Anglo-American and British traditions of literary and artistic scholarship there is a tenuous agreement that some names and works *must* be included in any putatively comprehensive account of modern writing and art. Further, there seems to be an identifiable pleasure in listing features of art and writing that begin to predominate (by Virginia Woolf's time line) on or about December 1910.

The names and techniques of the "modern" that are generally set forth constitute a descriptive catalogue resembling a natural philosopher's curiosity cabinet. In such cabinets disparate and seemingly discontinuous objects share space because that is the very function of the cabinet—to house or give order to varied things in what appears a rational, scientific manner. Picasso and Pound, Joyce and Kandinsky, Stravinsky and Klee, Brancusi and H.D. are made to form a series. Collage, primitivism, montage, allusion, "dehumanization," and leitmotifs are forced into the same field. Nietzsche and Marx, Freud and Frazier, Jung and Bergson become dissimilar bedfellows. Such naming rituals have the force of creative works like *Ulysses* and *The Waste Land*. They substitute a myth of unified purpose and intention for definitional certainty. Before succumbing to the myth, however, perhaps we should examine the "change" that, according to Woolf's calendar, occurred on or about December 1910.

Surely that change is most accurately defined as an acknowledgement of radical uncertainty. Where precisely anyone or anything was located could no longer be charted on old maps of "civilization," nor could even the most microscopic observation tell the exact time and space of day. The very conceptual possibilities of both time and space had been dramatically refigured in the mathematics of Einstein and the physics of Heisenberg. A war of barbaric immensity combined with imperialism, capitalism, and totalitarianism's subordination or extermination of tens of millions to produce a reaction to human possibilities quite different from Walt Whitman's joyous welcoming of the modern. Whitman in the nineteenth century exalted: "Years of the modern! years of the unperform'd!"

For T. S. Eliot, the completed and expected performance of mankind scarcely warranted joy. There was, instead, the "Murmur of maternal lamentation" presaging

> Cracks . . . and bursts in the violet air
> Falling towers
> Jerusalem Athens Alexandria
> Vienna London
> Unreal.[4]

Eliot's speaker, however, is comforted by the certainty that there are millennia of "fragments" (artistic shrapnel) constituting a *civilization* to be mined, a cultured repertoire to act as a shore against ruins. That is to say, Fitzgerald's Tom Buchanan in *The Great Gatsby* seems to be a more honestly self-conscious representation of the threat that some artists whom we call "modern" felt in the face of a new world of science, war, technology, and imperialism. "Civilization's going to pieces," Tom confides to an assembled dinner party at his lavish Long Island estate while drinking a corky (but rather impressive) claret. "I've gotten to be a terrible pessimist about things," he continues.[5]

Now, I don't mean to suggest that Anglo-American, British, and Irish moderns did not address themselves with seriousness and sincerity to a changed condition of humankind. Certainly they did. But they also mightily restricted the province of what constituted the tumbling of the towers, and they remained eternally self-conscious of their own pessimistic "becomings." Tom's pessimism turns out to be entirely bookish. It is predicated upon Stoddard's (which Tom remembers as "Goddard's") racialistic murmurings. What really seems under threat are not the towers of civilization, but

rather an assumed supremacy of boorishly racist, indisputably sexist,

and unbelievably wealthy Anglo-Saxon males. One means of shor-
ing up oneself under perceived threats of "democratization" and a
"rising tide" of color is to resort to elitism—to adopt a style that
refuses to represent anything other than the stylist's refusal to represent (what Susan Sontag refers to as an "aesthetics of silence").

Another strategy is to claim that one's artistic presentations and
performances are quintessential renderings of the unrepresent-
able—human subconsciousness, for example, or primitive structural
underpinnings of a putatively civilized mankind, or the simultaneity of a space-time continuum. Yet another strategy—a somewhat
tawdry and dangerous one—is advocacy and allegiance to authoritarian movements or institutions that promise law and order. Regardless of their strategies for confronting it, though, it was
change—a profound shift in what could be taken as unquestionable
assumptions about the meaning of human life—that moved those
artists whom we call "moderns." And it was only a rare one among
them who did not have some formula—some "ism"—for checking
a precipitous toppling of man and his towers. Futurism, Imagism,
Impressionism, Vorticism, Expressionism, Cubism—all offered explicit programs for the arts *and* the salvation of humanity. Each in
its turn yields to other formulations of the role of the writer and
the task of the artist in a changed and, always, ever more rapidly
changing world.

Today, we are "postmodern." Rather than *civilization's* having
gone to pieces, it has extended its sway in the form of a narrow and
concentrated group of power brokers scarcely more charming, hu-
mane, or informed than Tom Buchanan. To connect the magnifi-
cent achievements, breakthroughs, and experiments of an entire
panoply of modern intellectuals with fictive attitudes of a fictive
modern man (Fitzgerald's Tom) may seem less than charitable. For
even though Tom evades the law, shirks moral responsibility, and
still ends up rich and in possession of the fairest Daisy of them all
(though he ends, that is to say, as the capitalist triumphant, if not
the triumphant romantic hero of the novel), there are still other
modes of approach to the works of the moderns.

Lionel Trilling, for example, provides one of the most charitable
scholarly excursions to date.[6] He describes modern literature as
"shockingly personal," posing "every question that is forbidden in
polite society" and involving readers in intimate interactions that

leave them uneasily aware of their personal beings in the world. One scholarly reaction to Trilling's formulations, I'm afraid, is probably like that of the undergraduates whom he churlishly suggests would be "rejected" by the efforts of Yeats and Eliot, Pound and Proust. It is difficult, for example, for an Afro-American student of literature like me—one unconceived in the philosophies of Anglo-American, British, and Irish moderns—to find intimacy either in the moderns' hostility to *civilization* or in their fawning reliance on an array of images and assumptions bequeathed by a *civilization* that, in its prototypical form, is exclusively Western, preeminently bourgeoisie, and optically white.

Alas, Fitzgerald's priggishly astute Nick has only a limited vocabulary when it comes to a domain of experience that I, as an Afro-American, know well: "As we crossed Blackwell's Island a limousine passed us, driven by a white chauffeur, in which sat three modish negroes, two bucks and a girl. I laughed aloud as the yolks of their eyeballs rolled toward us in haughty rivalry" (69). If only Fitzgerald had placed his "pale well-dressed negro" in the limousine or if Joseph Conrad[7] had allowed his Africans to actually be articulate or if D. H. Lawrence[8] had not suggested through Birkin's reflection on African culture that

> thousands of years ago, that which was imminent in himself must have taken place in these Africans: the goodness, the holiness, the desire for creation and productive happiness must have lapsed, leaving the single impulse for knowledge through the senses, knowledge arrested and ending in the senses, mystic knowledge in disintegration and dissolution, knowledge such as the beetles have, which live purely within the world of corruption and cold dissolution. (245–46)

Or if O'Neill[9] had only bracketed the psycho-surreal final trappings of his Emperor's world and given us the stunning account of colonialism that remains implicit in his quip at the close of his list of dramatis personae: "The action of the play takes place on an island in the West Indians, as yet un-self-determined by white marines." If any of these moves had been accomplished, then perhaps I might feel, at least, some of the intimacy and reverence Trilling suggests.

But even as I recall a pleasurable spring in New Haven when I enjoyed cracking Joycean codes in order to teach *Ulysses*, I realize that the Irish writer's grand monument is not a work to which I shall return with reverence and charitably discover the type of inquisition that Trilling finds so engaging: "[Modern literature] asks us if we are content with our marriages, with our family lives, with our professional lives, with our friends" (7–8). I am certain that I shall never place Ulysses in a group of texts that I describe, to use Trilling's words, as "spiritual" if not "actually religious." Perhaps, the reason I shall not is because the questions Trilling finds—correctly or incorrectly—intimately relevant to his life are descriptive only of a bourgeois, characteristically twentieth-century, white Western mentality. As an Afro-American, a person of African descent in the United States today, I spend a great deal of time reflecting that in the world's largest geographies the question "Where will I find water, wood, or food for today?" is (and has been for the entirety of this century) the most pressing and urgently posed inquiry.

In "diasporic," "developing," "Third World," "emerging"—or whatever adjective one chooses to signify the non-Western side of Chenweizu's title "The West and the Rest of Us"—nations or territories there is no need to pose, in ironical Audenesque ways, questions such as, Are we happy? Are we content? Are we free?[10] Such questions presuppose, at least, an adequate level of sustenance and a faith in human behavioral alternatives sufficient to enable a self-directed questioning. In other words, without food for thought, all modernist bets are off. Rather than reducing the present essay to a discourse on underdevelopment, however, or invoking a different kind of human being, what I want to evoke by emphasizing concerns other than those of "civilization" and its discontents is a discursive constellation that marks a change in Afro-American nature that occurred on or about September 18, 1895. The constellation that I have in mind includes Afro-American literature, music, art, graphic design, and intellectual history. It is not confined to a traditionally defined belles lettres, or to Literature with a capital and capitalist *L*.

In fact, it is precisely the confinement (in a very Foucaultian sense discovered in *Madness and Civilization*) of such bourgeois categories (derivatives of Kantian aesthetics) that the present essay seeks to subvert.[11] Hence, there will be few sweeps over familiar geographies of a familiar Harlem Renaissance conceived as an enterprise of limited accomplishment and limited liability—"Harlem Renaissance, Ltd." Instead, I shall attempt to offer an account of

discursive conditions of possibility for what I define as "renaissancism" in Afro-American expressive culture as a whole. I am, thus,
interested less in individual "artists" than in areas of expressive production. It is my engagement with these areas of Afro-American
production (intellectual history, music, graphic design, stage presence, oratory, etc.) that provides intimacy and that leads me,
through a specifically Afro-American modernism, to blues geographies that are still in search of substantial analysis—and liberation.

૨ઢ

The affinity that I feel for Afro-American modernism is not altogether characteristic. Scholars have been far from enthusiastic in
their evaluation of the "Harlem Renaissance" of the 1920s—an
outpouring of Afro-American writing, music, and social criticism
that includes some of the earliest attempts by Afro-American artists
and intellectuals to define themselves in "modern" terms. Few
scholars would disagree that the Harlem Renaissance marks a
readily identifiable "modern" movement in Afro-American intellectual history, and most would concede that the principal question
surrounding the Harlem Renaissance has been: "Why did the renaissance fail?"

Scarcely four years after "Black Tuesday," that awful moment
that plummeted America into depression, a prominent intellectual
and contemporary of the renaissance wrote:

> It is a good thing that [the editor] Dorothy West is doing in instituting a
> magazine [*Challenge*] through which the voices of younger Negro writers
> can be heard. The term "younger Negro writers" connotes a degree of
> disillusionment and disappointment for those who a decade ago hailed
> with loud huzzas the dawn of the Negro literary millennium. We expected
> much; perhaps, too much. I now judge that we ought to be thankful for
> the half-dozen younger writers who did emerge and make a place for
> themselves.[12]

James Weldon Johnson's disillusionment that the Harlem Renaissance "failed" finds its counterparts and echoes in the scholarship,
polemics, and popular rhetoric of the past half-century. An avatar
of Johnson's disillusionment, for example, is the scholarly dis-

approbation of Nathan Huggins's provocative study *Harlem Renaissance* (1971).[13]

Huggins charges that the Harlem Renaissance failed because it remained provincial. Its spokespersons unfortunately accepted the province of "race" as a domain in which to forge a New Negro identity. Mired in this ethnic provincialism, writers like Countee Cullen, Claude McKay, Langston Hughes, Alain Locke, and others failed to realize that they did not have to battle for a defining identity in America. They needed only, in Huggins's view, to claim "their *patria*, their nativity" as American citizens (309). The Harvard historian believes that Afro-Americans are—and have always been— inescapably implicated in the warp and woof of the American fabric. In fact, he holds that they are nothing other than "Americans" whose darker pigmentation has been appropriated as a liberating mask by their lighter-complexioned fellow citizens. Hence, Afro-Americans are fundamentally bone of the bone—if not flesh of the flesh—of the American people, and the intricacies of minstrelsy and the aberrations of the Harlem Renaissance are both misguided, but deeply revelatory, products of the way race relations have stumbled and faltered on the boards of progressive optimism in the United States.

While Huggins adduces provinciality and narrowness as causes for a failed Harlem Renaissance, his contemporary and fellow Afro-American historian David Levering Lewis takes a contrary view.[14] Lewis ascribes Harlem's failings to a tragically wide, ambitious, and delusional striving on the part of renaissance intellectuals. Writing ten years after Huggins, Lewis describes the appearance of Alain Locke's compendium of creative, critical, and scholarly utterances *The New Negro* (1925) as follows:

> Its thirty-four Afro-American contributors (four were white) included almost all the future Harlem Renaissance regulars—an incredibly small band of artists, poets, and writers upon which to base Locke's conviction that the race's "more immediate hope rests in the revaluation by white and black alike of the Negro in terms of his artistic endowments and cultural contributions, past and prospective." To suppose that a few superior people, who would not have filled a Liberty Hall quorum or Ernestine Rose's 135th Street library, were to lead ten million Afro-Americans into an era of opportunity and justice seemed irresponsibly delusional. (117)

Lewis suggests that this delusional vision was a direct function of a rigidly segregated United States. Unlike Huggins, who assumes *patria* as a given, Lewis claims that Afro-Americans turned to art during the twenties precisely because there was no conceivable chance of their assuming *patria*—or anything else in white America. Art seemed to offer the only means of advancement because it was the *only* area in America—from an Afro-American perspective—where the color line had not been rigidly drawn. Excluded from politics and education, from profitable and challenging areas of the professions, and brutalized by all American economic arrangements, Afro-Americans adopted the arts as a domain of hope and an area of possible progress.

Lewis's stunningly full research reveals the merits of his thesis. He provides a grim look at dire economic and social restrictions that hedged blacks round everywhere in the United States during the 1920s. Exceptional art—like effective and liberating social strategies—was, perhaps, a quite illusory Afro-American goal. In the end, all of Harlem's sound and flair could not alter the indubitably American fact that black men and women, regardless of their educational or artistic accomplishments, would always be poorer, more brutally treated, and held in lower esteem than their white American counterparts. The renaissance, thus, reveals itself in retrospect, according to Lewis, as the product of middle-class black "architects [who] believed in ultimate victory through the maximizing of the exceptional. They [members of the 'talented tenth'] deceived themselves into thinking that race relations in the United States were amenable to the assimilationist patterns of a Latin country" (305–6).

The gap between the Afro-American masses and the talented tenth could not have been manifested more profoundly than in the latter's quixotic assimilationist assumptions. For, ironically, the most acute symbol of Harlem's surge at the wall of segregation is not poems nor interracial dinner parties, according to Lewis, but rather the Harlem riot of 1935, in which thousands took to the streets and unleashed their profound frustrations by destroying millions of dollars' worth of white property. The riot, for Lewis, offers the conclusive signal that the strivings of the twenties were delusional and that the renaissance was fated to end with a bang of enraged failure.

Johnson, Huggins, and Lewis are all scholars who merit respect for their willingness to assess an enormously complex array of interactions spanning more than a decade of Afro-American artistic, social, and intellectual history. Thanks to their efforts, we have far more than a bare scholarly beginning when we attempt to define one of the seminal moments of Afro-American "modernism." Yet, the scholarly reflections that we possess are, unfortunately, governed by a problematic—a set of questions and issues—that makes certain conclusions and evaluations inevitable. For if one begins with the query that motivates Johnson and others, then one is destined to provide a derogatory account of the twenties. "Why did the Harlem Renaissance fail?" is the question, and the query is tantamount to the unexpected question sprung by a stranger as one walks a crowded street: "When, Sir, did you stop beating your wife?" Both questions are, of course, conditioned by presuppositions that restrict the field of possible responses. To ask "why" the renaissance failed is to agree, at the very outset, that the twenties did not have profoundly beneficial effects for areas of Afro-American discourse that we have only recently begun to explore in depth. Willing compliance in a problematic of "failure" is equivalent, I believe, to efforts of historians—black and otherwise—who seek causal explanations for the "failure" of the Civil Rights Movement.

It seems paradoxical that a probing scholar of Lewis's caliber—an investigator who implies strongly that he clearly understands the low esteem in which Afro-Americans will *always* be held—devotes three hundred pages to proving the "failure" of a movement that in the eyes of white America could never have been a success—precisely because it was "Afro-American." The scholarly double bind that forces Afro-Americanists to begin with *given* assessments of black intellectual history and thus laboriously work their way to dire conclusions is, quite simply, an unfortunate result of disciplinary control and power politics. The purely hypothetical injunction to an Afro-Americanist from the mainstream might be stated as follows:

> Show me, by the best scholarly procedures of the discipline, why the Harlem Renaissance was a failure, and I will reward you. By explaining this *failure,* you will have rendered an "honest" intellectual service to the discipline, to yourself, and to your race.

The primary evaluation where such an injunction is concerned remains, of course, that of the dominating society whose axiological validity and aptitude are guaranteed by its dictation of the governing problematic.

If, for the moment, we return to Anglo-American and British modernism, it is difficult to conceive of scholars devoting enormous energy to explicating the "failure" of modernism. Surely it is the case that the various "isms" of the first decades of British and American modernism did not forestall wars, feed the poor, cure the sick, empower coal miners in Wales (or West Virginia), or arrest the spread of bureaucratic technology. Furthermore—though apologists will not thank me for saying so—the artistic rebels and rebellions of British and American modernism were often decidedly puerile and undeniably transient. The type of mind-set that has governed a Harlem Renaissance problematic would be in force vis-à-vis British and American modernism, I think, if a scholar took Ranier Marie Rilke's evaluation in a letter to a friend as the indisputable truth of modernism's total effect on the world. Writing at the outbreak of World War I, Rilke laments

> that such confusion, not-knowing-which-way-to-turn, the whole sad man-made complication of this provoked fate, that exactly this incurably bad condition of things was necessary to force out evidence of whole-hearted courage, devotion and bigness? While we, the arts, the theater, called nothing forth in these very same people, brought nothing to rise and flower, were unable to change anyone.[15]

A too optimistic faith in the potential of art may, in fact, be as signal a mark of British and American modernism's "failure" as of the Harlem Renaissance. I suspect, however, that no group of British or white American scholars would take failure as their watchword and governing sign for an entire generation and its products. The predictable corollary of my suspicion is my belief that a new problematic is in order for the Harlem Renaissance. What is needed, I believe, is a reconceptualization of the questions we will ask in order to locate the efforts of the 1920s.

&

The new problematic that I am attempting to formulate begins with turn-of-the-century Afro-American discursive strategies and their motivation. My claim is that Afro-American spokespersons in late nineteenth-century America were primarily interested in a form of discourse—of public address and delivery—that would effectively articulate the needs, virtues, and strengths of a mass of Afro-Americans stranded by Jim Crow discrimination and violent lynch law in the "country districts" of the South. Both Booker T. Washington and W. E. B. DuBois set forth statements that define strategies of discourse—a black "discursive field," as it were—that are southern in focus and revolutionary in implication. For in *Up from Slavery* (1901) and *The Souls of Black Folk* (1903) alike, we find that the "subject" is the black masses of southern country districts; the goal of both works is the effective liberation of this mass group from feudal subsistence economies and legally reinforced conditions of ignorance and illiteracy. In order to be recognized and heard as Afro-American spokespersons, however, both Washington and DuBois had to assume a discursive stance in relation to the signal white American *form* for representing blacks—the minstrel mask.

Briefly, minstrelsy is a perduring legacy and strategy of representation when blacks appear in white discourse. It offers a form of appropriation, a domestic space for taking, hearing, and containing the black OTHER. Only by assuming a posture relative to this space could turn-of-the-century, Afro-American spokespersons become effectively articulate.

While the options of such spokespersons were not as clear-cut as a simple duality would suggest, I claim that Washington and DuBois, in their deployment of a "mastery of form" and a "deformation of mastery," respectively, set the contours of a field of Afro-American phonics that marks the birth of Afro-American modernism.

"Mastery" is such a common term in colleges and universities with the M.A. and M.Ph. degrees that the first strategy—"mastery of form"—is easily understood. But "deformation" is a more difficult concept.

What I intend by the term is akin to what the deconstructionist Jacques Derrida calls the "trace." The deformative sounds of Afro-America are the group phonics and common language of the masses, sounds that are traditionally labeled "substandard," "nonsensical," or "unlearned" by white speakers. But such commonly understood sounds, under a linguist's scrutiny, reveal themselves as normal, standard, literate components of one dialect. The provisional and dialectical character of black English infects, as it were, assumptions by all speakers in the United States that their language variety is anything other than a quite provisional dialect. It is impossible to sustain a master, standard, or absolute position in the face of the radically demonstrated provisionality of one's position. When Caliban knows himself as a usurped king, it is time for Prospero to depart the island.

Deformation, then, is the putative bondsperson's assured song of his or her own exalted, expressive status in an always coequal world of sounds and soundings. Anecdotally, one can image Paul Whiteman trying to sustain the title "King of Jazz" in the presence of Louis Armstrong. In the context of the present discussion, it is very difficult to imagine ninety-nine percent of the Anglo-American population of the years between 1899 and 1920 attempting to convince itself that it sounded in any way as brilliant as W. E. B. DuBois, who takes apart—or de-forms—illusions of such equality through the lyrical brilliance of his prose and his deliberately ironical and satirical mockeries of such illusion.

Washington intersperses *Up from Slavery* with outrageous darky jokes, caricatures of elderly black southern men and women, aspersions against overly ambitious northern blacks, and insulting stereotypes of the race, including a portrait of his own mother as a CHICKEN THIEF. But he also devotes a quarter of his autobiography to the art of public speaking, and his outlandish portrayals of the folk of the "country districts" reveal themselves, finally, as means of holding the attention of an audience that knows but one sound—minstrelsy—of the Negro. In effect, Washington employs sounds of the minstrel mask, or form, to create a space and audience for black public speaking. That public speaking, in turn, is employed to secure philanthropic funds for a black vocational educational institution that constitutes a moral skills center for the black folks of the country districts. Tuskegee Institute is the ultimate result of Washington's sounding on, and mastery of, the minstrel form. His mastery of form is, in fact, signified by the transcendence of minstrel *non-sense* represented by Tuskegee.

In contrast to Washington's mastery of form is DuBois's deformation of mastery. Refusing the sounds of minstrelsy, DuBois instituted black song, specifically the Afro-American spiritual, as the carrier of a black folk energy from southern country districts. Fisk University, built, in part, by monies obtained from concerts of spirituals presented by the Fisk Jubilee Singers, becomes a symbol of the type of educational centers that are needed to move Afro-Americans into the first ranks of twentieth-century life. For DuBois, the black university is the site where black folk energies and Western high culture merge, producing a sound that surpasses all traditional American music, or minstrelsy. In its emphasis on the symbolic weight of black folk spirituality and spiritual singing, *The Souls of Black Folk* stands as a singing book.

The defining discursive models of mastery and deformation provided by Washington and DuBois produce not a binary opposition, but, rather, a type of Cartesian plane—a system of coordinates in which any point on, say, a horizontal axis of mastery implies a coexistent point on a vertical axis of deformation. Hence, the notion of a discursive field.

Alain Locke, a key Afro-American spokesperson of the 1920s, seems to have possessed a brilliant comprehension of this field— his anthology *The New Negro* (1925) represents Afro-American discourse in its myriad stops and resonances. Locke's collection is a blend of businesslike mastery and lyrical and intrepid deformation. It is a public document geared toward specifically in-group and distinctively racial ends. Its purpose is to sound a comprehensive Afro-American voice, one capable of singing in the manner of spirituals (Locke himself wrote the very centerpiece essay on the Afro-American spirituals), yet adept in the ways of southern education and vocation. There are essays devoted both to Hampton-Tuskegee vocationalism and to black business enterprise in the South. Moreover, *The New Negro* employs a rich array of African and Afro-American graphics in order to frame its claims for the emergence of a "New Negro" with venerable visuals drawn from centuries-old traditions. The result is a landmark in Afro-American discourse: a collection that sounds a resonantly new note as both a public speaking manual and a deeply racial (and vernacular) singing book.

High cultural and vernacular expressivity merge in the office of moving Afro-America from subservience, low esteem, and dependency to the status of respected and boldly outspoken nation. What is signal in Locke's venture is the unabashed coalescence of mass and class, "standard" dialect and black vernacular, aesthetic and political concerns. A long and probing essay addressed to the cause of African decolonization and written by DuBois is the concluding section of Locke's work.

If *The New Negro* is representative of efforts of Harlem Renaissance spokespersons (and I believe it is), then the discursive results of Harlem in black intellectual history can scarcely be deemed failures. For Locke's work both enjoins and represents a successful expressive moment in the field constituted by a mastery of form and a deformation of mastery. *The New Negro* is a kind of manual of maroonage, a voice of a northern, urban black population that has radically absented itself from the erstwhile plantations and devastated country districts of the South. Combining a panoply of folk sounds with traditional artistic forms and entrepreneurial and practical concerns of black liberation, *The New Negro* projects an articulate, nationalistic, and independent black voice. That voice—if at times too sanguine, overly self-conscious and self-confident— constitutes a high point for energies set in motion at the turn of the century.

Further, the voice of the New Negro comprised a model for subsequent generations. When Sterling Brown, who is preeminently a poet and critic of the 1930s, assumed the mantle of "folk poet" as a natural wrap, he demonstrated the efficacy and effects of a successful Afro-American modernism. For what the Harlem Renaissance, as a masterfully achieved space within a black discursive field, enabled was a speaking or sounding place where a middle-class, Phi Beta Kappa, college-bred poet like Brown could responsibly play a distinctive note. DuBois's black, country folk as university pupils find their voice and representation in the Jubilee Singers of Nashville. The urbane Sterling Brown met the blues singer Gertrude "Ma" Rainey in Nashville (home of Fisk University). He was in the company of the famous black musicologist and Fisk faculty member John Work when they encountered Rainey at a Nashville club. What the two men drew from the tradition of folk sound represented by Rainey is now a matter of black discursive history.

Brown's *Southern Road* (1932) is one of the most outstanding collections of modern, black verse in existence. Work's collections and analyses of black song *(Folk Song of the American Negro, Jubilee, Ten Spirituals)* are unsurpassed. The productions of the two men not only guaranteed their own recognition, reward, and employment, but also brought new perspective to the group portrait of the Afro-American that had been in formation since the turn of the century. This perspective was a usable construction for writers like Richard Wright and Zora Neale Hurston who had their maturation in the thirties.

❧

The success of the Harlem Renaissance as Afro-American modernism's defining moment is signaled by *The New Negro*'s confidently voiced plays within a field marked by the mastery of form and the deformation of mastery. Only by reconstructing or remembering a discursive history of Afro-America and its socioeconomic and sociopolitical motivations and objectives can one see Harlem and its successors as articulations that carry a population not away from querulous literary ancestors, but rather *up from slavery*. Modernism for Afro-America finds impetus, empowerment, and inspiration in the black city (Harlem). No cracks and bursts in the violet air here, only soundings designed to secure the highest available social, economic, and artistic rewards for a generation that moved decisively beyond the horrors of old country districts.

A blues sound rolled forth, producing the sense of a moment's speaking, an augury of possibilities for finance and even fusion (jazz) that surely became orchestrated during the 1960s and 1970s, the period of a black arts movement that referred to itself in energetically self-conscious ways as "Renaissance II."

Perhaps the eternally modern in Afro-American discursive and intellectual history is not so much signaled by the single "Harlem Renaissance" as by a more inclusive "renaissancism" defined as an ever-present folk or vernacular drive that moves always up, beyond, and away from whatever forms of oppression a surrounding culture next devises. "Renaissancism" is, finally, the sign of the modern that joins Harlem and the *Indigene* movement of Haiti and African Negritude. One might say that the success of Afro-American renaissancism consists in its heralding of a countermodernism, as it were, a drive unlike the exquisite disillusionment and despair of Britain and Jazz Age U.S.A. I use "counter" just as advisedly as I earlier employed "modernism" alone, for now I believe the complexities—a very peculiar set of expressive manifestations and critical and theoretical issues—of Afro-American twentieth-century expression should be comprehensible. Recognition of such complexities leads to the recognitions of a trace, a something not accounted for in traditional, Anglo-American definitions of modernism. One definition of what can be recognized is a "counter-modernism."

This countertradition found its socioeconomic and sociopolitical groundings in what the sagacious Franz Fanon called "dying colonialism." *The New Negro*, as stated earlier, concludes with an essay by DuBois that sings, figuratively, this death of colonialism and sounds a note of liberation to which hundreds of millions of formerly colonized, darker peoples of the world can march. This note from Harlem, as any scan of the global scene today will reveal, is, perhaps, the most thoroughly modern sound the United States has yet produced.

Notes

1. Harry Levin, "What Was Modernism?" *Massachusetts Review* 1 (1960): 609–30. All citations are marked by page numbers in parentheses.

2. Robert Martin Adams, "What Was Modernism?" *Hudson Review* 31 (1978): 19–33. Hereafter in my notes, I will list the full reference. Subsequent cites will be marked by page numbers in parentheses.

3. Ihab Hassan. "POSTmodernISM A Paracritical Bibliography," *New Literary History* 3 (Autumn 1971): 5–30.

4. T. S. Eliot, "The Waste Land," in Maynard Mack et al., eds., *Modern Poetry,* 2nd ed. (Englewood Cliffs, N.J., 1961), 157–58.

5. F. Scott Fitzgerald, *The Great Gatsby* (New York, 1953), 13.

6. Lionel Trilling, "On the Teaching of Modern Literature," in *Beyond Culture* (New York, 1965), 327.

7. I refer, of course, to Conrad's "Heart of Darkness."

8. D. H. Lawrence, *Women in Love* (New York, 1974).

9. The reference is to Eugene O'Neill's *The Emperor Jones.*

10. Wystan Hugh Auden's ordinary citizen as "Modern Man" is coldly described by the speaker of "The Citizen (To JS/07/M/378 This marble Monument Is Erected by the State)," a 1940 poem, as "in the modern sense of an old-fashioned word, he was a saint." Quoted from Mack, *Modern Poetry,* 206. The speaker is not undone when his/her report is broken by someone's question about such exemplary conduct: "Was he free? Was he happy?" The speaker answers: ". . . The Question is absurd:/Had anything been wrong, we should certainly have heard."

11. In *Madness and Civilization*, Michel Foucault argues that it is de rigueur for a rational, bourgeois, capitalist state to "confine the poor, the criminal, and the insane in order to know the boundaries of affluence, sanity, and innocence." It is, however, *confinement* in itself that enforces the categories; if you are an inmate of a "total institution" (like a prison, or American Slavery as the "Prisonhouse of Bondage"), then you are automatically classified according to the defining standards of that institution. The Kantian reference is, of course, to the *Critique of Judgement* (1790). Once "ART" and "AESTHETICS" are distinguished from "popular culture" and "low taste," then one has effected a confinement that can be enforced merely by mentioning a word. Such distinctions—resting on Western metaphysics—can be used to defend and preserve canons of literature and to protect "artistic" masterpieces from all criticism. Only "*men* of Taste" are held to possess the developed "aesthetic sense" and sensibility requisite to identification and judgment of genuine works of "art." If such men declare that a product is *not* ART but a product of some other category, there is no escape from their authority of confinement—except subversion.

12. "Foreword," *Challenge* 1(1934): 1.

13. Nathan Huggins, *Harlem Renaissance* (New York, 1971). Subsequent citations appear in text.

14. David Levering Lewis, *When Harlem Was in Vogue* (New York, 1981). Subsequent citations appear in text. The phrase "when Harlem was in vogue" is drawn from the section of Langston Hughes's autobiography *The Big Sea* (1940) devoted to the Harlem Renaissance. Hughes writes of the renaissance as a mere "vogue" set in motion and largely financed by white downtowners while Negroes played minstrel and trickster roles in it all. A time of low-seriousness and charming high jinks is what Hughes (one hopes ironically) portrays. In fact, I think Hughes's characterization is as much a product of the dreadful disappointment he suffered when his patron (Mrs. R. Osgood Mason) dumped him because he decided to write an "engaged" poem, a "socialist" response to the opening of a luxury hotel in New York when so many were starving. He reads treacherous patronage over the entire Harlem Renaissance. Further, to say, as Hughes does, that you were "only funning" is to dampen the pain that results if you were really serious and your patron was "funning" all along. In any case, I believe Hughes's account (partially because he lived and produced wonderful work through subsequent generations) has had an enormous effect on subsequent accounts of the renaissance. In many ways, this effect has been unfortunate.

15. Quotes from Miklos Szabolcsi, "Avant-garde, Neo-avant-garde, Modernism: Questions and Suggestions," *New Literary History* 3 (1971): 75.

ॐ

Getting Spliced: Modernism and Sexual Difference

Carolyn Burke
University of California, Davis

SINCE THE PUBLICATION OF HUGH KENNER'S *THE POUND ERA*, EZRA POUND
has increasingly displaced T. S. Eliot as the representative American
modernist poet, especially among writers and critics who see continuity between the early days of modernism and its recent Postmodernist permutations. Pound also occupies a central position
from the related perspective of those who, in Marjorie Perloff's
words, "read synchronically, against the backdrop of the avant-garde
arts of Europe in the period *entre deux guerres*," for whom "Pound's
structures seem quintessentially modern." In this view, *how* the
poem is put together is of greater interest than *what* it says:

> If poetry teaches us how to talk to ourselves, it is not because it provides
> us with a vision of Reality but because its processes imitate the processes
> of the external world as we have come to know it.[1]

Moreover, as Perloff observes, Poundians adopt the vocabulary of
their poet. They pay close attention to Pound's formal strategies,

I am most grateful to Janice Radway, Daniel J. Singal, and Janet Wright for their
help with the "splicing" of this article.

chief of which is parataxis or juxtaposition, the constellation of "luminous details" in a pattern of energies that Kenner has described at length (for example, in his claim that in Pound's *Homage to Sextus Propertius* [1919], "the words lie flat like the forms on a Cubist surface").[2]

One can argue, however, that paratactic modernism is first and most clearly seen in the prewar writing of Gertrude Stein, and furthermore, that Stein's version of collage poetics offers an alternate model to Pound's. Already before the war, Stein was more attuned than Pound to the parallels suggested by Cubist collage to writers who wanted language to imitate the changing conditions of the outside world or for whom questions of sexual difference could be figured as elements within writing. From our own vantage point, moreover, her example suggests ways of reading the women writers whose work has not always seemed to conform to modernist tradition as defined by Pound's (and the Poundians') criteria. Cyrena N. Pondrum asks us to "wonder about the adequacy of our definitions of modernism" when these have difficulty situating women writers:

> We have too much shaped these definitions to describe Eliot, Pound, Joyce and Yeats alone, without accounting, in these broader definitions of literary history, for what modernism meant in the hands of Stein, H. D., Sitwell, Woolf. . . . When we do take such account, we may find ourselves understanding the male modernists better as well.[3]

And if one adds Marianne Moore, Mina Loy, Djuna Barnes, Laura Riding, and others to this list of female modernists whose writing does not quite fit traditional definitions, we may find that their syntactical and rhetorical solutions to gender issues suggest to us more flexible, and imaginative ways of reading, offering new perspectives on the work of their male contemporaries. Pound's developing theories of modernist writing during the 1910s are of particular interest, then, given his attention to women poets during this period.

While Pound was composing *Homage to Sextus Propertius* between 1917 and 1919, he was also developing a critical theory that could justify and explain this new departure in his poetry. By 1918 Pound had turned from the vocabulary of the visual arts that generated his prewar theories toward the more intellectual idea of poetry that he called first "verbalism" and then "logopoeia." Distinct from the lyric's reliance on music ("melopoeia") and the imagist poem's dependence on the presentational strategies of the plastic arts ("phanopoeia"), logopoeia depends upon language itself: it is "the dance of the intellect among words . . . the latest come, and perhaps most tricky and undependable mode" of poetry.[4] It was, moreover, a modern "attitude of mind," typified by the self-mocking irony and literary sophistication that Pound admired in the poetry of Jules Laforgue and in T. S. Eliot's Laforgue-inspired writing. In such poetry, this kind of self-referential irony, "the citadel of the intelligent,"[5] revealed a new poetic sensibility that was at once highly literate and critical. "It is language commenting upon its own possibilities and limitations as language,"[6] or as contemporary critical language would have it, poetry that is both "metalinguistic" and "intertextual." Finally, logopoeia requires the use of an analytic intelligence in both writer and reader, with the reader supplying the missing connections to join different levels of style and diction all set in juxtaposition without benefit of transitions. A sign of intelligence in writing, logopoeia could, then, perform the kind of cultural critique that Pound felt necessary given the state of society in the postwar years. But, Pound feared, because such poetry demanded strenuous intellectual activity on the part of the reader, "this process being unnatural to the majority of mankind, the way of the ironical is beset with snares and with furze-bushes."[7] It was practiced by, and appealed to, a self-conscious elite.

It is rarely observed that Pound first set forth his definition of "logopoeia" in a 1918 essay on Marianne Moore and Mina Loy, where he called it "poetry that is akin to nothing but language, which is a dance of the intelligence among words and ideas." He insisted, furthermore, that both poets were "possibly in unconsciousness, among the followers of Jules Laforgue"[8]: presumably they, like Laforgue and Eliot, also wrote "not the popular language of any country but an international tongue common to the excessively cultivated."[9] However, although Pound in this first definition of logopoeia had categorized a crucial aspect of what we now call "modernism" (and anticipated important strains in contemporary poetry), until recently it has been mentioned as no more than another quirky idea from his post-Vorticist years, and never in connection with the issue of gender that its origins would suggest. For example, although Perloff's *The Dance of the Intellect* proposes that we see the break with lyric, the use of collage poetics, and the logopoeic "attitude of mind" as the essence of Poundian modernism, no mention is made there of Pound's suggestive and problematic linkage of logopoeia with the female poets whose "sinuosities and mental quirks"[10] inspired him to formulate the theory. Yet Pound's sponsorship of the two women is notable precisely because he appears to have ignored the fact that they *were* women.

In the midst of his praise for their distinctly modern poetic intelligence, Pound nevertheless failed to notice other features of their poetry: their different uses of what he called "melopoeia" and "phanopoeia," and their differently inflected awareness of how sexual difference can matter as both the "what" and the "how" in modernist poetry. In other words, because of Pound's self-imposed limitations of thought about the links between gender and creativity (which will be explored briefly in a later section), he could not see that logopoeia in the hands of a female poet might produce a different kind of cultural critique, one that focused on issues of gender. By this time, Pound was already certain that "genius" was coded "masculine," and seems to have felt that, unlike the sentimental poetesses of the nineteenth century, intelligent modern women like Moore and Loy wrote just like men. Before probing the reasons behind his blindness to gender as an element within modernist poetry, we should first identify an important counterstrain of modernist poetics—centered on the modalities of joining and separation, union and disunion—that was first exemplified in the paratactic and gender-conscious writing of Gertrude Stein.

&

Gertrude Stein remembered Pound "as a village explainer, excellent if you were a village, but if you were not, not." [11] It is hard to imagine Stein tolerating rival claims to genius, let alone Pound's logopoeic theories, since she had had to struggle with her own earlier association of masculinity with genius until her discovery of "female" modes of creativity in her domestic relations with Alice Toklas and in women artists like Isadora Duncan. She and Pound came at the central modernist question of the link between language and representation from different angles and under different psychosexual pressures. Furthermore, by the early 1920s, Pound had only begun to integrate into the structure of the *Cantos* the implications of what Stein had learned from Cézanne and the Cubists before the war, that juxtaposition could be utilized as the formal principle of sustained modernist writing.

When Stein wrote in *G.M.P.*, "a splice is something that causes a connection," [12] she was probably thinking about the uses of syntax to "cause connections"—first, between the disparate objects in the world and the words used to signify them, and then, among the words themselves. At the same time, she may have been thinking about connections of another kind; in Richard Bridgman's words, "when Gertrude Stein spoke of the sentence, she was likely to be making symbolic formulations that referred to human relationships as well as verbal ones." [13] As an attentive reader of the nineteenth-century English novel, Stein undoubtedly knew the slang use of the word "splice" as a synonym for "marriage," and she must have pondered the implications of "getting spliced" as an account of "getting married." Since *G.M.P.*, written during Stein's 1912 summer holiday in Spain with Alice Toklas, asserts that "one bed was used" and celebrates "that pleasure in all union," it is not surprising that the words "wedding," "marriage," and "union" recur like a joyous leitmotif that confirms the initial splicing of their lives in the conclusion of "Ada," Stein's portrait of Toklas. The splice that joins separate elements edge to edge (as in the splicing of film) provided Stein with the means to imag[in]e a union that was simultaneously syntactical and erotic. Although such implicit punning lurks within many of her remarks about syntax, it has not often been noticed that Stein's formulation of modernist technique—for the splice makes possible one kind of juxtaposition—contains a poetics of gender hidden within its apparently formalist concerns. Moreover, Stein's implicit parallel between verbal connectives and the modes of human intercourse raises important questions about the participation of women writers in literary modernism and the sexual poetics of its projects.

Although Stein's infrequent remarks about the traces of gender within writing are typically enigmatic, they nevertheless hint at ways in which the two were linked in her mind. Stein had a long conversation with Dashiell Hammett, during the California swing of her 1934–35 American tour:

I said to Hammett there is something that is puzzling. In the nineteenth century the men when they were writing did invent all kinds and a great number of men. The women on the other hand never could invent women they always made the women be themselves seen splendidly or sadly or heroically or beautifully or despairingly or gently, and they never could make any other kind of woman. From Charlotte Brontë to George Eliot and many years later this was true. Now in the twentieth century it is men who do it. The men all write about themselves as strong or weak or mysterious or passionate or drunk or controlled but always themselves as the women used to do in the nineteenth century.[14]

She also told an interviewer during this trip that "literature—creative literature— unconnected with sex is inconceivable," then observed cautiously "but not literary sex, because sex is a pan of something of which the other pans are not sex at all." [15] Although sex is "a part" of a larger "something," it is perhaps best seen as the splicing or the glue that holds that "something" together. It is to be found "below" or "behind" or "within" creative literature.

Several years before she toured the United States as a celebrity, Stein began to formulate her ideas about this larger "something," which she called "composition." When she lectured at Oxford and Cambridge in 1926, in response to Edith Sitwell's appeal for her help in the modernist cause, Stein was already taking a historical view of the cause and her role within it. She explained that, although successive generations were "all alike," what differed for each generation was "the way life is conducted," which is "authentically speaking, composition." Those who live within a particular "composition" do not normally recognize its representative patterns, and, for this reason, reject art that embodies or re-creates them. As a result, it usually happens that "those who are creating the modern composition authentically are naturally only of importance when they are dead because by that time the modern composition having become past is classified." However, because the Great War altered the way that her contemporaries understood reality, "every one became consciously became aware of the existence of the authenticity of the modern composition" [*sic*]. In fact, the "war may be said to have advanced a general recognition of the expression of the contemporary composition by almost thirty years." [16] Since Stein's account of this "modern composition" includes the patterns of relationships of those who live within it, we may assume that these comprise the patterns of connection evoked in *G.M.P.* and celebrated in *Tender Buttons*: the many "weddings," "marriages," and "unions," as well as their opposites, the mismated pairings and disunions of works like "Miss Furr and Miss Skeene," "Two Women," and *Two*. Moreover, Stein's phrase implies a parallel between what we now call the culture of an era and the way in which the people of that era write: the cultural "composition" of a given society is reflected in the formal structures of its literary "compositions." In this view, writers like Stein (and Moore and Loy) express the changing psychosexual modalities of their lives in the "connectedness" or "disconnectedness," and especially in the connective tissue, of their work.

Even if most critics agree that "modernism is our inevitable art—as Gertrude Stein put it, the only 'composition' appropriate to the new composition in which we live, the new dispositions of space and time," [17] they are far from agreement about the nature of its formal dispositions, its poetics. Stein herself pointed the way to the familiar account of collage as the modernist poetic when she recalled how the "modern composition" first attracted public attention in 1915:

> I very well remember at the beginning of the war being with Picasso on the boulevard Raspail when the first camouflaged truck passed. It was at night, we had heard of camouflage but we had not yet seen it and Picasso amazed looked at it and then cried out, yes it is we who made it, that is cubism. [18]

Seen against the backdrop of continental "compositions" at this time, only writing that explores the syntactical constraints and the collision between conceptual and perceptual elements in the process of signification seems thoroughly modern. From this perspective, as David Antin argued in an influential essay, Stein "is our only pure modernist," and *Tender Buttons* "the only language work that lives in the same time as Picasso's Cubism." [19] Both Marjorie Perloff and Jayne Walker recently followed Antin's lead to show that Stein's modernism does not derive from Picasso's experiments with collage but is, in Walker's words, "a logical product of Stein's parallel investigation of the same fundamental issue that preoccupied first Cézanne and then Picasso and Braque: the problem of representation, redefined in terms of the distinctive resources of their medium." [20] But these critics have relatively little to say about gender as an element within the collage poetics that both describe so well, perhaps because we have only begun to speculate about the ways in which, for Stein, the splices, seams, and joints that connect nouns and pronouns (the equivalents of *papiers collés* in her medium) also evoke psychosexual joining.

Yet surely both Picasso and Stein knew the colloquial use of the French word "collage" to mean a couple living together without benefit of marriage, in an arrangement that had been "pasted" together (as in Zola's novels):

> The word collage is derived from *coller* (to paste or glue) and means pasting and, by extension, that which is pasted. The name, like the pictures, had carried a shock, the word collage having the slang meaning of an illicit love affair, which must have delighted Braque and Picasso with its inference of shameful cohabitation between nobly born oil paint and the streetwalker newspaper. . . . Behind the shock was wit: first in the basic form of disparates coupled in surprising and revealing combinations, and second, the use of newspaper clippings as verbal or visual puns. [21]

Since by 1912, when Picasso invented collage and Stein wrote *G.M.P.*, both artists were living in differently choreographed but equally unconventional "menages à la colle," they must have been amused by the wit implicit in the new term for what Stein would later call "the modern composition." If you couldn't get spliced, you could still "cause connections," in life as in art.

ૐ

Although Pound often asserted links between sexuality and writing, his theories about these matters could not have been more unlike Stein's. For example, commenting on Rémy de Gourmont's "sexual intelligence" in 1919, Pound asserted that "sex, in so far as it is not a purely physiological reproductive mechanism, lies in the domain of aesthetics, the junction of tactile and magnetic senses." [22] But he focused here on the individual artist's sensibility rather than on the possibility that linguistic processes may be seen to parallel relational processes in the external world. Furthermore, his idea about relations between the sexes can only be described as increasingly phallic in emphasis.

In 1919 Marianne Moore received a letter from him with a poem in place of a salutation; it began: "The female is a chaos/the male/ is a fixed point of stupidity." [23] A later postface to his translation of Gourmont's *Physique de l'amour* explains why the categories "woman" and "intelligence" coexisted with difficulty in Pound's mind. Asserting that "it is more than likely that the brain itself, is . . . only a sort of great clot of genital fluid held in suspense or reserve," he posits that the act of thought occurs with "man really the phallus or spermatozoide charging, head-on, the female chaos." Creativity, then, is "an act like fecundation, like the male cast of the human seed." "Even oneself has felt it, driving any new idea into the great passive vulva of London," [24] Pound concludes. It would have been hard for any woman to take comfort in finding her writing praised for its intelligence if this was the critic's definition of intellect.

What role remains for "the female chaos" as subject in Pound sexual poetics? She is "a sort of negation of action," [25] a passive material receptivity awaiting fulfillment, a Molly Bloom as "Penelope, la femme . . . vagin, symbole de la terre, mer morte dans laquelle l'intelligence male retombe." [26] She exists only to nurture the gushes of "cerebral fluid," which, "striking matter, force[s] it into all sorts of forms." Pound seemed to believe that by ascribing this "complementary" role to the female, he had protected himself against the charge of "writing an anti-feminist tract," even though, in his view, a woman's social role is not to create but to give support to the men who do what she is incapable of doing: "woman, the conservator, the inheritor of past gestures, clever, practical, as Gourmont says, not inventive, always the best disciple of any inventor." [27]

Yet it is a paradoxical fact of modernist literary history that in spite of these theories, Pound was an important supporter of Moore and Loy, particularly during the years when he *was* most vulnerable to the charge of antifeminism. Although Pound promoted women poets in the same spirit with which he worked for the recognition of their male counterparts, he championed them for the wrong reasons, or rather, for reasons extraneous to what they were doing. Because he saw their writing in the context of his program for the improvement of the artist's status and the modernization of poetry, he was blind to the ways in which an awareness of gender informs their work. After the war, his chief concern was to make intelligence, rather than emotion, the energizing power behind poetry, to rain its verbal arsenal—irony, satire, and analytic scrutiny—on the inert stupidities of mass culture. He enlisted Moore and Loy, therefore, in his newly discovered logopoeic "tradition" of writers who use "the weapon of their intellect to 'drive' intelligence into society in an act of social reform." [28]

Pound formulated the idea of logopoeia during the period in which, according to Ian Bell, his "major battles were conducted . . . to cultivate an appropriate vocabulary for the modernist enterprise," and his scientific analogies developed from his "concern with the status and the public acknowledgement of the writer's situation, predominant interests of Pound's modernity." [29] Thus, Pound's phallic poetics may be seen in part as a response to his own situation as an expatriate in literary London, where, according to Ford Madox Hueffer (Ford), "a man of letters [was] regarded as something less than a man." [30] Already at a disadvantage as a "colonial," an exile, and a man of letters, Pound's sense of himself as a member of the more powerful sex was further challenged by the apparent threat posed by the suffragists' political and literary agitation. Like the aggressive dress and behavior that he adopted in these years, his recourse to theories about the passive nature of the female may have functioned to shore up some of his uncertainties about his place in the world.

When in 1914, for example, Pound entertained the sculptor Henri Gaudier-Brzeska and his companion Sophie Brzeska, the conversation focused on abstraction in art, by which Pound meant the internal aesthetic arrangements of a poem or a painting; these produced abstract "emotions" that were different from the personal "feelings" expressed in more traditional forms. Gaudier-Brzeska responded to Sophie's difficulty with this distinction by insisting that women should not dabble in art. Pound agreed and added, "Why do [women] trouble themselves about these matters—why worry about their battle for emancipation—since they're strong enough to dominate us." He then described the sort of "strong" woman whose "genius" he so admired that he once planned to make her the heroine of an epic: the tenth-century Roman matron Marozia, who, through her three marriages to important men, "became the most powerful person in Rome." As if inspired by Pound's declaration of respect for "genius above all," Gaudier-Brzeska decided that evening to sculpt the bust of Pound that would illustrate his subject's theories.[31]

For Hugh Kenner, this understanding between poet and sculptor (and the bust that resulted from it) is a crucial and heroic moment in the development of Pound's aesthetic. But one can also interpret this incident as emblematic of Pound's increasing anxiety about the connections between artistic genius and sexual difference. Because women already dominate, their "battle for emancipation" does not deserve attention, and, in any case, the only woman worthy of notice resembles the men whose genius for order Pound will celebrate in the *Cantos*. It was fitting, furthermore, that Gaudier-Brzeska approached the monumental three-foot marble block that Pound gave him for the bust as if it were a megalith from the Easter Islands, endowed with primitive sexual energy. His "Hieratic Head of Ezra Pound," or "Ezra in the form of a marble phallus" (Wyndham Lewis's words), takes literally the idea of "Pound as the seminal figure of modern poetry," as well as his theory of the link between masculinity and creative genius.[32]

The "Hieratic Head," which became a kind of fetishistic personal emblem for Pound according to Alan Durant,[33] also seemed to prefigure his post-Vorticist call for a modern poetic language that would be "harder and saner . . . 'nearer the bone' . . . as much like granite as it can be," a masculine language free from the "emotional slither" of nineteenth-century poetry.[34] This opposition between masculine and feminine modes of writing had already been crystallized, however, as one of the bases of Vorticism in Pound's 1914 remarks about the different artistic stances implied in Impressionism and Imagism. He posits

> two opposed ways of thinking of a man: firstly you may think of him as that toward which perception moves, as the toy of circumstance, as the plastic substance *receiving* impressions; secondly, you may think of him as directing a certain fluid force against circumstance, as conceiving instead of merely reflecting and observing.[35]

This distinction appears to deal with a social situation in which the literary man, who is suspected of being "effeminate if not a decent

kind of eunuch," [36] asserts that he is not a womanlike "toy of cir-
cumstance," but an active, productive member of society. Pound's
postwar emphasis on the conceptual dimension of modernist poetry—logopoeia—developed from this inherently voluntarist idea
of the artist's role and the phallic theories of creativity enshrined
in Gaudier-Brzeska's tribute to his fellow Vorticist.

Seen in this light, Pound's sponsorship of Moore and Loy is
paradoxical, to say the least. If poetic intelligence is the forceful
emanation of the poet's mental capacity, then, like Marozia, intelligent women poets must also be seen as honorary men, "geniuses
above all." In his *Little Review* essay on Moore and Loy, Pound assumes that both women are university educated, because their poetry is "the utterance of clever people in despair, . . . a mind cry,
more than a heart cry." Their writing is "neither simple, sensuous
nor passionate," but it does exhibit "the arid clarity . . . of *le tem-
perament de l'americaine,* . . . a distinctly national product." [37] This
account sets them up as sisters in logopoeia but cannot recognize
the ways in which their awareness of themselves as women writers
produced poetry that is at once part of the overall modernist
project, yet distinct from it; consequently, it cannot make adequate
distinctions between the different kinds of logopoeia "au féminin"
that these two poets display. If we recall the principles of Stein's
"modern composition," especially the "splice . . . that causes a connection," however, we may learn to read the female modernists on
their own terms and respond to their joining of intellectual work
with a female subjectivity.

≈

Mina Loy, herself a sympathetic reader of Gertrude Stein's unpublished manuscripts in the years before the war, reached conclusions
much like Stein's, but with very different results. In the special
sense in which one may call Stein's writing Cubist in this period,
one might also describe Loy as the only English-language Futurist
poet, even though she denied membership in that band of aesthetic radicals and later satirized their theories and behavior. Just
as Picasso's example had encouraged Stein, the Futurists'
reorientation of artistic attention to the modes of modern life

prompted Loy's turn from a fin-de-siècle aestheticism to an engagement with modernist art and poetry. Her first published work bears witness to the catalyzing way in which Marinetti's program for the transformation of "passatista" habits of mind provoked by Loy's own realization that her contemporaries were experiencing a "crisis in consciousness." A manifesto set like a long poem, "Aphorisms on Futurism" appeared in the January 1914 issue of *Camera Work*, along with writing by Stein; in it Loy speaks as a Futurist prophet, proclaiming that the social and artistic conventions of the past are inadequate to express the complexity of modern life:

> TODAY is the crisis in consciousness.
>
> CONSCIOUSNESS cannot spontaneously accept or reject new forms, as offered by creative genius; it is the new form, for however great a period of time it may remain a mere irritant—that molds consciousness to the necessary amplitude for holding it.
>
> CONSCIOUSNESS has no climax.[38]

While Loy's declaration shares some of Pound's faith in the power of "creative genius," it also anticipates Stein's idea of the "modern composition," or the "new form."

As an artist trained in London, Munich, and Paris and a member of the influential Salon d'Automme, Loy approached the blank page as if it were a canvas. She was like Apollinaire, a "poète fondé en peinture." [39] While Pound's sense of the artist's relation to form focused on the poet-sculptor's forceful mental imprint upon matter, both Loy and Stein were more concerned with the physical properties of language as the "belle matière" itself. By 1912, although resident in Florence, Loy was sufficiently familiar with Cubism and had read enough of Stein's manuscripts to grasp the implications of these "new forms," for both poetry and prose. When the Futurists arrived there in 1913, she had already been thinking about a kind of writing in which point of view, like perspective in painting, could be displaced, the structure of the line or sentence loosened, and punctuation discarded so that words might lie side by side. In a sense, Stein's writing had prepared the way for Loy's response to Futurism, while Marinetti's volatility and contradictory assertions about woman's role in the transformed future stimulated her to write. (Not long after dismissing Marinetti in 1920 as a "conjuring commercial traveller" with "novelties from/Paris in his pocket," [40]

Loy published her poetic homage to Stein as "Curie/of the labora-
tory/of vocabulary" in *the transatlantic review*. This appropriately
unpunctuated tribute suggests that the modernist project to un-
earth in writing some liberating linguistic energy could, in fact, be
combined with a "feminist" project of changing consciousness.)[41]

Loy's vision of psychosexual and syntactic connection was, however, the negative or other side of Stein's more positive view in the
years 1913 to 1915, most likely because her marriage unravelled
during these years and she became involved in a complicated emotional dialogue with the Futurists. Unlike Stein's poems in celebration of the domestic happiness suggested in *G.M.P.* and *Tender Buttons*, the broken syntax of Loy's 1915 "Love Songs" embodies a
disillusioned vision of psychosexual relations that reflects their period of composition, during the first year of the Great War. Loy's
syntactic strategies take into account Marinetti's *parole in libertà*
(words set free from the constraints of poetic and grammatical
conventions), without, however, espousing his voluntarist and mi-
sogynistic ideology. Where Marinetti rejects romantic love as a
"passatista" idealization of sexual relations, Loy writes instead of
the psychic and social disconnectedness that results from a love
affair come apart at the seams.

With none of the Futurists' *modernolatria* (worship of the modern), Loy nevertheless incorporates the imagery of the modern city
as the cultural context of this failed attempt at union. But like the
sexual "collage" that comes unglued in "Love Songs," these urban
images also prove unstable in their new configurations within the
poems. Although Pound, at this time, appears to have had faith in
the image, or artistic form in general, as numinously given, Loy, as
a trained artist, knew that images were inherently unreliable and
no more numinous with meaning than anything else. She also knew
that images could dissolve, shatter, break into their components,
fade out, or prove unrecognizable from different angles of vision.
Her contacts with the futurist painters Carrà and Balla, who broke
images and figures in motion into a painterly version of the successive frames in a cinematic sequence, demonstrated that the poetic
image was what the mind determined it could be: it had no fixed
objective reality.[42] It might or might not be mimetic or representational, and more likely than not, it resembled those unstable mental pictures being discussed by the new theory of psychoanalysis.
For Loy, images partook of the other reality that in "Aphorisms"

she called "mental spatiality," an autonomous realm quite unlike
Pound's model of intellectual activity as the mind's forceful im-
printing upon matter. Where his "logopoeia" emphasizes the energizing consciousness of the artist's mind, her "mental spatiality"
suggests, rather, a model more like a painterly version of the
Freudian unconscious, in which images and meanings lie dormant
yet accessible to the artist through a creative process that is a kind
of self-analysis. Appropriately, Loy began her sequence of what
would become thirty-four "Love Songs" within this subjective "mental spatiality":

Spawn   of   Fantasies
Silting the appraisable
Pig Cupid   his rosy snout
Rooting erotic garbage
"Once upon a time"
Pulls a weed   white and star-topped
Among wild oats   sewn in mucous-membrane[43]

Although one recognizes some of the familiar images and language
of romantic love, an unsettling effect is created by their extreme
dispersion. Not only are there no clear subject-verb relations to
provide us with a sense of statement being made, but there is also
no apparent speaker or lyric voice, as we might have expected from
the title of the sequence. To whom these love songs are addressed
is also unclear: neither partner in the love relationship appears to
be present within the first poem. Furthermore, there is no punctuation except for the quotation marks around "Once upon a time"
and the hyphens connecting the two compound words. Syntactic
modes such as agency, subordination, and completion of statement
are lacking. Words and phrases float on the white space of the
page in a loosely connected pattern, like a free-floating collage in
which the elements stick onto the surface with relative and changing degrees of adhesiveness. These images may themselves be
spawned by fantasy and thus undergoing the process of appraisal
or sorting ("silting") by a speaker who seeks to understand them.

In the next stanza, the tentative way in which the first-person
speaker makes an appearance works to identify the difficulties of
knowing with the uncertainties of perception:

I would   an   eye in a bengal light
Eternity in a sky-rocket
Constellations in an ocean
Whose rivers run no fresher
Than a trickle of saliva

Although this desiring "I" is crossed chiasmically with its homonym,
the "eye," the speaker knows that the images seen are the spawn of
the fantasy, and, therefore, in flux and unreliable. The experiences
of sexuality—the encounter with the phallic Pig Cupid and the
descent from the garden of romance to the very physical geographies of "mucous membrane" and "saliva"—have resulted in a flash
of illumination (probably orgasmic fulfillment) that is too quickly
deflated. It is then seen as only another illusion following a moment of heightened consciousness. Critics who try to identify one
image or another with the "male" and "female" of this momentous
but deflationary sexual encounter typically run into trouble, since
Loy's love song itself envisions the momentary loss of fixed identi-
ties—a blending or exchange of "images" that then fall back into
their old oppositions.

The speaker then makes the first declarative statement in this
poem, which characteristically voices a wary distrust:

These are suspect places

I must live in my lantern
Trimming subliminal flicker
Virginal to the bellows
Of Experience
    Coloured   Glass

Two things only may be stated: first, the "places" of love, and reflection upon it in poetry, are "suspect," not only because of their
nature but also because of the rhetoric of "once upon a time" with
which the speaker has been taught to understand romance. Second, she—for we may now offer a qualifier of this unknown "I"—
decides therefore to be a wise virgin, preparing her lantern (once
again the apparatus for perception and vision) for her god's return.
The unusual setting of the phrase "coloured glass" off to the right

with a marked space between the words suggests that, although the first poem places its colors, textures, and allusions like so many shapes in a stained glass window, its juxtapositions more nearly resemble the temporary image patterns of a kaleidoscope; for without the divinely given illuminations that shine through a church window, meaning comes only in "subliminal flickers."

In a series of abrupt changes of focus that resemble those of a kaleidoscope or a cinematic montage, the next poem moves from the "I's" withdrawal from the "suspect places" of sexuality to a close-up look at another image of Pig Cupid, the male principle, and then shifts back to a more idealizing interpretation of the lover's mind, the sanctuary on whose threshold she is forced to wait:

The skin-sack
In which a wanton duality
Packed
All the completions of my infructuous impulses
Something the shape of a man
To the casual vulgarity of the merely observant
More of a clock-work mechanism
Running down against time
To which I am not paced
    My finger-tips are numb from fretting your hair
A god's door-mat
On the threshold of your mind

The "wanton duality" may be the primary fact of sexual difference, the source of the insurmountable division between "I" and the "you" addressed in the last three lines. Their different conceptions of sexual love, as well as their different desires and natures, keep her at the threshold of what she imagined to be the kingdom of heaven, where she would find completion. As in the first love song, however, the dominant mode is that of incompletion: no whole or complete statement is possible given this vision of sexual nonconnectedness until the speaker steps back from the experience in the final section of the first poem. Here, too, the emphasis on vision as opposed to "the casual vulgarity of the merely observant" contrasts the ideal of romantic love and mutual divinity with the actual failure of sexual union and the difficulty of overcoming this primary division. Nonunion is reflected on the page in the poem's incomplete statements and nonclosure. In contrast to Pound's voluntarist theories of the poet's intellectual powers at this time, Loy's scepticism considers the mind's conscious efforts insufficient to bridge such gaps, let alone create a "happy" ending.

The third poem posits a "we," the lovers as a couple, and a form of communion set in an imaginary past that never was attainable, thereby mocking the naiveté of "Once upon a time."

> We might have coupled
> In the bed-ridden monopoly of a moment
> Or broken flesh with one another
> At the profane communion table
> Where wine is spill't on promiscuous lips
> We might have given birth to a butterfly
> With the daily news
> Printed in blood on its wings

Through the repeated use of the past perfect subjunctive, Loy conveys the idea of a psychosexual completion imagined but unreachable. "We might have coupled . . ./We might have given birth. . . ." These verb forms suggest possibilities that are even more out of reach than those envisioned by the conditional "I would" of the first poem. What might have been a form of sacred communion has been profaned by their mechanical coupling, the "broken flesh" of this disunion that is the sexual act shorn of all emotional and spiritual meaning (much as the Futurists imagined it in their denunciations of romance).

"Love Songs" concludes on a note of self-mockery in its final poem (which consists of one ironic line: "Love————the preeminent literateur"). Loy returned to the ideal of the union that might have been in "The Effectual Marriage," which Pound offers as an example of logopoeia. In this poem, the scholarly Miovanni and his adoring wife Gina are seen with withering detachment as the incarnation of traditional relations between the sexes.[44] But, as Virginia Kouidis remarks, "the ideal fails in Miovanni's haughty isolation and Gina's enslavement to love. Their marriage possesses only a negative completeness; each supports the other's self-deceptions. . . ." [45]

So here we   might dispense with her
Gina   being a female
But she was more than that
Being an incipience   a correlative
an instigation of the reaction of man
From the palpable to the transcendent
Mollescent irritant of his fantasy[46]

We infer all is not wedded bliss from the speaker's ironic use of the pompous polysyllables that Miovanni himself might favor, a pedantic magniloquence that undermines itself and stresses both partners' isolation in what could have been a complementary relationship: "What had Miovanni made of his ego/In his library/What had Gina wondered among the pots and pans/One never asked the other." When Pound reprinted this poem in 1920 and again in 1931 (in an edited version, which he cut as he had cut *The Wasteland*), he retitled it "The Ineffectual Marriage" and observed that it was one of the poems "which may possibly define their epoch."[47] One wonders to what extent Pound's praise for Loy's portrait of a marriage reflects an understanding that its author used the wit of logopoeia to treat the thematics of sexual [dis]union from a feminine, not to say feminist, perspective.

❧

In the May 1918 issue of *The Egoist*, T. S. Eliot referred to Pound's comparison of Moore and Loy and quoted his definition of logopoeia. Although he praised "The Effectual Marriage," Eliot preferred Moore because he thought Loy tended to become "abstract," while "Miss Moore is utterly intellectual, but not abstract; the word never parts from the feeling."[48] The possibly "unconscious" French influence on the two women's writing was again offered as an explanation for their "logopoeic" approach to language. Although Moore kept insisting to Pound that "I know of no tangible French influence on my work,"[49] Pound nevertheless continued to mention the French connection as the source of both Moore's and Loy's "whimsicalities" in his next discussion of the new American poetry, as if this "inheritance" accounted for their tendency to write logopoeia. Pound also declared "there are lines in

[Loy's] 'Ineffectual Marriage' perhaps better written than anything I have found in Miss Moore," and found in Moore's "Pedantic Literalist" "a verbalism less finished than Eliot's." [50] It was as if Pound took Loy as his smart female poet because Eliot chose Moore.

Given the ways in which their names were coupled as the leading female figures of American modernist poetry, it is not surprising that Moore and Loy regarded each other with wary respect. William Carlos Williams, a good friend of both women, probably exacerbated the situation by writing in the prologue to *Kora in Hell* (1918): "Of all those writing poetry in America at the time she was here, Marianne Moore was the only one Mina Loy feared." Williams also recalled that Moore "once expressed admiration for Mina Loy . . . because Mina was wearing a leopard-skin coat at the time and Marianne had stood there with her mouth open looking at her." [51] In his view, Loy's sense of needing to compete with Moore's poetry was matched by Moore's lack of assurance in the presence of the better dressed, more sophisticated and socially adept poet. Moore's only published mention of Loy situates her work within the context of what Louis Untermeyer called the "vers libertine" produced by the *Others* poets:

> the emphatic work of William Carlos Williams . . . a sliced and cylindrical, complicated yet simple use of words by Mina Loy; [poems] by Walter Arensberg which corroborated the precisely perplexing verbal exactness of Gertrude Stein's "Tender Buttons." [52]

But it is likely that Moore's "Those Various Scalpels," a riddling analytic portrait of a woman whose "dress" she admired, written in 1918 or 1919, subjects Mina Loy's sophistication to discreet but ironic scrutiny.[53]

In a witty dissection of both her subject and the Renaissance blazon tradition, Moore's speaker in the poem studies the woman's hair, ears, eyes, hands (one is raised in "an ambiguous signature," the other, "a bundle of lances all alike") and costume in order to pose the questions, "Are they weapons or scalpels?" (which could also be asked of the poet's own, very different verbal ammunition). Although the other woman's ornaments are admired as "rich instruments with which to experiment," the speaker concludes with another question that could serve as Moore's warning to herself:

"but why dissect destiny with instruments/more highly specialized than components of destiny itself?" Bonnie Costello discusses "Those Various Scalpels" as an example of Moore's "relentless verbal intelligence," the fierce wit that Pound praised as logopoeia.[54] If the poem's original subject *is* Mina Loy, then it may be seen as both a consequence of Pound's (and Eliot's and Williams's) insistent coupling of the two women, and an implicit comment on their differences and similarities. For the wit of logopoeia also "dissects" its subjects with "instruments more highly specialized" than may be necessary, and Moore is as much on guard against her own tendency to dissect as she is against "the hard majesty of that sophistication which is superior to opportunity" exhibited by her subject, in both senses of the word.

It is, moreover, quite possible that Loy's "The Effectual Marriage" was in Moore's mind as she composed her long poem "Marriage," where the beautiful, sophisticated woman as a type makes another appearance ("Eve: beautiful woman—/I have seen her/when she was so handsome she gave me a start"), only to be subjected to Moore's satire. One critic has suggested that the question of marriage in general, and the famous Bryher-McAlmon marriage in particular, were on Moore's mind when she composed "Marriage,"[55] which reads like a renunciation of this "institution/perhaps one should say enterprise" as too likely to impinge upon the integrity of the female self. Furthermore, it is not merely accidental that this poem was published in 1923, not long after women's suffrage was finally achieved in the United States. For by this time, "Hymen" is "unhelpful/a kind of overgrown cupid/reduced to insignificance/by the mechanical advertising/parading as involuntary comment." In contemporary America, marriage—"this amalgamation which can never be more/than an interesting possibility"— seems to require "all one's criminal ingenuity to avoid." It would be difficult to imagine a greater contrast to Loy's "Pig Cupid," and her speaker's complex, but interested attitude toward the possibility of union. Stylistically as well as thematically, the two women's uses of collage poetics to explore the theme of sexual union in the modern world could not be more dissimilar.

Moore's speaker inspects the "enterprise" as an outsider who has, nevertheless, understood some of its appeal as well as its dangers. Fluctuating from the impartial stance of "one" ("all one's •

criminal ingenuity to avoid") to the meditative, reflective "I" ("I wonder what Adam and Eve/think of it by this time"), the speaker also lets the participants talk in their own voices, the better to convict themselves of vanity and self-interest. Her Eve, handsome and demanding, declares: "I should like to be alone," but allows herself to be tempted by Adam's suggestion, "why not be alone together?" This subversive satire shifts, however, just at the point of greatest fierceness, to an erotically charged passage that evokes what is lost when one determines to be alone:

> Below the incandescent stars
> below the incandescent fruit,
> the strange experience of beauty:
> its existence is too much;
> it tears one to pieces
> and each fresh wave of consciousness
> is poison.

Although R. P. Blackmur insists that there is "no element of sex or lust" in "Marriage," [56] I think he misses the regretful tone of these lines. Even though the rest of "Marriage" examines the "enterprise" with the cold eye of an anthropologist among "savages" ("What can one do for them?"), this detachment occurs almost as if by default.

In his 1918 essay on Moore and Loy, Eliot praised the "fusion of thought and feeling" [57] in Moore's poetry in the same terms that he soon would use in praise of Donne and the metaphysicals, his own standards for wit. Moore herself was aware that a "metaphysical" quality informed her poetry at all levels, thematic, syntactical, and formal, and hinted at this quality in "Diogenes" (1916), a poem that she never reprinted. In the voice of the original cynic, the poem ponders:

> Day's calumnies,
> Midnight's translucencies.
>   Pride's open book
> Of closed humilities—
>   With its inflated look;
> Shall contrarities
> As feasible as these
>   Confound my wit?[58]

The question of how the poet's wit is to deal with "feasible contrarities" is at the heart of Moore's sexual poetics in "Marriage," which Pamela White Hadas calls "a rhetorical response to the idea of marriage as a confrontation of opposites." [59] Sexual difference is perhaps the central "contrarity" for a poetics based on what Kenneth Burke calls "the motif of the spinster . . . and the theme of the spirited feminine independence." [60] The confrontation of opposites figured in Adam and Eve surfaces throughout "Marriage" in unresolved oxymoronic structures of thought and feeling: for example, the "imperious humility" with which the ladies greet the men at tea, the impossible attempt at "amalgamation" of the sexes' need to be "alone" yet "together," and the "public promises/of one's intention to fulfill a private obligation."

Of course, this "structure of overt or implicit chiasmus" informs her poetry in general, as Costello observes: "the antithetical structure of her thought is relentless and will not rest in simple oppositions." [61] Not for Moore the splice as syntactic or social connective. Her opposites stare at each other across the gap between their individual solitudes: "One sees that it is rare—/that striking grasp of opposites/opposed each to the other, not to unity." This meditation on sexual difference as the model of how opposites seek to "grasp" the other or opposing self concludes with the cynicism of a Diogenes reflecting on a final contrarity: "Liberty and union/now and forever" (the inscription on Daniel Webster's tomb, a fitting commentary on the impossibility of amalgamating firmly opposed "states" such as North and South, male and female).

When Adam, Eve, the speaker, and the various authorities cited and undercut in "Marriage" are seen as participants in a "chiasmic square dance," [62] the poem perfectly illustrates Pound's description of logopoeia as a "dance of the intelligence among words and ideas." At the same time, however, like many of Moore's poems, "Marriage" is also informed by a slyly gendered awareness of the respective power positions of male and female ("the spiked hand/ that has an affection for one/and proves it to the bone"). Not wishing to collaborate in an enterprise that works according to the principle of "that which is great because something else is small," [63] Moore's sexual poetic abjures amalgamations and prizes the separate integrities of its component elements. If Moore's is a variety of the collage poetics that has been linked with Poundian logopoeia and with modernist poetry in general, it is surely an idiosyncratic, separatist version of this practice. Williams better than Pound described its peculiarities by insisting on Moore's love of words, images, and structures that retain their "edges," poems "where there is almost no overlaying at all." In his view, when Moore used a word, she did so "in such a way that it will remain scrupulously itself, unnicked beside other words in parade."[64] This poetic is perfectly matched to a mind that "is not matrimonially ambitious,"[65] presumably persuaded that "liberty and union" cannot coexist. Williams also remarked, "the only help I ever got from Miss Moore toward the understanding of her verse was that she despised connectives."[66] Her dislike of connectives keeps all the partners in the verbal dance at a discrete (and discreet) distance from each other—"unnicked"—while the intelligence moves them about in new choreographies, without, however, resolving their figures back into the two-steps of social dancing.

ટૂ

As practiced by Stein, Loy, and Moore, the poetics of collage is flexible enough to express homosexual, heterosexual, and asexual models of the links between sexuality and writing. By contrast, from the perspective of our poststructuralist, deconstructive ideas about writing, Pound's theories leading up to the *Cantos* would have to be described as "phallogocentric." In Jacques Derrida's *Spurs: Nietzsche's Styles*, this neologism joins "phallocentric" with "logocentric" to assert Lacanian psychoanalysis' dependence upon a conceptual system in which the phallus is identified with the Logos as a double powerful transcendent signifier or unexamined (and unexaminable) ground of meaning. But as philosopher and psychoanalyst Luce Irigaray has shown, this double centrism has had a long history in Western theoretical traditions where the female is posited as absence, other, or lack.[67] Pound's extreme disillusionment with the postwar situation of Western culture may have intensified his search for some ground of meaning, his turn to a version of the Logos or intellectual self-conscious as the modern replacement for God's "I am that I am." However, his related desire to identify this source of value with masculine-oriented qualities of hardness, aggressivity, and a particularly voluntarist mode of intellectual activity links his notion of logopoeia with the "phallogocentrism" of Western philosophic tradition. The "feminine" could have its place in writing only as the matter or "chaos" to be shaped by the fecundating masculine intelligence.

Although Marianne Moore revered Pound as a teacher of modern prosody and praised his "unerring ear," she observed astringently that the *Cantos* had certain flaws:

> Unprudery is overemphasized . . . and apropos of "feminolatry," is not the view of woman expressed by the Cantos older-fashioned than that of Siam and Abyssinia? Knowledge of the femaleness of "Chaos," of the "octopus," of "Our mulberry leaf, woman," appertaining more to Turkey than to a Roger Ascham?

Moore also appeared to share the view of T. S. Eliot, who "suspects Ezra Pound's philosophy of being antiquated." [68] Nevertheless, she continued to appreciate his efforts as "the 'new' poetry's perhaps best apologist" and his technical "concern for exact definition," which she glosses as "a neatening or cleancutness, . . . as caesura is cutting at the end." [69] In other words, she admired not Pound's "philosophy" but his poetic technique, which could be adapted to her own project of keeping words cut off from each other by poetic design.

But is it possible, finally, to separate the designs of modernist poetry from its philosophy, and has the latter rightly been seen as impelled by a longing for unitary order, as in the transcendental quest of Eliot or the more earthbound poetics of Williams and Pound? Although Williams saw Pound and Stein "as phases of the same thing," [70] I would suggest that we think about the female modernists as involved in a revisionary project that critiques the (perhaps unconsciously) phallogocentric principles implicit in male modernisms. If, as Marjorie Perloff observes of our contemporary poetic scene, "the Romantic and Modernist cult of personality has given way to what the new poets call 'the dispersal of the speaking subject,' the denial of the unitary, authoritative ego," [71] it seems likely that such poets draw on Stein's radical decentering of authorial perspective (as in, say, *Tender Buttons*) as much as or more than on Poundian logopoeia. Stein learned to let the "I" become just one element among many in a text by submitting her conscious mind to the rhythms of the external world in order to re-create those rhythms on the page. Pound later abandoned the attempt to "drive" his own intelligence into the world, perhaps because of his reduction to a more "feminine" position during his cruel incarceration near Pisa. There, according to Richard Sieburth, Pound no longer saw woman or nature "as an 'exterior formlessness' onto which shape must be cast, but rather as integral to the process: 'stone knowing the form which the carver imparts it.' " [72] Just the same, it is still difficult to imagine a reversal of positions between stone and carver in Pound's vision.

Margaret Homans has clearly stated the assumptions shared by many feminist literary critics:

> Poets' themes have implications for formal and rhetorical problems, and, conversely poets use rhetoric to model solutions to those social or cultural issues that their poems may be said to be "about." . . . The cultural construction of gender is at once a formal and a thematic issue. It shapes both the forms and the rhetorical modes poets have available to them and the wider social and cultural milieu that provides their subject matter. [73]

This contemporary statement of principles reads like a gloss on Stein's idea of "composition" (as I understand it) and suggests that we put the "constructions of gender" occulted or ignored by older accounts of modernism on our own critical agenda. The work of recognizing and specifying these poetic constructions has begun only recently, possibly because what women wrote "about" has not been understood as modernist in the same way that Pound and Eliot have been defined as modernist. Increasingly, critics are looking to the rapidly changing social and cultural milieux of the early twentieth century to situate gender issues within large-scale historical developments, such as the changes wrought by the Great War in societal structures in general and in relations between the sexes in particular. The rise of women's suffrage movements, the possibility of expatriation, the conditions of modern city life, and the influence of the new theories of religion, anthropology, and psychoanalysis are all being studied in relation to modernist "constructions of gender," with implications for new readings of both male and female writers. [74] Furthermore, numerous critical studies of particular modernist women writers have already demonstrated the need for rewriting our definitions of modernism to make them more responsive to issues of this kind.[75]

But until very recently, less attention has been paid to the other half of Stein's equation, the formal "compositions" that may distinguish the work of female modernists or the rhetorical and syntactic strategies described in this essay. Although Stein's writing is increasingly discussed from poststructuralist and deconstructive perspectives, the poetry of H.D., Laura Riding, and Lorine Neidecker, as well as Moore and Loy, merits such attention. Critics would also do well to look into the work of contemporary women poets who see themselves as the literary descendants of these female modernists. Already, some feminist and postmodern practices in both poetry and criticism appear to have joined hands in their preferences for decentered, antihierarchical modes of writing. Furthermore, a greater play of linguistic, biographical, sexual, and historical elements is included within their verbal choreographies, as in the writing of Beverley Dahlen, Susan Howe, and Kathleen Fraser, among others. Fraser, whose own work could be said to splice feminine poetics with a logopoeic attention to language, recognizes the importance of the female modernists to this contemporary project and believes that many women writers feel a need for poetry that permits "a backing off of the performing ego to allow the mysteries of language to come forward and resonate more fully." [76] Poets who see their poetry as part of the tradition that began with Stein, Loy, and Moore often published in *HOW(ever)*, a journal edited by Fraser. Although the journal's title was suggested by the "however" in the second line of Moore's famous "Poetry" ("Reading it, however, with a perfect contempt for it, one discovers in/it, after all, a place for the genuine"), this antithetical turn in Moore's thought is further broken down into its linguistic components, as if a Gertrude Stein had been examining the word for other possible resonances. The title wittily enacts Fraser's recognition of "our collective female experiences of multiplicity and fragmentation and our wanting to *locate* that, structurally, in the look and sound of our poems." [77] In spite of his idea of the "female chaos," Pound might have been pleased to know that the energizing wit he praised in the poetry of Moore and Loy still sashays through the writing of their postmodern descendants.

Notes

1. Marjorie Perloff, *The Dance of the Intellect: Studies in the Poetry of the Pound Tradition* (Cambridge, Eng., 1985), 23, 22.

2. Hugh Kenner, *The Pound Era* (Berkeley, 1971), 186, 325, 12. "Luminous details" is Pound's term for the words to be set in juxtaposition: see his *Selected Prose, 1909–1965*, ed. William Cookson (New York, 1973), 21, 24.

3. Cyrena N. Pondrum, "Gertrude Stein: From Outlaw to Classic," *Contemporary Literature* 27:1 (1986): 113.

4. *The Literary Essays of Ezra Pound*, ed. T. S. Eliot (New York, 1954), 25.

5. Ibid., 281.

6. Richard Sieburth, *Instigations: Ezra Pound and Remy de Gourmont* (Cambridge, Mass., 1978), 66. See also the helpful analysis of logopoeia in Marianne Korn, *Ezra Pound, Purpose/Form/Meaning* (London, 1983), 93–99.

7. Eliot, *Literary Essays*, 281.

8. The essay appeared as " 'Others' " in *The Little Review* 4 (March 1918): 57, and was reprinted in Pound's *Selected Prose*, 424–25.

9. Eliot, *Literary Essays*, 283.

10. Pound refers to their "sinuosities and mental quirks" in *Instigations* (1920; Freeport, N.Y., 1967), 241.

11. Gertrude Stein, *The Autobiography of Alice B. Toklas*, in Carl Van Vechten, ed., *Selected Writings of Gertrude Stein* (New York, 1972), 189.

12. Gertrude Stein, *G.M.P.*, in *Matisse, Picasso and Gertrude Stein with Two Shorter Stories* (1933; Barton, Berlin, Millerton, 1972), 258, cited in Jayne L. Walker, *The Making of a Modernist: Gertrude Stein from Three Lives to Tender Buttons* (Amherst, 1984), 133. I am indebted to Walker's excellent study of Stein's prewar writing, which stimulated the development of my argument in this article.

13. Richard Bridgman, *Gertrude Stein in Pieces* (New York, 1970), 197. Bridgman further comments on Stein's "loyalty to the noun" in *How to Write*: "if nouns were people and things, then sentences expressed the possibility of their union."

14. Gertrude Stein, *Everybody's Autobiography* (New York, 1937), 5.

15. Stein, quoted in John Hyde Preston, "A Conversation," *Atlantic Monthly* 156 (1935): 191, cited in Catharine R. Stimpson's thoughtful discussion of the body in writing, "The Somograms of Gertrude Stein," *Poetics Today* 6:1, 2 (1985): 73.

16. Stein, "Composition as Explanation," in *Selected Writings*, 513–23. On Sitwell as a supporter of Stein's writing, see Marjorie Perloff, *The Poetics of Indeterminacy: Rimbaud to Cage* (Princeton, 1981), 79–85.

17. Malcolm Bradbury and James McFarlane, "The Name and Nature of Modernism," in Bradbury and McFarlane, eds., *Modernism 1890–1930* (London, 1970), 23.

18. Stein, "Picasso," in Edward Burns, ed., *Gertrude Stein on Picasso* (New York, 1970), 18. See also Stein's account of the First World War as a Cubist composition, 18–19.

19. David Antin, "Some Questions About Modernism," *Occident* 8 (1974): 11, 14.

20. Perloff, *The Poetics of Indeterminacy*, 67–108; Walker, *The Making of a Modernist*, xvi–xvii.

21. Hamet Janis and Rudi Blesh, *Collage: Personalities, Concepts, Techniques* (Philadelphia, 1969), 21. Curiously, Janis and Blesh re-create a kind of sexual bias in their description of the collage materials as "masculine" and "feminine."

22. Eliot, *Literary Essays*, 341.

23. *The Letters of Ezra Pound*, 1907–1941, ed. D. D. Paige (New York, 1950), 146.

24. Ezra Pound, "Postscripts to *The Natural Philosophy of Love* by Rémy de Gourmont," in *Pavannes and Divagations* (New York, 1958), 203, 204, 207.

25. Ibid., 205.

26. Pound, in *Pound/Joyce: Letters and Essays*, ed. Forrest Read (New York, 1967), 208, cited in Sieburth, *Instigations*, 189, n. 31. Sieburth observes that "Pound's vision of woman as an agent both of disorder . . . and of revelation . . . is so broad and so complex as to require a monograph in itself" (143).

27. Pound, "Postscript," 205, 204, 213.

28. Korn, *Ezra Pound*, 94.

29. Ian F. A. Bell, *Critic as Scientist: The Modernist Poetics of Ezra Pound* (London, 1981), 2, 86.

30. Ford Madox Hueffer, *Ancient Lights* (London, 1911), 243; cited in ibid., 87.

31. For a full account of this incident, as noted in Sophie Brzeska's diary, see Timothy Materer, *Vortex, Pound, Eliot, and Lewis* (Ithaca, N.Y., 1979), 70–73.

32. Lewis is quoted in Kenner, *The Pound Era*, 256; cf. his account of the bust's significance, 248–50. Materer's comment appears in *Vortex*, 94.

33. See his Lacanian analysis of Pound's phallic theories: Alan Durant, *Ezra Pound, Identity & Crisis* (Brighton, Eng., 1981).

34. Eliot, *Literary Essays*, 12.

35. Ezra Pound, *Gaudier-Brzeska: A Memoir* (New York, 1959), 89.

36. Hueffer, *Ancient Lights*, cited in Bell, *Critic as Scientist*, 87.

37. Pound, " 'Others'," 57: their femininity asserts itself, however, in "l'americaine."

38. Mina Loy, "Aphorisms on Futurism," *Camera Work* 45 (1914): 13–15; reprinted in Loy, *The Last Lunar Baedeker*, ed. Roger L. Conover (Highlands, N.C., 1982), 273.

39. Roger Shattuck describes Apollinaire as a "poète fondé en peinture" in *The Banquet Years* (New York, 1968), 319. On Loy's artistic training, see my "Becoming Mina Loy," in *Women's Studies* 7:1, 2 (1980): 136–58, which also reprints her "Aphorisms on Futurism" and other poems.

40. These phrases appear in Loy's satire of the Futurists, "Lions' Jaws," in *The Little Review* 7 (1920): 39–43; reprinted in Loy, *The Last Lunar Baedeker*, 57–61.

41. See my "Without Commas: Gertrude Stein and Mina Loy," in *Poetics Journal* 4 (1984): 43–52, where their artistic association is treated more fully.

42. On Loy's response to Futurist painting, see my "Becoming Mina Loy," and Virginia M. Kouidis, *Mina Loy, American Modernist Poet* (Baton Rouge, 1980), 49–59.

43. Loy's "Love Songs" are cited here from the 1917 texts as published in Kouidis, *Mina Loy*, and not in *The Last Lunar Baedeker*, where her spacing and line breaks are often regularized in ways that minimize the collage aspect of her modernism. For the complete text of "Love Songs" and a balanced discussion of the sequence, see Kouidis, *Mina Loy*, 59–85.

44. "Gina" and "Miovanni" are clear inversions of "Mina" and "Giovanni," presumably the scholarly critic Giovanni Papini, with whom Loy was involved during Papini's Futurist period (1913–15) and for whom her "Love Songs" were written.

45. Kouidis, *Mina Loy*, 35.

46. Loy, "The Effectual Marriage," in Alfred Kreymborg, ed., *Others: An Anthology of the New Verse* (New York, 1917); reprinted in *The Last Lunar Baedeker*, 31–35.

47. Pound printed this edited and retitled version first in *Instigations* (1920), 240, and then in his *Profile: An Anthology Collected in Milan* (Milan, 1932), 67–68.

48. T. S. Apteryx [Eliot], "Observations," *The Egoist* 5 (1918): 70.

49. See Paige, *Letters of Ezra Pound*, 143–44, and Moore's reply, in *Marianne Moore, A Collection of Critical Essays*, ed. Charles Tomlinson (Englewood Cliffs, N.J., 1969), 17.

50. Pound, *Instigations*, 238–40.

51. William Carlos Williams, *Kora in Hell: Improvisations*, in Williams, *Imaginations*, ed. Webster Schott (New York, 1971), 10; *Selected Essays of William Carlos Williams* (New York, 1969), 292. Cf. Williams's description of Moore "in awe of Mina's long-legged charms," in *The Autobiography of William Carlos Williams* (New York, 1951), 146.

52. Marianne Moore, " 'New' Poetry Since 1912," in Patricia C. Willis, ed., *The Complete Prose of Marianne Moore* (New York, 1986), 121.

53. That Loy may be the subject of "Those Various Scalpels" was suggested to me in a personal communication (24 January 1984) by Patricia C. Willis, Curator of the Marianne Moore Collection at the Rosenbach Museum and Library, and editor of Moore's *Complete Prose*. The poems appear in *The Complete Poems of Marianne Moore* (New York, 1981), 51–52.

54. Bonnie Costello, *Marianne Moore: Imaginary Possessions* (Cambridge, Mass., 1981), 164, 175 (where Costello also observes that the conclusion of "Those Various Scalpels" can serve as Moore's own motto).

55. Laurence Stapleton, *Marianne Moore: The Poet's Advance* (Princeton, 1978), 40–41. "Marriage" is reprinted in *The Complete Poems*, 62–70.

56. R. P. Blackmur, "The Method of Marianne Moore," in Tomlinson, *Marianne Moore*, 84, 85, where Blackmur claims "there is no sex anywhere in her poetry."

57. Eliot, "Observations," 70. Costello makes this point in *Marianne Moore: Imaginary Possessions*, 40.

58. Moore, "Diogenes," *Contemporary Verse* (1916); reprinted in Pamela White Hadas, *Marianne Moore: Poet of Affection* (Syracuse, 1977), 184–85.

59. Hadas, *Marianne Moore: Poet of Affection*, 148.

60. Kenneth Burke, "Motives and Motifs in the Poetry of Marianne Moore," in Tomlinson, *Marianne Moore*, 95.

61. Costello, *Marianne Moore: Imaginary Possessions*, 164. I am indebted to Costello's insightful analysis of Moore's chiasmic strategies: see especially 160–66, and cf. 236, where she notes that "Moore's is a 'genius for disunion' like that of [the] Irish grandmothers' in 'Spenser's Ireland.' "

62. Ibid., 165.

63. Moore, "When I Buy Pictures," in *The Complete Poems*, 48.

64. Williams, *Selected Essays*, 128–29.

65. Moore, as cited in Donald Hall, "An Interview with Marianne Moore," *McCall's* 92 (1965): 182.

66. Williams, *Selected Essays*, 124.

67. See the bilingual edition of *Spurs/Eperons* (Chicago, 1978), 247–48, where "phallogocentrisme" is, unfortunately, translated as "phallocentrism"; Luce Irigaray, *Speculum*, trans. G. Gill, and *This Sex Which Is Not One*, trans. C. Porter with C. Burke (Ithaca, N.Y., 1985).

68. Willis, *The Complete Prose*, 272.

69. Ibid., 122, 447.

70. Williams, *Selected Essays*, 162.

71. Perloff, *The Dance of the Intellect*, x.

72. Pound, *Instigations*, 147. Idem, *Cantos* LXXIV/430, 457. See Sieburth's sensitive account of this shift in Pound's sense of his own place in the natural universe as expressed in the Pisan *Cantos*, 147–58.

73. Homans, " 'Syllables of Velvet': Dickinson, Rossetti and the Rhetorics of Sexuality," *Feminist Studies* 11:3 (1985): 569.

74. Among these are Sandra M. Gilbert, "Soldiers' Heart: Literary Men, Literary Women, and the Great War," *SIGNS* 8:3 (1983); Alicia Ostriker, *Writing Like a Woman* (Ann Arbor, 1983); Susan Squier, ed., *Women Writers and the City: Essays in Feminist Literary Criticism* (Knoxville, 1984); Elyse Blankley, "Daughters' Exile: Renee Vivien, Gertrude Stein, and Djuna Barnes in Paris," diss. Univ. of California, Davis, 1984; Susan Gubar, "Sapphistries," *SIGNS* 10:1 (1984):

91–110; Rachel Blau DuPlessis, *Writing Beyond the Ending: Narrative Strategies of Twentieth-Century Writers* (Bloomington, 1985); Carolyn Burke, "The New Poetry and the New Woman: Mina Loy," in Diane W. Middlebrook and Marilyn Yalom, eds., *Coming to Light: American Women Poets in the Twentieth Century* (Ann Arbor, 1985), 37–57; and Shari Benstock, *Women of the Left Bank: Paris, 1900–1940* (Austin, 1986). Gilbert and Gubar's forthcoming *No Man's Land: The Place of the Woman Writer in the Twentieth Century* will be a major reexamination of female modernism in historical context.

75. In addition to studies already mentioned, see also, among others: Jeanne Kammer, "The Art of Silence and the Forms of Women's Poetry," in S. Gilbert and S. Gubar, eds., *Shakespeare's Sisters: Feminist Essays on Women Poets* (Bloomington, 1979), 153–64; Carolyn Burke, "Supposed Persons: Modernist Poetry and the Female Subject," *Feminist Studies* 11:1 (1985): 131–48; Susan Stanford Friedman, *Psyche Reborn: The Emergence of H.D.* (Bloomington, 1981); Claire Buck, "Freud and H.D.—Bisexuality and a Feminine Discourse," *m/f* 8 (1983): 53–66; Rachel Blau DuPlessis, *H.D.: The Career of That Struggle* (Bloomington, 1986); Marianne DeKoven, *A Different Language: Gertrude Stein's Experimental Writing* (Madison, 1984); Randa Dubnick, *The Structure of Obscurity: Gertrude Stein, Language and Cubism* (Urbana, 1984); Catharine R. Stimpson, "Reading Gertrude Stein," *Tulsa Studies in Women's Literature* 4:2 (1985): 265–71; and Taffy Martin, *Marianne Moore: Subversive Modernist* (Austin, 1986). The special issue of *Contemporary Literature* devoted to H.D. (27:4 [1986]) and the three panels at the 1986 MLA meeting devoted to modernism in Stein, H.D., and Moore indicate the growing critical interest in this question.

76. Kathleen Fraser, "The Tradition of Marginality," unpub. man., 12. See also Beverley Dahlen, *A Reading* 1–7 (San Francisco, 1985); articles by Gayle Davis and Rachel Blau DuPlessis on Dahlen in *Ironwood* 27 (1986): 148–53, 159–69; and Susan Howe's "Steinian" reading of Dickinson as a precursor of modernist writing, *My Emily Dickinson* (Berkeley, 1985). Cf. the account of modernist and contemporary women's poetry in Alicia Ostriker, *Stealing the Language: The Emergence of Women's Poetry in America* (Boston, 1986).

77. Fraser, "The Tradition," 13. Marianne DeKoven has discussed the poetry of Fraser, Dahlen, and Frances Jaffer, as well as a number of contemporary women poets writing in this tradition, in "Gertrude's Granddaughters," *The Women's Review of Books* 4:2 (1986): 13–14.

Modernism Mummified

Daniel Bell
Harvard University

for uunm ?

IN HIS INTRODUCTION TO *THE IDEA OF THE MODERN,* IRVING HOWE QUOTES the famous remark of Virginia Woolf, as everyone does since hyperbole is arresting, that "on or about December 1910 human nature changed." Actually, Mrs. Woolf had written that "human *character* changed." She was referring (in her famous essay "Mr. Bennett and Mrs. Brown," written in 1924) to the changes in the position of one's cook or of the partners in marriage. "All human relations have shifted—those between masters and servants, husbands and wives, parents and children. And when human relations change there is at the same time a change in religion, conduct, politics and literature." [1]

This essay is a reprise and a reflection on themes I advanced in *The Cultural Contradictions of Capitalism* (1976) and the essay "Beyond Modernism, Beyond Self," a memorial essay for Lionel Trilling, in the volume *Art, Politics and Will,* edited by Quentin Anderson, Stephen Donadio, and Steven Marcus (1975) and reprinted in my collection of essays, *The Winding Passage* (1980).

This search for a transfiguration in sensibility as the touchstone
of modernity has animated other writers. Lionel Trilling, in tem-
perament ever cautious and complex, while persuaded in his reading of the *Iliad* or Sophocles that human nature does not change
and that moral life is unitary, nevertheless came to believe, as he
stated in the opening pages of *Sincerity* and *Authenticity*, that in the
late sixteenth and early seventeenth centuries "something like a
mutation in human nature took place," and that a new concern
with the *self*, and being at one with one's self, "became a salient,
perhaps a definitive, characteristic of Western culture for some four
hundred years." [2]

The answer to when and how what we call "the modern"
emerged has a large historical canvas. One can date it with the rise
of the museum, where cultural artifacts are wrenched from their
traditional places and displayed in a new context of syncretism:
history mixed up and consciousness jumbled by will, as when Napoleon ransacked Egypt and Europe to stuff the Louvre with his
trophies; and yet vicarious emperors have always displayed their
power by placing their heels on culture. For Jacob Burckhardt, the
modern begins, of course, in the Renaissance, with the emphasis
on individuality, originality, and putting one's name in stone. One
can say, and I would place great weight behind the argument, that
the modern begins with Adam Smith and the proposition that the
economy is no longer subject to the household or moral rules but
is an autonomous activity, just as in this extension of liberalism one
has the autonomy of law from morality (to be regarded principally
as a set of formal procedures), and the autonomy of the aesthetic
from all constraints so that art exists for art's sake alone. And if
one believes that the fundamental source of all knowledge and
sensibility is epistemological, one would have to date the creation
from Kant, with the proposition of an activity theory of knowledge
(as against the classical contemplative theory deriving knowledge
from preexisting Forms), so that, as Kant says in the *Prolegomena*,
"The understanding does not derive its laws (a priori) from, but
prescribes them to, nature," a theorem that is carried out in modern art and in politics.[3]

What is clear, out of all these variegated elements, is that what
defines the modern is a sense of openness to change, of detachment from place and time, of social and geographical mobility,

and a readiness, if not eagerness, to welcome the new, even at the
expense of tradition and the past. It is the proposition that there
are no ends or purposes given "in nature," that the individual, and
his or her self-realization, is the new ideal and *imago* of life, and that
one can remake one's self and remake society in the effort to
achieve those individual goals. Revolution, which had once been a
ricorso in an endless cycle, now becomes a rupture with the endless
wheel, and is the impulse to destroy old worlds, and for new worlds
to create.

In all this it is clear that *capitalism* and *modernism* have common
roots. Both were dynamic in their restless kneading of the dough;
for both there was "nothing sacred"; for both there were no limits
on the efforts of rugged individualism or the unrestrained self to
tear up the past and to make it new.

Yet what is also clear, and this is the history still to be unraveled,
is that brothers though they may have been in the womb, there
was a deep fratricide whereby the rising bourgeoisie, sublimating
its energies into work, feared the excesses and the flouting of conventions and cultural forms by the new *bohème*, while the avatars of
modernism despised and held in contempt the money-minded
bourgeoisie, for whom culture was only a commodity and a source
of display, status, and consumption.   *modern + the world*.

Capitalism and cultural modernism also had different trajectories. At its extreme, capitalism became concerned with efficiency,
optimization, and maximization as it subordinated the individual
to the organization. Cultural modernism opened an attack, often
an unyielding rage, against the social order; became concerned
with the self, often to a narcissistic extent; denied art the function
of representation; and became unusually absorbed with the materi-   *created*
als alone—textures and sounds—which it used for expressiveness.   *Two art*

I have tried, in my work, to relate cultural modernism to changes   *classes*
in social structure. I have argued that in modernism—in painting,   *high +*
literature, music, and poetry—there was a common syntax, which I   *low.*
have called the "eclipse of distance," and that in these varied genres
there was a common attack on the "rational cosmology" that had   *if picks*
defined Western culture since the Renaissance; that of foreground   *unfilled*
and background in space through mathematical perspective; of beginning, middle, and end, as the ordered chronology of time; and
of a "correspondence theory of truth" in the idea of *mimesis* or the

semantic relation of word to object.[4] I had tried to show that where
the aesthetic was joined to politics, particularly in the twentieth
century, the "world-view" of modernism had been principally reactionary or revolutionary (whether Stefan George and Gottfried
Benn, or the German expressionists in theatre and art; whether
Pound, Eliot, Yeats, and Wyndham Lewis and the ambiguous politics of a Lawrence, or the early revolutionary stance of Auden, etc.,
etc.). And I had argued that contemporary bourgeois society, seeing its inflated, decorative culture collapse under the onslaught of
cultural modernism, had in an astonishing *tour de force* taken over
cultural modernism and flaunted it as its own culture—this being
the cultural contradiction of capitalism.

Today, according to the winds of the *Zeitgeist*, modernism has
ended. We have "postmodernism" wrenching modernism from its
historical context, and jumbling it with different cultural styles (old
hat, nouveau, and deco) in a new, bizarre syncretism (such as
Philip Johnson's pediment to the AT&T tower on Madison Avenue), and academics ransacking the texts to deconstruct the past
and create a new presence. So the hoot owl of Minerva screeches
in the false dawn.

II

What of America? Lacking a past and having made itself in a revolutionary act, America has been the only pure capitalist society we
have known. But has there been an American Modernism? And if
so, what was it?

Modernism in the United States existed in *form*, not in *content*.
Not only is this an arbitrary distinction, but I am necessarily using
these words in an arbitrary way. And it is by exposition, rather than
definition, that this distinction can be made clear and, perhaps,
useful.

In *content*, American culture (leaving aside nineteenth-century
New England and the twentieth-century South—yet this remains a
large country) was primarily small-town, Protestant, moralizing, and
anti-intellectual in the sense that Richard Hofstadter has used this
term. If, as Santayana once remarked, Americans were innocent of
poison, they were even more so of sexuality (not sex). Can one
imagine a Huysmans, a Swinburne, or an Aubrey Beardsley (though

The Yellow Book was initiated by an American expatriate) or any other ("dandy aesthete") (to use Martin Green's phrase) on the American scene?

American modernists, as is obvious from the history, could flourish principally only in Europe: James leaving New York and Boston, Pound from Idaho, Eliot from St. Louis, Gertrude Stein from Baltimore, Hemingway from the Illinois suburbs, and the "lost generation" of the twenties going earlier to London or later to Paris. The little magazines took their cue from Europe. The painters, beginning with the Armory Show, again hailed from Europe. The composers, again, spent the obligatory period abroad.

The two innovative American writers, Dos Passos and Faulkner, were experimental and modernist, but they were not part of a native *modernist culture* in the sense that such writers as Mallarmé, Rimbaud, and Proust were able to place their imprints deeply on a French culture. Dos Passos introduced a style of montage close to cinema and, to some extent, the political Expressionist theater of Germany, but his influence was largely in the radical milieu of his time. And though Dos Passos continued his montage techniques when he abandoned his radicalism, he was written off by the critics as *passé*. Faulkner wrote powerful experimental novels, derived from the French influences (*The Sound and the Fury* can rank with any of the great modernist *romans fleuves*) yet he received little critical attention. Faulkner was revived only in 1945 when he sketched for Malcolm Cowley the map of Yoknapatawpha County, and Cowley then redefined Faulkner in the sociological context of the struggle between the Sartorises and Snopeses for the soul of the South— not as a modernist writer.

The two distinctive modernist innovations—as cultures—were jazz and photography, but jazz was outside the mainstream, regarded as sinful even in the jazz age of the twenties, and only became a major influence in American culture in the forties with the larger commercial jazz bands, while photography, despite Stieglitz, was aesthetically marginal to American concerns. The one great technical innovation, film, was regarded as "the movies" in the United States, a form of mass entertainment, and as "the cinema" in France, where it became an aesthetic and so provided the route back to critical commentary in the United States.

In these senses, while there were *modernists* in the United States, there was no *modernist culture* in content. The one place where there was a modernist culture in the United States was in *form*—and this was the machine aesthetic. And, as the old saying goes, this was no accident. The machine aesthetic excluded the self and the person, it was abstract and functional, and it was fused with industrial design. Photography came into its own not with the periodical *Camera Work*, but with the business scene; the *Fortune* pages provided its showcase. The great functional factories and the huge functional skyscrapers, as well as the curving ribbons of the new concrete motorways, became the emblematic symbols of the new culture. The key term that defined its form was *functional*. Modernist artists such as Charles Sheeler, in his "precisionist" paintings and photographs, reflected these abstract geometrical designs. Abstract artists, such as Stuart Davis, fused the rhythms of jazz with the linear forms of the machine age.

A modernist culture began to appear in the United States after World War II with the collapse of the small-town Protestant hold on American life, the distinctive imprint of urbanism as the focus of economic activities, and the flood of French-European Surrealists (Breton, Masson, Ernst) who influenced the new art of a Gorky or a Pollock; the Russian emigrés such as Stravinsky and Balanchine, who shaped developments in music and dance; the large number from Central Europe such as Erwin Panofsky and Roman Jakobson, who influenced art history and linguistics; and the many German refugees who brought in continental sociology and philosophy (as well as physics and other sciences). The complete story of all those myriad influences remains to be told.

III

What of modernism today? It has become what culture usually becomes in periods of luxury and decadence, a decorative commodity or the last duchess on the wall. On the one hand, there are the *culturati* who make up the new industry of galleries and museums and magazines, as well as entertainment, the purveyors and transmitters and cicerones of culture. And on the other, the corporations and banks that line their corridors with the requisite Newman,

Motherwell, Noland, Morris Louis, or Kline, where the thick impasto and the rivers of color sag and go limp against the neutral beige carpets and the whitewashed walls.[5]

Modernism today is the "official" high culture—because it is dead and stuffed. And its high taxidermist is Hilton Kramer and his magazine, *The New Criterion,* who identify modernism *with* capitalism and bourgeois society. In a recent *tour de farce,* "Modernism and Its Enemies," Kramer sets the glow of high culture in the Sixties, "which witnessed an extraordinary expansion in cultural life ... the era that saw the building of a great many new museums and the expansion of a great many existing museums," the spread of "a public that was large and growing." As the capstone, *The New York Times* appointed him as its cultural critic because, "As the then executive editor of *The Times,* Turner Catledge, explained to me (with something of a sigh), 'Our readers are now a lot smarter about all this than we are.' To keep these readers and win still others the managers of the paper felt it necessary to redress the balance, and this meant—in some fields at least—joining the modernist tide instead of opposing it." [6]

There are two striking points in this exposition: one, modernism is to be explained by its audience, and by the existence of museums. Historically, it has always been the artist who establishes and writes the culture. The artist may have been adversary or entwined with court or church, but culture was defined by the artist. The museum was the place the artist avoided. If one turns to the bombastic outriders of modernism, the repeated cry in the Futurist manifestos of Marinetti is that the museums are "cemeteries of empty exertion, calvaries of crucified dreams, registries of aborted beginnings," and Marinetti urges the "gay incendiaries with charred fingers [to] set fire to the library shelves," and flood the museums.[7]

Second, other than the genuflections to the Abstract Expressionists of the postwar period (now thirty years in the past), there are few references to contemporary artists or writers who exemplify the creativity and vitality of high culture today. In fact, this modernist culture, the only true "high culture," must guard the portals against the new radicals—e.g., a Beuys—who beat at the gates, while defending a huckster like Julian Schnabel. Culture is high culture only when it is calcified in the museums of Modern Art.[8]

Who are the enemies of modernism? According to Mr. Kramer, there are the radicals who feel betrayed because modernism, instead of remaining revolutionary, has "turned out to be a coefficient of bourgeois capitalist culture." And there are the *philistines* (Mr. Kramer's, not Arnold's, designation), such as this writer, who identify modernism as the begetter of the counterculture of the sixties. Mr. Kramer, as a veteran polemicist, skews his targets and misstates positions. The Marxists who have attacked modernism have not thought of it as revolutionary but as a derivative of bourgeois life. In my writings, I call the counterculture a "conceit" in its claims to be modernist, but say that the liberal culture was unable to draw the line between a modernism (and fantasies of murder and bestiality) lived out in the imagination, and the claim to justify the erasure of any distinction between art and life and to act out (albeit in street theater) the lifestyles of outrage.

There are also two striking omissions about the critics of modernism: Mr. Kramer completely ignores the large group of conservative intellectuals, followers of Russell Kirk, who have described Modernism as the invention of the Devil, and the source of *all* political heresy in the contemporary world. Yet, as "old believers," they are as fervent as Mr. Kramer in their defense of capitalism and have even attacked the "neo-conservatives" for still clinging to the modernist heresy, something that is not true of that group—except for Mr. Kramer.

The second omission is Mr. Kramer's amnesia about his own past. Writing in 1959, on the threshold of the hallowed sixties, Mr. Kramer remarked in the socialist magazine *Dissent*:

> Everything in our economy and in the social organization of the arts conspires against the privacy and independence which would be indispensable if the spirit of the avant-garde were to survive. Once we find ourselves in a situation, as we do today, in which society has assigned vast bureaucracies to the task of seeking out and exploiting the last word in all the arts, and when the artists themselves have joined as eager accomplices in this orgy of self-exploitation—in this situation I think it is mere piety to deny that the avant-garde is dead. *The fact of the matter is that since 1945 bourgeois society has tightened its grip on all the arts by allowing them a freer rein.*[9]

Old polemical apparatchiks never die, they only change their targets.

Much of this would be merely sectarian if not for the fact that Mr. Kramer, almost alone, remains a defender of Modernism—at least in its petrified state. Irving Kristol and Peter Berger have conceded the point that capitalism is often a gross and unlovely system, to be defended primarily on the ground that it is an engine for increasing material standards of life and that it is "a necessary but not sufficient condition of democracy under modern conditions." But neither Kristol nor Berger has defended modernism in the terms of Mr. Kramer.

Mr. Kramer defends Modernism not only as an aspect of capitalism, but also of democracy, and writes that "what is really at stake, then, in this attack on modernism [is] something central to the vital cultural life of our democratic society. . . ." But this is intellectually confusing and historically invalid. The avatars of modernism themselves have been overwhelmingly antidemocratic (and often as not, anti-Semitic); and Mr. Kramer, like an inverted Marxist, conflates his realms. Democracy is *not* dependent on capitalism, but on a set of traditions and legal concepts, such as the common law, that antedate capitalism, while capitalism itself has been compatible with fascism and authoritarianism, as in Italy or Chile.

Mr. Kramer writes: "The truth is, the culture of modernism has served all along as the aesthetic and spiritual conscience, and sometimes even the moral conscience, of middle-class life, and it is this which has made it pre-eminently the culture of democratic society."

But this is a slippery glissade. Modernism has been a savage and often destructive force *against* middle-class life (need one repeat the litany of Baudelaire, Verlaine, Rimbaud, Pound, et al.?), and if modernism serves as an "aesthetic and spiritual conscience," Mr. Kramer clearly wears a hair shirt to bed at night. To say that modernism is preeminently the culture of democratic capitalism is to have embalming fluid rather than blood in one's veins. And if so, Mr. Kramer remains the walking mummy of modernism.

IV

The "sense of an ending," as Frank Kermode has remarked, is a recurrent theme in cultures that move toward an eschatological climax or are mired in cultural despair. If we have no fixed time as to when modernism began—one's starting point, as I have noted, can be based on sensibility, or self, or on the autonomy of institutions, economic or aesthetic—it is clear that "cultural modernism" has come to a close. As Octavio Paz, himself a child of the modern, stated in his Charles Eliot Norton Lectures at Harvard:

> Modern art is modern because it is critical. . . . Today we witness another mutation: modern art is beginning to lose its powers of negation. For some years now its rejections have been ritual repetitions: rebellion has turned into procedure, criticism into rhetoric, transgression into ceremony. Negation is no longer creative. I am not saying that we are living at the end of art: we are living the end of the *idea of modern art*.[10]

Was modernism "co-opted" by capitalism, as Herbert Marcuse has suggested, or was it a contradiction of capitalism, as I have argued? Marcuse stated the problem from the standpoint of culture, yet one can argue that the psychological force that became dissipated in this last century was not culture but capitalism. Marcuse claimed (in his *One-Dimensional Man*, published in 1964) that all aspects of life—art, technology, working-class rebellion, black resentment, youth *Sturm und Drang*—had been flattened out by the technological rationality of society, only to find himself hailed, a few years later, as the Pied Piper of Revolution by the raucous students of Berlin and Paris.[11] Capitalism, said Marcuse, was based psychologically on "surplus repression," imposed by the severity of the superego through the agency of the family. (In the United States today, almost one out of every two children will spend some period of their youth in a one-parent or a fatherless family!) Yet, if one looks at capitalism today, one can put Marx on his head. It is culture with its varying demands that has become the substructure of Western capitalist society and the production system reorganized to meet its voracious appetites—material; erotic and aesthetic; high, middle, and low; punk and rock; *Hollywood Squares* and TV bang-bang.

A society demonstrates its vitality through wealth, power, and culture, high and low. Power alone breeds sterility, as we see today in the Soviet Union, North Korea, or Albania. Wealth alone breeds decadence. And culture? A culture derived from religion and sustained by its commanding faith can give us the great Buddhas of the Orient or the Christian art of the Middle Ages. A period of

great expansion, nineteenth-century Paris, an era open to change
and discovery, to geographical and social mobility, can break from
mythology for the vivacity of *plein air*, the excitement of the spectacle, the presentation of the self.

Bourgeois society (not early adventure capitalism, the capitalism
described by Sombart) forced a cleavage between high and low culture, deploring the adventurousness of the one and the vulgarity of
the other. Modernist culture was extraordinarily creative because it
lived, sociologically, in tension with bourgeois society, and because,
as Paul Tillich once observed, it reached down to the taproots of the
demonic and transmuted those surging impulses into art. Today,
bourgeois society has collapsed and the demonic cavorts everywhere, for there are few taboos. Alfred Jarry could open his *Ubu Roi*
with the clownish king saying "Merdre," but how much of a shock is
that today against the desecrations of a Genet or a Burroughs?[12]

Today we have a culture that is eclectic and syncretistic because
the rational cosmology and the mirror of nature have been shat-
tered. The disjunction of forms, growing out of the tension with
mimesis, has vanished, and formalism has become largely self-
referential. The disjoined and alienated experiences (articulated
now largely by women writers) too often are expressed in sociological cliches, or lack "shape" (to use the term of Jean Rhys), and fail
to engage society other than through narcissistic reflection.

The new vogue term is "postmodernism." Its meaning is as amorphous as modernism itself, but the term also contains a set of para-
doxes as startling as the engagement of modernism and capitalism
in the past two hundred years. Postmodernism—if we date it from
the subterranean writings of Michel Foucault and, in the United
States, of Norman O. Brown (with a small nod to Norman Mailer)—
proclaimed not only the "de-construction of man" and the end of
the Enlightenment Credo of Reason, but also the "epistemological
break" with genitality, and the dissolution of sexuality into the poly-
morph perversity of oral and anal pleasures.[13] For them, this was the
liberation of the body, as modernism had been the liberation of the
imagination. The sexual revolution that followed broke into the gay
and lesbian movements as one current, and the somewhat overlapping rock-drug culture as another. Imagination had come out of
the closet and lived out its impulses openly.

REASONS WAS NORMAL TO SAY ABOUT ART

WERE NEVER STILL TABOOS?

Foucault and Brown had gone "beyond," a transgression of the taboos, a posthumous rendering, so to speak, of modernism. But by a strange twist of fate, the term "postmodernism" itself was appropriated through the media by a successive generation of artists who, often conventionally, reacted against modernist formalism and expressionism, and were immediately hailed by the chic *culturati* ready to follow the new winds of fashion. The practitioners of "postmodernism," by and large, have substituted pastiche for form and cleverness for creativity. In architecture, Michael Graves mixes Moorish fantasy with heavy Byzantine arches, as in his Portland, Oregon, building, and his proposed superstructure to the Whitney Museum. In literature, there is the affectless flat prose of Ann Beattie. In painting, we see the reintroduction of shadowy figuration, like X-ray images, in the canvases of the neo-expressionists. And on the stage, there are the hypnotic dream imagery and dissociated slow-motion tableaus by Robert Wilson, underscored by the monotonic minimalism of Philip Glass. *John Adams* *these is also postmodernist*

Much of this was foreshadowed by Pop Art, an art that largely recycles images through collage or juxtaposition, on silkscreen or phosphorescent acrylic. Some original artists like Jasper Johns or Jim Dine can subdue the image by expressing it through the tension of technique and texture, as in their prints. But with a Rauschenberg, the technique becomes too obvious; with a Warhol, the image too blatant. In both cases the outcomes finally become tiresome. *modernism is my shadow of modern culture + culture as culture culture*

What passes for high culture today lacks both content and form, so that the visual arts are primarily decorative and literature self-indulgent babble or contrived experiment. Decoration by its nature, no matter how bright and gay, becomes, in its finite and repetitive patterns, mere wallpaper, a receding background incapable of engaging the viewer in the renewable re-visions of perception. Self-referential literature, when both the self and the reference repeat the same old refrains, becomes a tedious bore, like Uno showing that he can stand on one finger in a circus. A culture of recycled images and twice-told tales is a culture that has lost its bearings.

"Whether ritualized or not, art contains the rationality of negation," Herbert Marcuse wrote in *One-Dimensional Man*. Paradoxically, the only cultural currents of negation, *as an irrational form,* have been segments of popular culture that have broken all boundaries, set themselves up against the traditional social values of American society, and are marketed wildly and successfully, as sex and rebellion, by the purveyors of capitalism and mass culture.

Today, television soap operas are the Streets of Libido, the softcore pornography deliberately titillating the viewers with a fantasy life they can act out in their own homes. Heavy Metal and hardcore rock appeal to youths who feel angry and discouraged about the dead-end prospects of earning a living. Sex-obsession as exhibited by a Madonna or Prince takes an ever more explicit form. One can imagine the grafitti on the walls: Genet lives!

Is this so different from the rock-and-roll initiated by Elvis Presley in the late 1950s, or the sweet inducements of LSD sung by the Beatles, or the hard stomp of Mick Jagger's Rolling Stones? In one sense, as with any enlargement of a cultural phenomenon, there has been a "widening gyre" in which more and more of what has been assaulted continues to crumble, and more and more of what had been forbidden now goes on publicly. But what also seems to be true is that the youth culture, and especially lower-class culture, now is exploited more crassly by the commercial interests. With regard to sex and violence, the appetites of the young turned out to be voracious, and as Martha Bayles, a critic on the *Wall Street Journal,* has written: "After all, raw sexuality and anti-social anger are the two preferred weapons of the adolescent against his elders. And when the entertainment industry discovered how endlessly marketable these distillations of black culture were, it ceased to see reasons for restraint." [14]

For the entertainment industry—movies, TV, rock music records, and publishing—all of this is free enterprise and free speech, and the government must not be allowed to interfere with the libertarianism/libertinism of the marketplace. Again a cultural contradiction of capitalism? A century and a quarter ago it was Baudelaire and the bourgeoisie condemning *Les Fleurs du Mal* as an outrage against public decency. Today is it Foucault and *Hustler* magazine as brothers in "negation"?

Cultural fashions, especially in popular culture, come and go in spasms. With the rising threat of AIDS, the campaigns against drugs and tobacco, the sheer exhaustion of the ugliness of sexual violence, as demonstrated in the film *Sid and Nancy,* we may be on the verge of a "new sobriety." That remains to be seen, and that is also another story. "Never call retreat" is a maxim of the ideologue, not of culture.

If this is the case, when all is said and done, we can now be grateful for modernism as a culture that itself was once committed to shock. It is safely in the museums, and on the corporate walls, ready for the closets of History. Such old contradictions never die; they just fade away.

Notes

1. Virginia Woolf, *Collected Essays* 1 (New York, 1967), 320–21 (italics added). When I first read this phrase and quoted it in my book, I wondered what may have happened to Mrs. Woolf herself in 1910 to give rise to this startling assertion. In 1910, if one follows the detailed events in Quentin Bell's biography, Mrs. Woolf began to speak up for the feminist cause, signaled the importance of Roger Fry's "First Post-Impressionist Exhibition," and bathed naked with Rupert Brooke by moonlight in the Granta. While Bloomsbury had become "licentious in its speech by 1910" as Mr. Bell notes, as a sociologist I was relieved to find that it was primarily in social situations that this momentous change had occurred.

2. Lionel Trilling, *Sincerity and Authenticity* (Cambridge, Mass., 1972), 19.

3. *Kant's Prolegomena*, ed. Paul Carus (La Salle, Ill., 1945), 82. If the reference to politics seems strange, I have in mind simply the view one finds in classical Greek thought that the natural order, the moral order, and the social order are all akin in having an entelechy defined by the *telos*, and that the proper ends of nature, morality, and the social are given in the unity of purposes that exist in the constitutive structures of *physis* and *nomos*. Modernity, beginning with Hobbes, dirempts that unity, and insists that ends are individual and varied.

4. This theme was first stated in my essay "The Eclipse of Distance," in *Encounter* (May 1963). Needless to say, I have not tried to write a general "theory" of modernism, but to look at these aspects that relate to "external" forces, rather than its own immanent trajectories.

5. I have no objections, per se, to corporations or museums or collectors buying the canvases of these worthwhile artists for display on their walls. How could one? What becomes objectionable is that the buying of "modern art" is by now obligatory as a means of demonstrating "support for the arts," or as a way of showing that one is "with it." It is in that sense that the Museum of Modern Art becomes the "seal of Good Housekeeping" for the corporations, and the arbiter of taste for the society. A Duncan Phillips, exercising his own independent judgment, was able to build a marvelous gallery (including the first purchases of Morris Louis) in Washington. But a Joseph Hirschorn, buying art by the carload, gets his name emblazoned on the malls of Washington as a benefactor of culture. Fortunately, the sifting of taste will make

such collections leaner, and in the years to come, few people will know of the vulgarity of Hirschorn, as few today recognize Frick as the ruthless head of the Carnegie Steel works who ordered the shooting of the workers in the Homestead strike of 1892.

6. Hilton Kramer, "Modernism and Its Enemies," *The New Criterion* (March 1986): 5.

7. "The Founding and Manifesto of Futurism," in R. W. Flint, ed., *Marinetti: Selected Writings* (New York, 1973), 43.

8. And not only the museums. New York's "newest antiques and decorative-arts fair," reports *The New York Times* in a cultural front-page article of November 21, 1986, is "Modernism: A Century of Style and Design, 1860–1960." "It's the most exciting 'antique' show I have ever seen," burbled Christopher Wilk, assistant curator of decorative arts at the Brooklyn Museum. Those artists shown include Hector Guimard, Frank Lloyd Wright, Russel Wright, and Charles Eames. "Although there are some selections at $100 or less— perfume bottles, early plastic jewelry, ceramic plates—" writes Rita Reif, "the majority of offerings are from $500 to $10,000, and master works command as much as $235,000." High, high culture, indeed.

9. Hilton Kramer, "To Hell with Culture," *Dissent* (Spring 1959): 166 (emphasis added).

10. Octavio Paz, *Children of the Mire: Modern Poetry from Romanticism to the Avant-Garde* (Cambridge, Mass., 1974), 148–49.

11. In 1970, Marcuse appeared on the stage of the Free University of Berlin and was hailed rapturously by the students who chanted rhythmically, "Her-bert, Her-bert, Her-bert." And when they broke into the singing of the *Internationale,* Marcuse whipped off his coat, raised his elbow with a clenched fist, and joined in the singing of the last chorus. When the noise finally died down, he stepped forward and cried: *"Studenten! . . ."* At which an angry volley shouted back: *"Studenten? Es heisst Genossen!"* Old professors never die. The story is told in Melvin J. Lasky's collection, *On the Barricades and Off.*

12. *Ubu Roi,* with sets elaborated by Bonnard, Vuillard, and Toulouse-Lautrec, was the first of the public utterances of obscenity. The word, *merdre,* set off a pandemonium that lasted throughout the evening. Presented in 1896, it could not be staged again until 1908. Yet even Jarry had given a spin to the word merde by adding one letter, so that the word has been translated, variously, as *shite* or *pshit.* Though used privately as the *mot de Cambronne,* a remark of one of Napoleon's generals at Waterloo, the public utterance of the word in 1896, as Roger Shattuck has observed, was "unthinkable." Compare this *scandale* with Genet's graphic depiction of homosexual rape in *Notre Dame des Fleurs* (and the film made of his fantasies) or Burroughs's description of the sexual ejaculation of a man while being hanged, in *Naked Lunch. Merde,* of course, is now the commonplace word for good luck for a student going off to an academic examination or a talisman for a friend going on a journey. Does everything, in time, become tamed?

For a discussion of Jarry and *Ubu Roi* see Roger Shattuck, *The Banquet Years* (London, 1959), ch. 7, esp. 161. The play has been fully translated under the strange title of *King Turd* by Beverley King and G. Legman (New York, 1953).

13. For a previous and more extensive discussion of Foucault and Norman O. Brown as going beyond modernism, see my *Cultural Contradictions of Capitalism*, 51–52.

14. I take this comment from the prospectus for a book on popular culture that Ms. Bayles will be writing for The Free Press. I am grateful for her permission.

ॐ

Uneasy Courtship: Modern Art and Modern Advertising

Jackson Lears
Rutgers University

HISTORIANS OF ART IN ADVERTISING MIGHT PONDER THE SEX LIFE OF INSECTS. The male praying mantis approaches the female warily. A successful leap means he can pass on his genes to the next generation, then, with luck, slip away unharmed. If he misses or is detected too soon, he is likely to lose his limbs or his head. A headless mantis can perform sexual feats undreamt of by the whole insect; he becomes a technically superb mating machine—until copulation is over and the female devours him completely.

The sexual cannibalism of mantises illuminates a century of uncertain courtship between artist and advertiser. It especially captures the ambivalence of artists themselves: eager to enter the

The first version of this article appeared under the title "The Artist and the Adman" in *Boston Review*, April 1986, vol. 11, no. 2. It was part of the "Culture in the Works" series published with the support of the Rockefeller Foundation. For helpful comments and criticisms, I wish to thank Nicholas Bromell, Daniel Singal, Janice Radway, Dominick LaCapra, Annette Igra, and especially Karen Parker Lears.

agency, make a fast buck, and depart with independence intact; fearful that if they linger too long or make one misstep, they may acquire technical prowess but ultimately disappear in the maw of the organization. The entomological analogy may be particularly appropriate for American male artists: it embodies the sexual anxieties that pervade republican and romantic traditions of artistic potency, especially the fear that art in the service of commerce unmans the artist by reducing him to an agent of effeminate luxury; it also suggests the lure of risk and struggle that has attracted many artists to the practical world of men. The artist may have more in common with the mantis than he knows.

Sociobiological analogies, to be sure, are always suspect, and in the current "postmodern" atmosphere, this one may be obsolete. The phrase "selling out" has acquired an antique glaze; the best and brightest art school graduates aspire to become Creative Persons for the big agencies. And nearly all critics agree that the conflict between modernist art and modern advertising has disappeared—if it ever existed. The cruder version of this argument asserts that modernist art has always reflected the cultural style of capitalist modernization: the restless experimentation, the unrelenting contempt for established forms and values. The subtler version suggests that modernism has lost its cutting edge: as Fredric Jameson writes, "what was once an oppositional and anti-social phenomenon in the early years of this century, has today become the dominant style of commodity production . . . a once scandalous 'perceptual art' has found a social and economic function in supplying the styling changes necessary to the *société de consommation* of the present." Undermining referentiality, celebrating self-absorbed fantasy, the modernist media (according to Gerald Graff) provide "a model by which social powerlessness can be experienced as gratification." The notion that modernism and capitalism are (witting or unwitting) accomplices has become a newly minted critical commonplace.[1]

One aim of this essay is to question that commonplace. To begin, we have to acknowledge the ambiguities of the shopworn word *modernity*—especially in considering the role of art in the marketplace. An incident recalled by Stephen Spender illustrates the problem. During the 1920s, Harrod's (the London department store) asked three literary luminaries—George Bernard Shaw, Arnold

Bennett, and H. G. Wells—to write testimonials for the store. They declined for a variety of reasons but took the proposal seriously, sympathetically, and at such length that their letters of refusal were ultimately printed by Harrod's as advertisements. These were all modern writers in the sense that they were in fundamental sympathy with modernizing tendencies: the hegemony of technical expertise and bureaucratic organization, the mass production and marketing of consumer goods (though Shaw and Wells might have entered a few Fabian quibbles about ownership of the means of production or inequalities of distribution). Still, all held to a modern faith in progress through scientific and technological advance.[2]

But there was another sort of modern (or "modernist") sensibility—the sensibility of Joyce, Lawrence, Eliot, Woolf. One should try to imagine, Spender suggests, their response to Harrod's request for a testimonial. To a man and woman, they would have treated it as a preposterous joke. Shaw, Wells, and Bennett felt responsible to a public composed of modern consumers: the same constituency as Harrod's. But Joyce & Co. felt "an entirely different kind of responsibility. They would feel responsibility to a past which had been degraded by commerce, a past of realer [*sic*] values betrayed by advertising. They would feel that their responsibility was as artists, and not as money-makers producing a consumers' product."[3]

The point of the anecdote should be clear. What literary critics and cultural historians call "modernism" or "modernity" has often been rooted in hostility toward modernization, and in particular the modernizing tendencies within nineteenth-century bourgeois society: its complacent faith in material progress, its positivism and philistinism, its alleged cultural enfranchisement of the untutored masses. It should not be surprising, then, that one finds modernist and anti-modernist sympathies coexisting, often within the same individual: a thirst for artistic novelty and experimentation, combined with longings for a sense of spiritual authenticity that seemed absent amid the everyday business of modern life. Those longings animated the visual as well as literary arts of early modernism. Among painters and poets alike, there was a dawning recognition that the forms provided by nineteenth-century bourgeois culture were inadequate to contain the ineffable mysteries of life. A drive to recover "primitive" motifs of myth and magic united artists as diverse as Lawrence, Picasso, and Gauguin—to mention only a few.[4]

According to conventional wisdom, the high seriousness of the early modernists began to dissipate around the middle of the twentieth century. Angst gave way to gamesmanship, the self-conscious employment of artifice for its own sake; preoccupation with the terrors of the inner life became passé; the skillful manipulation of surfaces became the mark of artistic genius. Nabokov, not Eliot, was the prophet of this "postmodern" age. Small wonder that a "poststructuralist" criticism deconstructed the inner self as a bourgeois illusion, and encouraged acquiescence in what Graff called "the agreeably meaningless surfaces of mass culture."[5] In such a cultural climate, one would expect the commercial artist to prosper like a dung beetle, not die like a mantis.

Yet artists' ambivalence toward advertising persists even in the contemporary atmosphere. Many film directors, for example, commute between movies and ads, seeking vocational fulfillment outside the agency. Tony Scott, director of Diet Pepsi ads and movies like *The Hunger*, puts the conflict succinctly: "I do thirty seconds for the money and ninety minutes for the ego." In recent years, a number of social scientists have systematically interviewed people in the creative departments of agencies and discovered that most still claim they would prefer to be crafting their own films, plays, or music but that "the money" makes advertising irresistible. Some refer to it in the familiar idiom as a "game" (fun, but not really appropriate activity for serious adults); others describe it as "poison gas." Maybe these doubts imply a vestigial belief that there ought to be some tension between the claims of the marketplace and the pristine soul (or even merely the "ego") of the artist.[6]

The nature of that tension remains unclear. Certainly, the relationship between modern art and modern advertising is too complex to be reduced to any linear scheme of progress or decline. Advertising has employed vendors of high fashion like Richard Avedon but also artists with more idiosyncratic personal visions, from Maxfield Parrish and René Magritte to Leo Lionni and Joseph Cornell. The courtship of art and advertising has been clouded by distrust and only fitfully consummated. It has produced pain and pleasure both, and it deserves a closer look.

The prevailing idiom in modern advertising, as in modern political propaganda, has long been what Northrop Frye calls "stupid realism"—"a kind of sentimental idealism, an attempt to present a conventionally attractive or impressive appearance as an actual or attainable reality." It parodies the prophetic realism of Brueghel, Hogarth, Goya, or Daumier; it evokes the scrubbed social vision presented by AT&T or the Young Communist League. The first piece of high art directly appropriated by an advertiser was squarely in the stupid realist tradition; John Everett Millais's *Bubbles* (1886), a work of unimpeachable sweetness, was turned to commercial advantage (amid critical uproar) by Pears Soap.[7] Innumerable examples since have all embodied the nineteenth-century conventions of representation that the early modernists found inauthentic.

"Stupid realism" is such a polemically loaded term that it requires some justification. It is meant to apply to corporate advertising and political propaganda—"official" discourses that legitimate existing structures of power. It is not meant to characterize all forms of mass-marketed commercial entertainment, many of which can powerfully dramatize the messy actualities of human experience. But in advertising, those actualities are systematically sanitized. The darker dimensions of life are airbrushed out of the picture. The term "stupid realism," loaded though it may be, helps us to distinguish popular culture from the propaganda of commodities, to separate the achievement of Billie Holiday from that of Batten, Barton, Durstine, and Osborne.

Yet stupid realism has never enjoyed unchallenged dominance in advertising art. From the circus posters and patent medicine advertisements of the mid-nineteenth century to the Beardsleyan posters of the 1890s, one can detect a strain of what might be called "magic realism," which later meshes with surrealism. The links between early advertising and popular magic are explicit and pervasive in American folklore: the confidence man has not only been a Barnumesque huckster but also an agent of the marvelous, an effector of miracle cures and supernatural transformations of the self. By the 1920s more professionalized advertising aimed to animate the inanimate commodity with the appearance of life, and sometimes explicitly with magical powers. At about the same time, the surrealist Louis Aragon was recognizing the semblance of "Egyptian divinities" in roadside gas pumps. Admaker and surrealist often shared a common fascination with the hallucinatory image, from Maxfield Parrish's work for Jello puddings in the 1910s to Salvador Dali's ads for Schiaparelli cosmetics in the 1940s.[8]

One impulse behind the fascination was the desire to fashion "eye appeal" that would stop the busy viewer in his tracks. As early as the 1910s, admakers were discussing the problem that the trade press now calls "clutter": too many advertisements crowded into the consumer's perceptual landscape, clamoring for attention. The need to attract attention led away from fact-filled "reason-why" copy and toward the halting, uncertain adoption of modernist aesthetic strategies.

During the early twentieth century, the basic affinity between adman and artist involved the effort to retrieve concrete images from the mists of Victorian rhetoric. Admakers who professed reverence for "the divinity of common things" would have applauded Ezra Pound's quest for solidity in language, and endorsed William Carlos Williams's slogan "No ideas but in things." Whether the early modernists called themselves imagists, cubists, or surrealists, they shared a sense that the exhaustion of nineteenth-century academicism required a return to "the things themselves." What they did with those things varied: cubists fragmented and reassembled the object; imagists and surrealists juxtaposed radically dissimilar images in alogical structures. Rejecting a literalist referentiality, they nevertheless sought a new precision of form. By the 1920s, Pound was redefining imagism as vorticism, seeking to capture dynamic movement in language. The culmination of this tendency was the technique of visual montage developed in the films of Sergei Eisenstein. In nearly every case, the modernist aim—which became the aim of more venturesome advertisers—was not to tell a story, but to create a cluster of images that would resonate with a reader or viewer.[9]

One need only switch on the television set to see the application of these formal innovations to contemporary advertising. As early as the 1920s, though, admakers were seeking attention through the use of startling juxtapositions and dynamic forms. By 1925, a *Printer's Ink* contributor asserted that "Futuristic Monstrosities are all the Rage." But the rage rarely went beyond a few cubist borders and elongated ladies in awkward postures. Futuristic fashion was mostly talk. In the 1930s even the talk was drowned out by the rejection of "artiness" (with only a few exceptions) under the sobering impact of the Great Depression. During the 1940s and 1950s, as agencies began to hire emigré designers, there was a partial but mostly subterranean resurgence of modernist strategies. The "creative revolution" of the 1960s brought the invasion of ironists with hand-held cameras, obsessed by quick cuts and staccato pacing. Modernist technique rose to full respectability in the advertising business.[10] Yet there was a persistent impulse toward referentiality, rooted not only in the preferences of clients and copy chiefs but also in the basic purpose of advertising: the need to send a message, however oblique, about a product. The literalist tradition could never be vanquished altogether.

The limits on modernism in advertising point to the inadequacies of current critical assumptions. The formalist approach can take us only so far in understanding the relationships between modernist art and modern advertising. Modernism has never been merely a matter of form; its creators have always been inspired by a particular social or personal vision. The advertised version strips the art of that vision, reducing it to mere technique. The point can be made with respect to surrealism as well as another major modernist tradition, the functionalist aesthetic associated with the Bauhaus. Following the example of Laszlo Moholy-Nagy's work for Container Corporation of America (CCA) in the 1930s and 1940s, functionalism has made itself felt in the bright primary colors of highway signs and the clean bold lines of corporate logos. Given the utopian hopes of the Bauhaus founders, this seems a pathetic denouement: an art that was meant to embody a whole way of life has been reduced to a meager promotional rule—or to an agent of labor discipline. By the 1960s, as Adrian Forty observes, functionalist office furniture was being designed "to create an illusion of equality while preserving hierarchies." Commercial use reversed the egalitarian and communal ideals of the Bauhaus.[11]

The fate of functionalism is symptomatic of broader tendencies. The key to any fruitful interchange between advertising and art (in modernist or more conventional modes) has always been the ascendance of formalism and professionalism. The rejection of all romantic dreams of transcendence, the dismissal of any vestigial sense of higher purpose, the acceptance of art as primarily a set of formal problems to be solved—all these developments smoothed the assimilation of art to advertising.[12]

This is not to say that the ultimate result—the advertisements themselves—lost all utopian connotations. Over thirty years ago the literary critic Leo Spitzer laboriously demonstrated the ways a Sunkist orange juice ad tapped ancient longings for communion with nature.[13] One can find other utopian ideals embodied in contemporary advertisements' images of work, fraternity, sexuality— take your choice.

But from the individual artist's point of view, advertising offers little possibility of creating a coherent personal vision from recalcitrant materials; instead, it demands that one perform one's craft smoothly enough to fit into the larger package prepared to please the corporate client. Even if one is content to reduce art to technique, this procedure violates the modernist shibboleth of artistic autonomy. According to Sid Ramin, who composed the "Come Alive" theme for Pepsi, "if you're a real purist, like most composers are, you don't really adjust to all the terrible things that writing music for commercials demands." The abbreviated format, the missed beats, the requirement to write for someone (in Ramin's case, for "a girl singer with a brassy voice" as well as for Pepsi)—all this is usually too much for a serious formalist to stomach. The artist who makes the necessary compromises risks becoming a stock figure in advertising lore: the abused, dyspeptic genius. Yearnings for autonomy surfaced in the trade press as early as the 1920s, when copywriters demanded the right to sign their ads—and agency executives indignantly refused, observing that the ad was meant to represent the client's "personality," not the copywriter's. Such an argument is difficult to imagine today, when most television commercials require an army of craft people, each concentrating on his or her own patch of expertise, to cooperate in a highly specialized division of labor. With a few exceptions, most can have little more sense of the overall plan than the average autoworker does of the car he or she is assembling. The process has grown far more complex than the making of magazine ads in the 1920s but the objective remains the same: to create a smooth, impenetrable surface, a seamless web of imagery that meets the needs of the client.[14]

Then why have so many twentieth-century artists been drawn to advertising, excited by its possibilities, awed by its achievements? "The money" has been crucial, but there have been other attractions as well. Advertising art has incorporated a fundamental avant-garde impulse, the rage for novelty, into the production of images with mass appeal. One key to successful advertising, agency people agree, is to stay a step ahead of your audience—but only a step. Make it new (as Pound advised), but not too new. Striving to be absolutely *au courant*, supported by the enormous institutional resources of the modern corporation, advertising has acquired an interpretive power quite apart from its capacity (or incapacity) for selling goods. Like the folktales and religious icons in traditional cultures, advertisements constitute a framework for making sense of life in a particular kind of society. As a result of this contextualizing function, advertising seems to perform many of the tasks accomplished by popular arts of the past. Marshall McLuhan, among others, has characterized advertising as the "folklore of industrial man." [15] The problems with this phrase ought to be immediately apparent: folk traditions often sought to embed cultural meanings in a coherent cosmology, while advertising always shuffles them arbitrarily according to the dictates of the market; advertising, moreover, does not issue from the "folk" but from corporate elites. But even if advertising is no more than a pathetic substitute for folk tradition, it offers artists a sense that they are participating in the popular life of their time.

The desire to merge with one's moment and milieu may also be fed by the accelerating technical sophistication of the advertising industry. In a society whose rulers are intoxicated by technological change, advertisements often epitomize state-of-the-art ingenuity. This is especially true of television. Given the complexity of the production processes involved and the superabundant variety of available talent, it's not surprising that the recent advertising scene is awash in technical virtuosity—drowning, one might almost say, in its own creative juices. Many formats are available: from high-tech special effects (Levi's) to "postmodern" quotations of mass culture, including ads from the 40s and 50s (Eastern Airlines, Sunsweet prunes); from in jokes directed at specific "taste cultures" (Miller Lite's repertory company of sports retirees) to straightforward stupid realism (the Old Milwaukee guys, squatting around the campfire, giving one another the somewhat frightening assurance that "it doesn't get any better than this").

Over an extended period, most campaigns mingle stupid realism with more experimental forms. The Pepsi Generation campaign offers a good example. The interviews suggest that the campaign was based less on detailed statistical research than on intuitive guesses about what one agency executive called "the pig in the python"—the demographic bulge of young people coming of age in the early 1960s. It was widely assumed that this group would revitalize a youth culture according to the patterns being cut in California.[16] The Pepsi Generation campaign, in other words, was a good example of a common interchange between advertising and the wider culture: advertising "creatives" make inferences about broad cultural trends, based on their own observation and pop sociological fashion; they inflate those inferences into assumptions and project the assumptions back into the wider culture, in the advertising imagery they create. Media-ridden trend-spotting acquires a life of its own, feeding on itself, replicating itself.

This may be one key to the distinction between a hegemonic culture stemming largely from elite sources and one with more genuinely popular roots. The elite-based culture, for all its dynamism and sensuous appeal, may acquire an aura of inauthenticity— at least from the vantage point of those outside the regnant historical bloc. It is at least arguable that ordinary people cannot *see* *themselves* in most billboards or commercials, any more than they catch sight of their own experience in textbook accounts of American history or government.[17] To be sure, admakers seek images that will resonate with their audience; a minimum of resonance is necessary if the images are to sustain any persuasive power at all. But the admakers' vision of that audience is narrowed by their own class insulation and the blinders of pop sociology.

So it was that the Pepsi Generation burst onto America's telescreens in 1964, nubile bodies cavorting in transports of joy so intense the kids might have required hospitalization if the ecstasy has lasted more than sixty seconds. All the scenes that have become the visual cliches of soft-drink advertising were beginning to fall in place. The sanitizing process that is so important to the idiom became especially apparent in 1969, when Batten, Barton, Durstine, and Osborn (BBDO—the agency handling the Pepsi account) hired a filmmaker named Ed Vorkapich to drive across the country, shooting film that could be used with Pepsi's new slogan: "You've got a lot to live, and Pepsi's got a lot to give." Vorkapich knew, first of all, that the scenes had to be uniformly upbeat; BBDO and Pepsi executives had decided that "the country was depressed" by protest

against the war in Vietnam. The long-standing desire to appropriate some of Coca-Cola's all-American iconography melded with a
more immediate impulse to create "an adult voice" lecturing rebellious youth (as a Pepsi staffer put it): "Hey for Godsakes, it ain't
too terribly bad what we've got going for us in the good U.S. of A.
OK, we do have a wonderful country." This was all fine with
Vorkapich; he was feeling "positive" about America too, and he was
perfectly willing to follow the explicit instructions: no jeans, no
long hair, and no "hippie types." [18]

Despite the thematic conventionality of the Pepsi campaign, it
displayed some aesthetic innovation, particularly in Vorkapich's
lighting techniques. To hear him tell it, he was a "gunfighter" in a
roomful of "organization men." The image retailored the artist's
role to meet familiar male anxieties: still a romantic outsider, he
was nevertheless tough and effectual amid the ball-less wonders of
Madison Avenue. When he shot his first commercial for Pepsi in
1963, Hollywood conventional wisdom held that you couldn't shoot
film after 4:00 P.M. because the light would look yellow. "But that's
the prettiest time!" Vorkapich protested. He proceeded to shoot in
the late afternoon, with the sun behind his subjects. "What the hell
is going on here? . . . We're not making art films! We're making
commercials!" a Pepsi executive complained when he saw the film.
But the new style prevailed; back-lighting and sun flares became
staples of commercial filmmaking.[19]

The yoking of formal experiment and thematic predictability
suggested that the relationship between modern art and advertising
could never be understood through purely aesthetic categories. Art
critics, in the tradition best articulated by Clement Greenberg, have
assumed that the birth of modernist sensibility occurred with the
appearance of paintings about painting and poems about poetry.
"In turning his attention away from the subject matter of common
experience," Greenberg wrote in 1939, "the poet or artist turns it
upon the medium of his own craft." A relentless concentration on
the materials and methods of the creative process constitutes what
Ortega called "the de-humanization of art": it shut out ordinary
citizens from the precincts of the avant-garde, leaving them vulnerable to the allure of Kitsch—which remained engaged with "the
subject matter of common experience." Greenberg wrote as if the
issues surrounding mass culture could be defined entirely in aesthetic terms, as if the distinction between avant-garde and kitsch

could be sniffed out only by the "cultivated individual" who could decode the difficulties of self-reflexive art.[20]

For nearly half a century, critical discourse was shaped by those assumptions. Under the aegis of aestheticism, the Marxian concept of alienation was transformed. For Marx it had implied an unjust set of power relations that separated the worker from the fruits of his work; for twentieth-century art critics it became a synonym for the emotional disaffection of the aesthete in a philistine world. From this view, the artist-turned-admaker had betrayed a sacred trust by pandering to the oafish sentiments of the mob. This critique was vulnerable from two directions. On the one hand, defenders of mass culture from Herbert Gans to Warren Susman could dismiss Greenberg et al. (with some justification) as a pack of snobs, unable to hear the pulsating heart of "the people" amid advertising jingles and Tin Pan Alley songs.[21] On the other hand, once advertising did begin to incorporate avant-garde techniques, formalists were forced to acknowledge that many advertisements were aesthetically superb; the basis of their critique began to melt away. We are left with the current situation: would-be critics feel a visceral sense of unease when confronted by advertising, but are silenced by the general celebration of its aesthetic brilliance.

But there are better criteria for criticism than the question of artistic excellence. The tension between advertising and art involves more than a matter of taste. At the risk of oversimplification, one might suggest that a basic impulse behind aesthetic activity is a desire to redeem everyday utilitarian drabness, to leaven the lump of the routine and commonplace, to glimpse a cosmos of hope amid the kingdom of necessity. This longing for a kind of transcendence, however brief and fragmentary, is at the root not only of high art but also of vernacular craft and decorative traditions. It is what led William Morris and other critics of industrial capitalism to celebrate household arts as a vanishing realm of freedom. Advertising art, in contrast, can never nurture a truly disinterested aesthetic involvement; it always pulls up short at the point of sale. Nor can advertising ever sustain a transcendent vision of life, beyond the performance principle of advanced capitalism; it is fated to serve as the iconography of mass production and the corporate system.[22]

There are several ways of characterizing the conflict between art and advertising without resorting to aesthetic snobbery. The poet Lewis Hyde, for example, explores the "spirit of the gift" that survives from precapitalist "gift cultures" and animates contemporary notions about the creativity of the gifted artist. Where the gift relationship persists in contemporary societies, objects engender feelings of mutual obligation and interdependence; where it has been suffocated by the atmosphere of commodity exchange, objects promote envy, animosity, and competitive status-striving. From Hyde's perspective, artists who try to separate their art from the work they do in the marketplace may be motivated by more than disdain for practical life; they may be trying to sustain the spirit of the gift in a culture dominated by commodities.[23]

There is another tradition, too, that can sustain a critique of advertising art: the tradition which holds that art, even when it does not transcend everyday life, offers a compelling interpretation of common experience. Art, in other words, is not merely a formal exercise but also a species of truth-telling. From this view the problem with stupid realism is not that it is tacky—it can often be technically superb—but that it strips realism of its nineteenth-century rationale: the attempt to tell the truth (or at least *a* truth) even when it is sordid or disturbing. Ever since the early twentieth century, when admakers first sought to shed their Barnumesque inheritance, ad industry spokesmen have pursued the grail of "Truth in Advertising." Yet advertising truth has always been defined negatively, as the absence of outright falsehood. The dominant tendency in the development of twentieth-century advertising strategies has been to render truth claims irrelevant by shifting attention from the product to the images of richer, fuller life surrounding it.[24]

Not that those images are to be lightly dismissed. They are designed to resonate with common experiences in American life, and they have become a central presence in that life. While other interpretive traditions (religious, political, communal) have slipped into bureaucratese or disappeared, advertising has displayed ever more dynamism and sensuous appeal. By assisting consumers to navigate a bewildering sea of commodities, advertising implicitly promises a broader orientation to everyday life in the late twentieth century. To a degree it has succeeded: it shows people how to fit into a society geared to galloping consumption. Corporate advertising, as Michael Schudson reminds us, has become the official art form of advanced capitalist culture.[25] But no official art form, however clever, presents a satisfying interpretation of actual experience. The tradition that art constitutes a kind of truth is much broader and richer than literalist devotion to "fact." It animates any art, religious or secular, that attempts to grasp and express something fundamental and intractable in the human condition, some experience not reducible to smooth surfaces, some unarticulated passion, some unresolvable conflict, some doomed desire for the infinite. For the early modernist, these were the experiential truths that eluded nineteenth-century cultural forms. And among modern artists in general, this tradition has nurtured resistance to the claims of advertising.

Within twentieth-century advertising, it's not surprising that literary folk have presented the strongest resistance. They are the heirs of a nineteenth-century print culture that idealized (even if it did not enact) a literalist notion of truth. Sherwood Anderson, walking home at the end of the day, could not remember the copy he had been writing; he sometimes felt "a sharp sense of uncleanliness" and longed to earn his living through "the joy of hands and mind combined in craftsmanship" rather than through "trickery." So after years of living in the agency but not of it, he left for New York to pursue his literary ambitions and discovered: "There is so much to unlearn. One who has spent so many years as I had just saying words to get a quick surface effect, as we advertising writers are always doing, are paid to do, has later to whip himself with much scorn." In part, these are the words of a Puritan plain speaker, in a voice brought to fullest force by George Orwell. The plain speaker's stance was characterized by a guilt-ridden distrust of artifice and a naive faith that language can become perfectly transparent. As Orwell said, "good prose is like a windowpane." [26]

Yet there is more in Anderson's critique than puritanical plain speaking. There is a dawning recognition that a new American culture had begun to emerge in the early twentieth century, a culture dependent on "quick surface effects" and standardized charm. Anderson wrote sympathetically of admen, in the midst of that new order. In "Milk Bottles" (1923), he tells of a copywriter in Chicago who cranks out orotund phrases for a milk company at the agency by day but breaks through that rhetorical facade into "real" prose one stifling hot night at home in his cramped apartment. He captures the strained faces in the buses, the smell of milk souring on windowsills. In the end, though, he lets the precious sheets flutter to the pavement below, and turns from the window with a shrug. [27]

Anderson sensed that modern advertising systematically excluded the more authentic forms of human experience from its verbal and visual discourse. It was no accident that this former adman, who had done his bit to create the new fake-cosmopolitan culture, turned in his fiction to write lovingly of people that culture had passed by—"grotesques" he called them in *Winesburg, Ohio* (1919), "the book of the grotesque." These were people in the interstices or on the outskirts of the urban corporate system: withered Victorian maidens disappointed in love; country doctors with pockets full of paper pills. To Anderson, they somehow seemed more substantial and admirable than their sleeker successors.[28]

A fascination with the grotesque is a major strain in modern literature, linking Anderson to William Faulkner and in turn to Gabriel Garcia Marquez and other Latin "magic realists." In every case, the author has concerned himself with defeated and despised cultural backwaters, with people who have been exploited or ignored by modernizing elites. Often these people are physically ugly by conventional criteria, but that is less important than their inability to conform to broader standards of normality. They are, it is agreed, a little "queer." Often there is an obsessive, single-minded quality to their lives—like that of the old carpenter in Winesburg, whose brother died of starvation in Andersonville prison during the Civil War and who remains immobilized by the memory forty years later. As Anderson said, "they have got hold of a single truth and tried to make it their own, to live their lives by it." [29] This refusal to become "sensible" or "well-rounded," to adjust to the demands of a routinized society, makes them failures in the eyes of the smart and up-to-date. Yet in their willingness to face grief and disappointment squarely, they endure (like Faulkner's Negro characters) and maintain a stoical dignity.

It is this elusive constellation of qualities, rather than ugliness *per se*, that keeps the grotesque out of the iconography of modernization. From freak show promoters to the producers of MTV, advertisers and other creators of mass culture have domesticated the physically aberrant to titillate a wide audience. The grotesques of Winesburg, Yoknapatawpha, or Macondo are less easily accommodated to the dominant culture. Nevertheless, sheer repulsiveness has acquired a special kind of symbolic power in the modern imagination, as an emblem of absolute deviance. Mass culture can market ugliness; it can even generate a grotesque critique of its own conformist ideals, as sometimes has occurred in film noir or rock music. Yet the dominant idiom of mass culture remains the high-gloss conventionalizing of human conflict and aspiration. And nowhere has that conventionality been more carefully embodied in images of physical perfection than in the realm of advertising. It's not surprising that modern writers and artists have sought alternatives to that world in images of physical deformity.

Frederick Exley's "fictional memoir," *A Fan's Notes* (1968), brings this strategy to its sharpest focus. The narrator shuttles drunkenly between advertising agencies and mental institutions, confronting the truth-telling power of the grotesque as he joins his fellow inmates at Avalon Valley State Hospital in their horror stories of mistreatment by the institution.

> These repeaters were the ugly, the broken, the carrion. They had crossed eyes and bug eyes and cavernous eyes. They had club feet or twisted limbs or—sometimes—no limbs. These people were grotesques. On noticing this, I thought I understood; there was in mid-century America no place for them. America was drunk on physical comeliness . . . [dedicated to the vision of normality embodied by] the carmine-hued, ever-sober "young marrieds" in the Schlitz beer sign. The sin of these repeaters was that they obtruded frightfully in the bill-board sign rather like fortuitously projecting Quasimodo into an advertisement to delineate the Male ideal (I saw Julie London, her sensual lips blowing the lazy smoke of Marlboros into the sexually smug and outrageously winking visage of Charles Laughton's "Quasi").

This passage does not imply a psychobabbling argument that madness is an essentially sane response to an insane world. The repeaters at Avalon Valley really are crazed, despairing; their suffering is genuine and there is nothing ennobling about it. But without sentimentalizing them, the narrator grants these deviants their true cultural significance—their function as a kind of collective Other for a society "drunk on physical comeliness" and bent on narrowing the boundaries of normality. The agent of that process is not mass culture in toto, since mass culture can at least produce grotesque alternative visions—the hunchback Quasimodo displacing the Marlboro Man, leering at Julie London. Rather, boundaries are standardized through the embodiment of demographic types (the Schlitz "young marrieds") in the iconography of advertising. From Exley's view advertising combined with sitcoms and soap operas in creating "a world to which the passionate and the singular aspiration were forbidden." [30]

The grotesque challenges that world, but the nature of the challenge is not always clear. Sometimes it is merely a cry of pain, sometimes it broadens and melds with the tradition of the "holy fool" or idiot savant, the truth-teller who stands outside organized society, lacking any of its laurels, commenting if only through example on its brutalities and hypocrisies, posing implicitly a redemptive alternative. The idea (like that of the "essentially sane" madman) risks sentimentality but has reaped rewards—from Dostoevsky's Prince Myshkin to J. M. Coetzee's Michael K. At its best, the tradition of the grotesque promises not only a critique but also a kind of redemption from what Cynthia Ozick calls "the wild and merciless power of inanity." [31] Redemption comes not through resort to a sacred realm of High Art but through immersion in the most fleeting, contingent, and even banal details of everyday life.

It is only a short step from an aesthetic of the grotesque to an aesthetic of the outmoded, which was pioneered by André Breton and the surrealists in the 1920s. As Walter Benjamin observed, Breton "was the first to perceive the revolutionary energies that appear in the 'outmoded,' in the first iron constructions, the first factory buildings, the earliest photos, the objects that have begun to be extinct, grand pianos, the dresses of five years ago, fashionable restaurants when the vogue has begun to ebb from them." [32] In referring to "revolutionary energies," Benjamin implied something more complex than orthodox Marxism envisioned. By recontextualizing the detritus of industrial capitalism within the sacrosanct realm of Art, the surrealist project sought a genuine transvaluation of value. This was perhaps clearest in the visual realm, in the collages of Kurt Schwitters and the Americans Joseph Cornell and Joseph Stella. Those alchemists of the quotidian gathered up the most forlorn, abused, and neglected fragments of commodity civilization—scraps of old newspaper advertisements, used railway tickets, theater programs for hopelessly passé ballerinas. They resituated the fragments in the architecture of the imagination, and, in the work itself, the fragments underwent "a sea change into something rich and strange." They acquired a redemptive aura, as part of a storehouse of cultural memory in a society that systematically erodes it. By defamiliarizing familiar objects, the aesthetic of the outmoded aimed at what Benjamin called a "profane illumination"—a moment that would call into question the given facticity of the existing social world and promote the hope of transcending it. These surrealists hoped to glimpse profounder truths than "the real world" had to offer. Unlike contemporary postmodern fashions that simulate outmoded styles, the surrealist aesthetic sought not to erase the boundaries between art and commodity culture, but to reassert and refine them.[33]

The contrast with advertising aesthetics could not be sharper. Superficially, the advertising artist also seeks to become an alchemist of the quotidian, to endow toasters and toothpaste with numinous significance. In practice he reverses the surrealist impulse: he locates commodities in a given symbolic universe decreed by current fashion. Rather than challenging the status quo, his work reinforces it, makes it seem natural, inevitable, inescapable. Rather than exalting the ignoble or grotesque, the process reaffirms existing hierarchies of economic power and cultural meaning.[34]

The surrealist aesthetic of the outmoded, implicitly rejecting the reverence for the new that has linked many avant-gardists with the world of advertising, preserved an older, profounder artistic tradition. Advertising, along with much of the avant-garde art that has been assimilable to it, exists in a kind of eternal present: denying the pull of the past, celebrating perpetual change, ignoring the destructive effects of the passage of time. It is no accident that death, the ultimate register of time, is rendered invisible in advertising—as invisible as the culturally "dead" style or commodity that has fallen out of fashion. The aesthetic of the outmoded, like the fascination with the grotesque, suggests an honorable modernist alternative outside the avant-garde "tradition of the new"—an alternative that neither trivializes nor evades the corrosive course of time, the pastness of the past.

Yet if this version of surrealism aimed to preserve the tension between art and advertising, there was another surrealist strain more easily adapted to the developing image empire. This strain was more representational and illusionistic, and surfaced most clearly in the work of Salvador Dali and René Magritte. Here, too, there was a defamiliarization process at work. As Magritte said, he wanted to "put the real world on trial" by subverting the mimetic assumption at the heart of realism: the identity of image and object. Attacking illusionism with illusionistic methods, Magritte used bizarre metamorphoses, incongruous juxtapositions, and well-placed captions (most famous: "This is not a pipe" beneath an illusionist image of a pipe) all to the same philosophical end: to emphasize the arbitrariness of representation. The basis of representation, he insisted, was not mimesis or resemblance but merely knowledge of the linguistic and visual conventions that constitute the rules of the game. The projected reversed established advertising strategies, which depended on an uncritical acceptance of those conventions (e.g., in perfume advertising, a picture of Catherine Deneuve depends for its meaning on the audience associating it with chic French beauty). Yet, despite his intellectual aims and well-advertised disdain for advertising, much of Magritte's work was commissioned as part of corporate publicity campaigns.[35]

The reason may lie in the narrow, intellectualist quality of Magritte's truth-telling—it was the kind of epistemological gamesmanship that lay behind so much Pop Art in the 1960s. The assimilation of Magritte may also stem from his determination to cling to an illusionist style even as he mocked its philosophical basis. The referent system behind Magritte's illusionism is ambiguous, displaced, or nonexistent: the "real world" is constantly "on trial." So it is not surprising that Magritte, like the less philosophically ambitious Dali, could be incorporated into the advertising that aims at stylistic daring, rejects literal representation, and calls attention to its own artifice. Seeking to supersede stupid realism, this brand of advertising nevertheless persists in exalting smooth-surface illusionism. From the advertisers' view, the surrealist fantasies of Dali and Magritte are little more than a set of "deceptive journalistic tricks" designed to arrest the attention of the unwary audience—a precursor to the high-tech high jinks of "special effects."

The phrase "deceptive journalistic tricks" is from the Abstract Expressionist painter Barnett Newman in 1946, contrasting the academic surrealism of Dali with the work of primitive Oceanic artists, then on display at the Metropolitan Museum of Art. According to Newman, the surrealists' "intent to make the real more so by means of the use of illusion resulted in theatricalism that is the ultimate reason for its failure."

> Eventually we unmasked the illusion and realized that to the artists it was also an illusion, that it was they who did not feel the magic. Realism [i.e., illusionist painting] including that of the imagination is in the last analysis deceitful. [For Oceanic primitives] deceptive journalistic tricks do not exist. The primitive artist gives us a vision, complete and naive.[36]

If one discounts the bathetic self-ennoblement and the bohemian posturing common to warring artistic sects, the passage is symptomatic of more important tendencies. From the view of Newman and other Abstract Expressionists, surrealist illusionism is—like advertising—the work of a con artist, a magician who does not "feel the magic" but only seeks to manipulate the audience through "theatricality" and "journalistic tricks." The distrust of theatricality, the celebration of naiveté as an alternative, make clear that Newman's statement was another salvo in the war between art and artifice. The determination to "feel the magic," to enter a re-enchanted world through cultivation of a primitive mentality, suggests the force of his recoil from modern, secular iconography.

The first generation of Abstract Expressionists offers a clear example of an effort to create art that would resist incorporation in the world of advertising and commodity culture. The basis of this resistance was their resolute antiformalism: nearly all insisted their problem was not how to paint, but what to paint. As Adolph Gottlieb put it in 1943: "there is no such thing as good painting about nothing. We assert that the subject is crucial." This preoccupation with subject matter is worth stressing because popularizers like Tom Wolfe have so often asserted that the Abstract Expressionists were engaged in a kind of formalist game, under the coaching of Clement Greenberg. Nothing could be further from the truth. In fact, Greenberg never really understood the Abstract Expressionists: he dismissed their preoccupation with myth as "something half-baked and revivalist," when for most it was at the heart of the matter. As Mark Rothko said in 1943: "The myth holds us, not through its romantic flavor, nor through the possibilities of fantasy, but because it expresses something real and existing in ourselves as it was to those who first stumbled on the symbols and gave them life." Robert Goldwater puts the matter succinctly. The Abstract Expressionists, he said, "were engaged in 'telling the truth' and they talked a good deal about it. This truth was an emotional truth which would emerge from themselves if they knew how to allow it." [37]

It was also a truth that was inadmissible to the symbolic universe of advertising. Henry James had called it "the imagination of disaster"; Adolph Gottlieb, writing a half century later during the Second World War, insisted on the need for the artist to cultivate the "constant awareness of powerful forces, the immediate presence of terror and fear, a recognition of the brutalities of the natural world as well as the eternal insecurities of life." This was what led the Abstract Expressionists to value primitive myth and magic as mediators and embodiments of those "powerful forces," and to capture the imagery of the unconscious in biomorphic abstraction; it was also what led them, far more surely than any aesthetic concerns, to reject the smooth surfaces and clean, finished edges of surrealist illusionism—which by the 1940s was being widely used in advertising campaigns for Pittsburgh Steel, Johnson Paints, Textron, RCA, and other corporate clients. Like the literature of the grotesque, Abstract Expressionist painting sought to grasp experiences that would never appear in corporate imagery: from insoluble sexual conflicts (Arshile Gorky) to impossible spiritual yearnings (Mark Rothko). This attempt to assimilate unassimilable subjects led to a quest for more "authentic" methods: a preoccupation with energy and spontaneity, with rough "unfinished" canvases, with encrustations and chaotic drips of paint. Surveying the results of this frenzy in 1957, Meyer Schapiro caught much of its cultural significance. In a culture dominated by mass production and the division of labor, he observed, paintings were among the last artifacts that still bore the marks of an individual self seeking communication with others; the Abstract Expressionists' preoccupations revealed their determination to create emblems of personal identity in a world where private selfhood seemed precarious and perhaps even obsolete.[38] Their work, despite its unevenness, can testify to a persistent tension between advertising art and an art that aspires to truth.

Ultimately Abstract Expressionism met an ironic fate. Despite its makers' determination to resist incorporation, by the early 1950s much of their work had become a lucrative investment opportunity for corporate collectors. The subject matter, which had been essential to the first generation, was obscure enough that it could be overlooked; style alone became the chief attraction for investors and even advertisers. By 1960 the work of Abstract Expressionist epigones had entered the referent system of commodity culture, signifying sophistication. One could find imitations of Pollock or Rothko serving as backdrops for corporate images of the good life set in minimalist urban apartments. Abstract Expressionist became another cultural prop, available for manipulation by the ever-alert "creatives" at the big agencies.

William Baziotes, *The Flesh Eaters,* 1952. Courtesy, Ethel Baziotes and Blum Helman Gallery, New York.

There was a further irony as well. The Abstract Expressionists wanted to capture an emotional truth that could be verified through personal experience. But their vision was so private that their truths sometimes risked an absolute subjectivity; in that case it could be judged only with reference to its "seriousness" or "sincerity." And as Irving Howe observed, "sincerity becomes the last ditch defense for men without belief and in its name absolutes can be toppled, morality dispersed, and intellectual systems dissolved." The desperate search for artistic truth may have been accelerated by the fear that there was no truth. The specter of nihilism may have haunted both the artist and the adman, whose key to success (the trade press agreed) was his "sincerity." [39] In the end, though, the Abstract Expressionists' willingness to acknowledge their own

doubt and despair made their art more than an exercise in corporate impression management, and sustained the tension between
their work and commercial propaganda.

Even the most determined efforts to relax that tension have met
with ambiguous success at best. In the early 1950s, for example,
Walter Paepcke, president of Container Corporation of America
(CCA), began to sponsor an advertising art that involved more than
spectacle or technical virtuosity The story of Paepcke's patronage is
worth at least passing scrutiny, because it illuminates the difficulties
inherent in any effort to move beyond a formalist definition of advertising art. Paepcke was more than just another businessman seeking the status of a modern Medici; he wanted to restore artists'
traditional interpretive power, to allow them to act as commentators
on substantive cultural issues that transcended the confines of commodity civilization. But his effort proved only partially successful.

An early devotee of Robert Hutchins's Great Books Program at
the University of Chicago, Paepcke inaugurated an ad campaign
for CCA that was designed to illustrate "Great Ideas of Western
Man." He hired Mortimer Adler to select quotations from his
Syntopicon (or index) of the ideas in the fifty-four Great Books.
The N. W. Ayer advertising agency, which handled the CCA account, then distributed several quotations to each of the artists it
commissioned. Each artist chose a quotation and interpreted it in
any medium or style he wanted. The range of artists commissioned
was extraordinarily wide, and some of the resulting works embodied
a powerful idiosyncratic vision. (One thinks, for example, of Roy
DeForest's painted fiberglass and wood construction, playful but
somehow haunting, that was meant to illustrate Carl Jung: "What
can I do? Become what you have always been.") For Paepcke, it was
a bold effort to break the boundaries of conventional commercial
art—in subject matter as well as style. Indeed, the very attempt to
engage a subject at all (other than the commodity for sale) was a
gesture toward a truth-telling art.[40]

Nevertheless, there were built-in limitations on the project.
Paepcke admitted in 1955 that he avoided controversial authors
whose names would reduce or distort the effect of their statements.
"Karl Marx, for example, could hardly have made a statement of
moral principle, no matter how true or sincere it might have been,
which could have been universally accepted at face value by the
American people." [41] The focus on truths that would be "universally

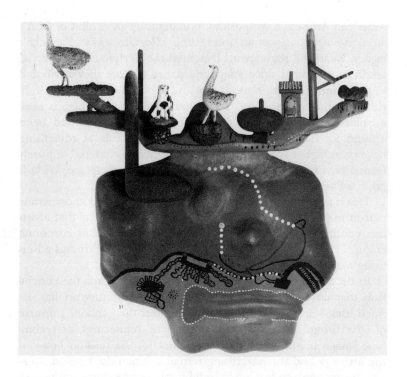

Roy Dean DeForest, *"What can I do?" "Become what you have always been."*
Carl Gustav Jung, Essays on a Science of Mythology, *1949*, 1967. Courtesy,
National Museum of American Art, Smithsonian Institution; Gift of the
Container Corporation of America.

acceptable at face value" led to broader difficulties than the predictable blacklisting of Marx; it ruled out the "profane illumination"
treasured by Benjamin and the surrealists; it ended by promoting a
pervasive blandness. The "Great Ideas" began to look like an indis-
criminate bunch of humanist bromides, in which Nietzsche
emerged as a burghermeister spouting aphorisms after a heavy meal.

Still, the series constituted a touching monument to Paepcke's
universalist vision—the hopeful rationalism that animated his earlier United Nations series as well as the Great Ideas of Western
Man. In retrospect his outlook may exude a kind of cultural imperialism, but its faith in reason, progress, and international toler-
ance was fundamentally benign. Recently the National Museum of

American Art held a symposium to inaugurate an exhibit of CCA's advertisements: it was an interesting effort to assess Paepcke's legacy. Nearly all participants lamented the decline of commercial aesthetic standards since Paepcke's day, a decline they attributed to the primacy of the bottom line and the swallowing of the individual by the organization. Yet in some ways the complaints were misplaced: the structural difficulties they described had been around for decades, while the aesthetic standards of advertising have risen higher than ever. Artistic brilliance, considered in purely formal terms, has not disappeared from the marketplace. What is gone is Paepcke's social hope.

This is not to deny that some other courageous and idiosyncratic patron might reappear in the future. Nor is it to deny that artists can continue to survive creatively in the interstices of corporate culture. From time to time, at least, the courtship of art and advertising may still be happily consummated.

In the final account, though, it is difficult to escape the conclusion that much of the profoundest twentieth-century art has defined itself—at least unconsciously— against the symbolic universe of advertising. The artist may appropriate, reinterpret, or recombine image fragments from that realm, but the tension between the art work and the advertising remains. When the tension slackens the art tends to lose some indefinable but fundamental power. This adversary relation involves more than a stylistic gap between avant-garde and kitsch; it embodies bedrock differences of purpose. Advertising can never escape a merely instrumental rationale for its existence. The admaker's social functions resemble those of a Soviet party hack: both serve as cogs in a vast cultural apparatus that justifies and celebrates the existing economic system. With rare exceptions, the smooth surfaces of advertising iconography conceal not only the actual conditions of production but also nearly all the conflicts that have served as grist for the great artist's mill—between the terror or tedium of existence and the passionate urge to transcend it, between the joys of earthly life and the certainty of its ending. In giving form and meaning to the muddle of experience, the artist has sought some sacred or profane illumination, some vision—however fleeting—of a world elsewhere, beyond the inane logic of getting and spending. It may be that the "real world" of postmodern entrepreneurship has extinguished that impulse forever. But I doubt it.

Notes

1. Marshall Berman, *All That Is Solid Melts into Air: The Experience of Modernity* (New York, 1982); Fredric Jameson, "Reflections in Conclusion," in Ronald Taylor, ed., *Aesthetics and Politics* (London, 1977), 209; Gerald Graff, *Literature Against Itself: Literary Ideas in Modern Society* (Chicago, 1979), 92.

2. Stephen Spender, "Moderns and Contemporaries," in *The Struggle of the Modern* (Berkeley, 1963), 71–75.

3. Ibid., 76.

4. For some interesting examples, see Robert Goldwater, *Primitivism in Modern Art* (New York, 1967), and Phyllis Rose, "The Case of Willa Cather," in Robert Kiely, ed., *Modernism Reconsidered* (Cambridge, Mass., and London, 1983), 123–45.

5. Graff, *Literature Against Itself*, 58. The argument is summarized in Bruce Robbins, "Modernism in History, Modernism in Power," in Kiely, *Modernism Reconsidered*, 229–45. Thomas Crow, "Modernism and Mass Culture in the Visual Arts," in Benjamin H. D. Buchloh, Serge Guilbault, and David Solkin, eds., *Modernism and Modernity* (Halifax, Nova Scotia, 1983), 215–64, offers a subtle account of developing interrelationships, but reaches the overstated conclusion that "the avant-garde serves as a kind of research and development arm of the culture industry: it searches out areas of social practice not yet completely available to efficient manipulation and makes them discrete and visible" (253).

6. K. Shapiro, "The Construction of Television Commercials: Four Cases of Interorganizational Problem Solving," diss. Stanford Univ. 1981, 38, 41, 398–99; J. B. Varcoe, "The Advertising Agency," in P. Zarry and R. Wilson, eds., *Advertising in Canada: Its Theory and Practice* (Toronto, 1981), 67. Also see William Leiss, Stephen Kline, and Sut Jhally, *Social Communication in Advertising* (New York, 1986), 131–43.

7. Northrop Frye, *The Modern Century* (Toronto, 1967), 26; Tim Shackleton, "Introduction," in Mike Dempsey, ed., *Bubbles: Early Advertising Art from A. & F. Pears, Ltd* (London, 1978); Ronald Berman, "Origins of the Art of Advertising," *Journal of Aesthetic Education* 17 (Fall 1983): 61–69. For a variation on Frye's theme, see Michael Schudson's witty discussion of advertising as "capitalist realism" in his *Advertising: The Uneasy Persuasion* (New York, 1984), ch. 7.

8. Louis Aragon, *Nightwalker*, trans. Frederick Brown (1926; Englewood Cliffs, N.J., 1970), 96–97; "Surrealism Pays," *Newsweek* (3 January 1944): 57–58.

9. William Carlos Williams, *Paterson* (New York, 1946), 6; F. S. Fling, "Imagism," and Ezra Pound, "A Few Don'ts by an Imagiste," *Poetry* [Chicago] 1 (1913): 198–206; idem, "Vorticism," in Richard Ellman and Charles Feidelson, Jr., *The Modern Tradition* (New York, 1965), 145–52; Sergei Eisenstein, "The Image in Process," in ibid., 163–69. In some ways the parallels are most apparent if we view advertisements not as individual artifacts but as an encompassing perceptual landscape that, taken as a totality, may create a "montage effect" on the viewer.

10. A commercial art manager, "Futuristic Monstrosities Are All the Rage," *Printer's Ink* 144 (12 November 1925): 57–58, 60; Jackson Lears, "Some Versions of Fantasy: Toward a Cultural History of American Advertising," in Jack Salzman, ed., *Prospects: An Annual of American Cultural Studies* (New York, 1984), 394–405, esp. 385–98; Roland Marchand, *Advertising the American Dream: Making Way for Modernity, 1920–1940* (Berkeley and London, 1985), esp. 140–47, 179–86, 300–306; Neil Harris, "Designs on Demand: Art and the Modern Corporation," in Martina Roudabush Norelli, *Art, Design, and the Modern Corporation* (Washington, D.C, 1985), 8–30; Stephen Fox, *The Mirror Makers: A History of American Advertising and Its Creators* (New York, 1984), chs. 4, 5, 6.

11. James Sloan Allen, *The Romance of Commerce and Culture* (Chicago and London, 1983), 3–77; Harris, "Designs on Demand"; Jeffrey Meikle, *Twentieth Century Limited: Industrial Design in America, 1925–1939* (Philadelphia, 1979); Adrian Forty, *Objects of Desire: Design and Society from Wedgewood to IBM* (New York, 1986), 149.

12. For examples of no-nonsense professionalism promoting assimilations, see John Atherton, "The Artist in Advertising," *Magazine of Art* 37 (March 1944): 100–103, and Egbert Jacobson, "Communication . . . versus Confusion," *American Artist* 17 (January 1953): 40–41, 44, 60–62.

13. Leo Spitzer, "American Advertising Explained as Popular Art," in his *Essays on English and American Literature* (Princeton, 1962), 248–77.

14. Sid Ramin, interview, Pepsi Generation Oral History Project, Archives Center, National Museum of American History, Smithsonian Institution, Washington, D.C.; Mac Artzt, "Should Copywriters Sign Their Copy?" *Printer's Ink* 150 (27 February 1930): 61–64; G. W. Freeman, "Let Copywriters Sign Their Copy? I Should Say Not!" ibid., 84–136. For the division of labor in contemporary advertising, see Michael Arlen, *Thirty Seconds* (New York, 1978).

15. Marshall McLuhan, *The Mechanical Bride: Folklore of Industrial Man* (New York, 1951).

16. Hilary Lipsitz, interview, Pepsi Generation Oral History Project.

17. On this point, see Jackson Lears, "The Concept of Cultural Hegemony: Problems and Possibilities," *American Historical Review* 90 (June 1985): 567–93, esp. 577.

18. Alan Pottasch, John Corbani, Ed Vorkapich, interviews, Pepsi Generation Oral History Project.

19. Vorkapich, interview, in ibid.

20. Clement Greenberg, "Avant-garde and Kitsch," *Partisan Review* 6 (Fall 1939): 34–49; Jose Ortego y Gasset, *The Dehumanization of Art*, trans. Helene Wehl (1925; Princeton, 1948), esp. 8–14.

21. Herbert Gans, *Popular Culture and High Culture* (New York, 1974); Warren Susman, "Introduction" to his *Culture as History* (New York, 1985), xix–xxx. The revaluation of Greenberg's theories is well underway: see, for example, nearly all the essays in Buchloh et al., *Modernism and Modernity*, and Francis Frascina, ed., *Pollock and After: The Critical Debate* (New York, 1985).

22. For a slightly different formulation of this position, see Peter Fuller, *Aesthetics After Modernism* (London, 1983). Morris's views are succinctly expressed in his "Of the Origins of Ornamental Art," in Eugene D. Lemire, ed. and comp., *Unpublished Lectures of William Morris* (1886; Detroit, 1969), 136–57. It might be argued that the quest for transcendence is powered by male discomfort in what has been culturally defined as the "female" world of day-to-day material (*mater*) reality. Given the pervasiveness of male anxiety in modernism, from Dostoevsky to Kafka and beyond, one has to wonder at the determination of Wassily Kandinsky (for example) "to free art from its traditional bonds to material reality." See Kandinsky, *Concerning the Spiritual in Art*, trans. Michael Sadler (London, 1914; rpt. New York, 1977), back cover. But to treat advertising as simply a celebration of the "female" world of sensuous objects is to overlook its functional role in a male-dominated bureaucratic system that depends on fear and anxiety rather than pleasure.

23. Lewis Hyde, *The Gift: Imagination and the Erotic Life of Property* (New York, 1982).

24. Lears, "Some Versions of Fantasy," esp. 381–83; Daniel Pope, *The Making of Modern Advertising* (New York, 1983), esp. chs. 5, 6, 7.

25. Schudson, *The Uneasy Persuasion*, 218–23.

26. Millicent Bell, *Marquand: An American Life* (Boston, 1979), 113; Sherwood Anderson, *A Story-teller's Story* (1924; Cleveland, 1968), 236, 196; George Orwell, "Why I Write," in *A Collection of Essays by George Orwell* (1947; New York, 1954), 320. On the origins of the Puritan plain speech tradition as a means of controlling the flood of deceptive meanings in market society, see Jean-Christophe Agnew, *Worlds Apart: The Market and the Theater in Anglo-American Thought, 1550–1750* (New York, 1986). Criticism of advertising and "postmodern" mass culture is still shaped by the plain speech tradition. See, for example, Graff, *Literature Against Itself*, and Raymond Williams, "Advertising: the Magic System," in his *Problems in Materialism and Culture* (London, 1980), 184, 198.

27. Sherwood Anderson, "Milk Bottles," in his *Horses and Men* (New York, 1923).

28. Sherwood Anderson, *Winesburg, Ohio* (1919; New York, 1960), 21–25.

29. Ibid., 25.

30. Ibid., 182.

31. Cynthia Ozick, "A Tale of Heroic Anonymity." Review of *The Life and Times of Michael K*, by J. M. Coetzee, *New York Times Book Review* (11 December 1983): 28.

32. Walter Benjamin, "Surrealism," in *Reflections*, trans. Edmund Jephcott (New York, 1978), 179, 181–82. Benjamin may have overlooked the most sustained literary use of the outmoded: Joyce's affectionately ironic treatment of Leopold Bloom, advertising canvasser, and Bloom's perceptual world of "charming soubrettes" and faded music hall extravaganzas.

33. I am indebted to Richard Wolin's lucid comments on these issues in his "A Theory of Aesthetic Experience," paper presented at Stanford University Conference in Honor of Leo Lowenthal, 16 November 1985.

34. See, for example, Marchand's discussion of the ways that modernist strategies reduced women to decorative objects while preserving men as avatars of
functional efficiency: *Advertising the American Dream*, 179–86. David Nye's
contrast between art photography and industrial/commercial photography
is also illuminating in this connection: see his *Image Worlds: Corporate Identi-
ties at General Electric, 1890–1930* (Boston, 1985), 49. The entire book, by
demonstrating the ways that mass-produced photography was bent to corporate purposes, offers a useful qualification to Walter Benjamin's stress on
the liberating potential of "mechanically reproduced" cultural forms. See
"The Work of Art in the Age of Mechanical Reproduction," in Benjamin,
Illuminations, trans. Harry Zohn (New York, 1969), 217–52.

35. Suzi Grabik, *Magritte* (Greenwich, Conn., 1970), esp. chs. 1, 8, 9; Michel
Foucault, *This Is Not a Pipe*, trans. and ed. James Harkness (Berkeley, 1983);
Georges Rogue, *Ceci n'est pas un Magritte: Essai sur Magritte et la Publicite*
(Paris, 1983). For the dependence of advertising strategies on dominant cul-
tural conventions, see Judith Williamson, *Decoding Advertisements* (London,
1978), 25.

36. Quoted in Irving Sandler, *The Triumph of American Painting* (New York, 1970),
185.

37. Adolph Gottlieb and Mark Rothko, letter, *New York Times* (13 June 1943), sec.
2: 9; Tom Wolfe, *The Painted Word* (New York, 1975); Clement Greenberg,
"Art," *The Nation* 165 (6 December 1947): 630; Rothko, quoted in Sandler,
Triumph, 65; Robert Goldwater, "Art and Criticism," *Partisan Review* 28 (May–
June 1961): 693–94. For a much subtler and more interesting version of
Wolfe's argument, see Casey Blake, "Aesthetic Engineering," *democracy* 1
(October 1981): 37–50, which provoked an illuminating response from
Karen Parker Lears in ibid., 2 (January 1982): 135–40. Serge Guilbaut, *How
New York Stole the Idea of Modern Art: Abstract Expressionism, Freedom and the
Cold War*, trans. Arthur Goldhammer (Chicago, 1983), describes some of the
ideological uses of Abstract Expressionism in the later Cold War period, but
does not catch the motives or the intentions of the painters themselves.

38. Gottlieb quoted in Sandler, *Triumph*, 64; Meyer Schapiro, "Recent Abstract
Painting," in *Modern Art, 19th and 20th Centuries: Selected Papers* (1957; New
York, 1978), 213–26.

39. Irving Howe, *A World More Attractive* (New York, 1962), 196–97; Lears, "Some
Versions," 367–68.

40. Allen, *Romance of Commerce and Culture*, 213–14; Harris, "Designs on Demand," 19.

41. Walter Paepcke, "'Great Ideas' Recall Our Heritage, Help Build Container,"
Industrial Marketing (January 1955), 86.

Modern Art and the Invention of Postmodern Capital

John Carlos Rowe
University of California, Irvine

The contact and habit of Tlön have disintegrated this world.
Enchanted by its rigor, humanity forgets over and again that it is a
rigor of chess masters, not of angels. Already the schools have
been invaded by the (conjectural) "primitive language" of Tlön;
already the teaching of its harmonious history (filled with moving
episodes) has wiped out the one which governed in my childhood;
already a fictitious past occupies in our memories the place of
another, a past of which we know nothing with certainty—not
even that it is false.
—Jorge Luis Borges, "Tlön, Uqbar, Orbis Tertius,"
trans. James E. Irby

MODERNISM CAN NO LONGER BE DISCUSSED APART FROM POSTMODERNISM.
The perplexing relations between the two terms have occupied a
central place in critical and theoretical discussions of the humanities for the past two decades. Until recently, however, the majority
of the literary discussions centered on the experimental writers of
the 1960s and early 1970s in North America, Latin America, and
Western Europe and the degree to which they derived from and/
or superseded their modernist heritages. The French sociologist
Jean Baudrillard and philosopher Jean-Francois Lyotard have posed
the question "What Is Postmodernism?" in socioeconomic terms,
in which literary experimentalism is simply one form of production
among others. Baudrillard's *The Mirror of Production* (1975) and *For
a Critique of the Political Economy of the Sign* (1981) and Lyotard's *The
Postmodern Condition* (1985) focus on an economy whose *basic* production is sign-systems—information, fashion, service, advertising,

entertainment—that govern material forms of production. Just how art and literature function in a postindustrial economy centrally dedicated to the production and reproduction of signs remains an important and still unresolved question for both Baudrillard and Lyotard. It is quite certain in the writings of both theorists, however, that *literary function* can no longer be understandable apart from everyday commercial activities, unless that very difference—between "high art" and popular culture, for example—is understood as part of general ideological aims. Baudrillard's and Lyotard's discussions of a postmodern economy merely focus a certain tendency in what has been loosely termed "poststructuralist" theory in the humanities and social sciences. The relation between relatively technical literary and philosophical issues and socioeconomics has been accomplished in large part thanks to Althusser, Foucault, and Derrida, each of whom has attempted to rethink the relation between abstract and material productions according to the controlling grammar of a particular cultural situation. Although poststructuralists have been criticized for essentializing certain characteristics of the sign—Derrida's *differance*, Lyotard's *differend*, Foucault's *archive*, for example—poststructuralism has remained profoundly historical in its efforts to understand the peculiar rhetoric of contemporary Western cultures. Even as their historical subjects vary widely— Derrida's onto-theological tradition in Western philosophy, Althusser's Marx, Foucault's focus on Enlightenment reason—these poststructuralists are always writing about the *history* that developed our postmodern culture. It is within this historical matrix of poststructuralist theory, then, that I will interpret the troubled relation of modern art to the emergence of a postmodern economy.

I will attempt to describe the current situation by way of an exaggerated structural formulation of the relation of modernism to postmodernism. In the late industrial and late colonial cultures of the West that we have come to call "modern," literary and artistic movements are generally characterized by their postmodern desires: quite simply, the guiding motivation for the artist is to exceed the boundaries and limitations of modern society and its discursive conventions. The modern artist stakes his/her claim by insisting upon the figural and connotative variety of literary style. By contrast, the "language of the marketplace" is simply denotative and suppresses figural play for the sake of useful, literal meanings whose references to things and concepts are established by consensus.

In a postmodern culture, the discursive relation of art and culture is significantly different; for the purposes of my rather schematic model, I shall contend that it perfectly inverts the modern situation. Postmodern, postindustrial societies in the West are characterized by an economy concerned with the production of representations. We speak commonly of the new "information" and "service" economies, but these two terms come from the rhetoric of an older, industrial society that insists upon defining *products* as *things.* When we speak of *representations* as products, we are referring more obviously to the *effects of certain processes,* in the same way that we understand a representation as always already the figuration of something prior to it or outside its discursive field. In a postmodern culture, the *representation* is always a *representation of a representation,* like the light on a computer screen that represents the hermeneutic and linguistic representations that belong to scholarly discourse. A postmodern economy accepts this condition for production— that which is produced reveals its derivation from some accepted pretext—and makes no effort to disguise or to *naturalize* the artificial qualities and conditions of its "product." Whereas industrial capitalism struggled to give some natural credibility to its products and the conditions of their manufacture, postmodern economy accepts the utterly fictive origins of human "information." Under these conditions, then, everything that belongs to social reality is always already understood to be highly figurative, charged both with its local significance and informed by its more general derivations.

Thus we should not be surprised that contemporary television advertising is extremely self-conscious about its own medium. An advertisement for an Isuzu automobile mocks the conventionally exaggerated claims of television ads for automobiles. An advertisement for Coors beer starring Mark Harmon, former quarterback for UCLA and a former star of the prime-time soap opera *St. Elsewhere,* is organized in several related narrative parts, in the manner of a soap opera, and draws on the convention of the football star as a natural, "no frills" human being. Both ads are fundamentally intertextual; both are extremely self-conscious about their forms and media. Neither advertisement, however, expresses any anxiety or even irony regarding this situation, even though *irony* may be used as a technical device, as it is in the Isuzu commercial. The *intertextuality* of language and the highly figurative *scene of representation* are accepted as the conditions of postmodern life, of an economy in which representation is the *proper* product. In this cultural situation, the claim for some sharp distinction between literary and ordinary language—such as that made by the high moderns—seems simply old-fashioned, anachronistic. In fact, it is *not* the characteristic *pose* of the contemporary artist, although it is fair to say that there are many survivors of the "experimentalism" of the 1960s and 1970s—John Barth, John Hawkes, Robert Coover, William Gass, et al.—who continue to write in an "experimental" mode that appears every day to be more *destylized,* more *realistic* as a representation of either the particulars or the general rhetoric of a postmodern condition.

Contemporary American fiction from about the mid-1970s to the present has been characterized by a stubborn insistence upon literature's special appeal to stable, generally philosophically credible, *human values* and to certain cognitive universals, often accessible only by way of some *literary* expression. John Gardner's *On Moral Fiction* (1978) was first greeted as an attack directed primarily at the "surfictionists" of the 1960s and 1970s, among whom he himself had at one time been counted.[1] Gerald Graff's *Literature Against Itself* (1979), John Aldridge's *American Literature and the Way We Live Now* (1984), and Charles Newman's *The Postmodern Aura: The Act of Fiction in an Age of Inflation* (1985) are similarly directed at the bankruptcy of countercultural artistic experiments and the superficiality of a "postmodern" literary aesthetic.[2] Each of these critics, despite radically different theoretical and political postures (from Aldridge's "liberal humanism" to Newman's Marxism), suspects that the decline of distinct "literary values" may be the result of a postmodern economy whose dizzying rhetorical performances (i.e., *products*) outstrip the most energetic efforts of conventional literary representation or criticism. In sum, each of these critics of postmodern experimentalism confirms Philip Roth's now famous dictum: "The American writer in the middle of the 20th century has his hands full in trying to understand, and then describe, and then make *credible* much of the American reality. . . . the actuality is continually outdoing our talents, and the culture tosses up figures almost daily that are the envy of any novelist."[3] Graff and Newman in particular attack the superficiality of the experimentalists' claims to the "essential fictionality" of reality, in part because what had been a bold claim on the part of moderns as diverse as Kafka and Henry James,

Proust and Gertrude Stein, Pound and Stevens had become the *condition* for a postmodern economy and its social reality.

These critics are not just isolated reactionaries; their respective cries for a literature that would revive the "critical edge" and subversive claims of "great literature" from the past have been joined by the artists themselves. What has come to be termed "metafiction" has in fact swerved from the modernist's celebration of literature's fictionality and figurality to a certain self-consciousness regarding the culture's *artistic capabilities*. Thus the "neo-realism" of Raymond Carver is already "metafictional," in the sense that it offers its own minimal realism as an alternative to a social reality that Geoffrey Hartman some time ago characterized as a world of "superfetated meanings," of "excess signification," a world in which the dizzying vertigo of the postmodern "novel" has become the condition of everyday reality.[4] In Marquez's *Autumn of the Patriarch*, the arts by which a brutal dictator maintains his precarious rule and those by which the narrative voice operates are nearly impossible to distinguish. By the same token, the psychic fabulation of the woman in D. M. Thomas's *The White Hotel* is disentangled by a psychotherapeutic narrative that finally reveals the "origin" of the fantastic in the Nazis' mass murder. More obviously, John Irving's *The World According to Garp* incorporates Garp's metafictional stories inside another metafictional frame—Irving's own narrative—that seems intent upon exposing the dangers of such fabulation and returning Garp to everything that his act of fiction-making had helped endanger: bourgeois individualism, the family, interpersonal relations, an apolitical "realism." The novels, stories, and theoretical writings of William Gass, often celebrated in the 1970s in conjunction with the surfictionists, have achieved new fashion, because their claims for a discrete and coherent fictional world—a world realized in the precise and formal language-games of the author—are understood properly as alternatives to the groundless and irrational textuality of postmodern reality.[5]

From neo-realism to the self-consciously metafictional, contemporary literature offers us the "alternative" to postmodern reality that a return to stable values, personal immediacy, and "unmediated" vision might fantastically bring. Postmodern experimentalism has, in fact, reproduced the literary and artistic equivalent of "modern culture," in which literal and stable meaning are given particular

*realism
or
Subversion?*

centrality. The so-called "postmodernism" of the experimentalists of
the 1960s and early 1970s was nothing other than the tail end of
high modernism, but now pushed into a cultural situation in which
the utopian project of modern literature has been *perversely* realized.
As a consequence of this changed and constantly changing cultural
situation (an *economy* of ceaseless change, in the Marxist's worst
nightmare of capitalism run wild), the literary experimentalists seem
to have been caught unexpectedly by an "imitative fallacy" occasioned by a new historical situation. Read in the 1980s, *Giles Goat-Boy*
or *The Lime-Twig*, for example, appear far more realistic than subversive of the terms by which social reality is maintained.

I have described rather reductively the relation of art to modern
and postmodern cultures, respectively, in terms of a rhetorical *chiasmus*, which I offer in the place of any more decisive demarcation of
the "boundary" separating modern and postmodern literatures:

> The Modern Age's literature and art are "Post-Modern"; The Postmodern
> Age's literature and art are "Modern."

Such a model suggests, of course, that the changed relations of
literature to the dominant culture are simply the effects of historical transformations occasioned by changes in the economic traditions. Vulgar Marxism, thus far. But my argument is considerably
more dialectical or *differential* in the sense that the artist's avant-
garde and utopian claims for literature produced in the modern
age helped *effect* the transformation of an industrial economy into
a postmodern, postindustrial economy of representation. The same
reading experience that gives us the uncanny sense that literary
experimentalists of the 1960s and early 1970s merely imitate
postmodern reality applies as well to the polemical utopianism of
the high moderns. The competing inner subjectivities of the characters in a Virginia Woolf novel, for example, are generally set
against the social formalities and conventions of ordinary London
life. It is the tedium of *la vie quotidienne* that drives her characters
deeper and deeper into imaginary worlds that can be "connected"
only by way of some intersubjective "reading," only by means of
some "sympathy" that is best metaphorized in the related *interests*
of writing and reading. But the subjective pluralism for which Mrs.
Dalloway longs or that might have kept Septimus Smith from the
shocks of the First World War (might have prevented that war it-

MODERN ART WAS A CRITIQUE OF "MODERN" CULTURE
THIS (1?) TO A COUNTER-CULTURE WHICH WAS
A LIVING CRITIQUE, THEN THE WALL
WAS DOWN WE SHOULD ASK.

self, Woolf often seems to argue) is in fact *realized* in the post-modern age of two-way communications and sophisticated telematics. "Another man's truth is only a dismal lie to me," Conrad complains, but the implied alternative is a world in which every man might have his *own* truth, and it is precisely *that* world which is promised and thus *marketed* in the shape-shifting technologies of postmodern culture.

I cannot hope to offer in this essay some far-ranging analysis of the ways that the high modernists contributed tangibly to the realization of a culture in which the figural qualities of experience, the play of competing subjectivities, the necessary stylization of art or "fashion" have become the common assumptions. I shall, then, simply *speculate* about the ways in which certain utopian impulses in Henry James and Ezra Pound helped give credibility to discursive strategies initially intended only to question the apparent "naturalness" of modern social reality. Yet, what made possible even the literary claim for such avant-garde discourse was a particular will for transformation informing the late age of industrialism and colonialism that we call "modern culture." In short, the modern literary avant-garde, so well represented in its beginnings by Henry James and in its heyday by Ezra Pound, was one manifestation of the ideological transformation from a modern material economy to a postmodern economy of immaterial "representations." My argument depends fundamentally on Fredric Jameson's far-reaching theory of modernism, which includes an inevitable account of the relation of modernism to postmodernism. Jameson's theory of modernism, especially as it is developed in *Fables of Aggression: Wyndham Lewis, The Modernist as Fascist* (1979) and *The Political Unconscious* (1981), is a coherent, powerful, and sophisticated approach. In my judgment, Jameson's theory of modernism is the most important and potentially influential approach since Georg Lukacs's "Ideology of Modernism" and *History and Class Consciousness*. And Jameson's theory has the advantage of Lukacs's not only in coming *after* the exhaustion of modernism as a literary mode, but also in a utopian orientation that is, unlike Lukacs's reactionary defense of nineteenth-century realism, genuinely oriented toward a social and literary future.

For Jameson, Henry James quite clearly figures the swerve into aestheticism occasioned by the exhaustion of nineteenth-century realism—an *exhaustion* occasioned by ideological contradictions so evident by the end of the nineteenth century as to frustrate the traditional legitimating functions of the realistic novelist. We should note here not only how James and Pound serve Jameson's general conception of modernism, but how each also represents a particular theoretical discourse that finds at least one of its respective origins in modernism. Ezra Pound, together with Joyce, represents for Jameson the aesthetic "mythography" that we associate with the archetypal criticism of Northrop Frye. Henry James quite explicitly figures in Jameson's narrative as the invention of the formalism drafted by T. S. Eliot and codified by the American New Critics.

Jameson's Henry James typifies the literary response to the crisis of the philosophical subject occasioned by the history of capitalism's alienation of the individual. Capitalism lays special claim to the individual subject as the figure capable of affirming, expressing, and reproducing itself in and through a capitalist economy. This may well be the fundamental irony of capitalism; it is in fact the great artistic *achievement* of capitalism: to turn into a philosophical origin and end the very individual that capitalist economic practices seem intent upon destroying. By now, the "solution" to this apparent paradox is familiar enough. Alienating workers from the coherent processes and products of their own labor-power, capitalism invents a philosophical and idealist "category" of the "subject" that defines itself just insofar as it can distinguish itself from its material circumstances. This idealist "subject," ceaselessly struggling to liberate itself from the wear and tear of time and the servitude of labor, finds its proper expression in the abstract discourse of philosophy. A bourgeois transcoding of the aristocrat's "natural rights" to property and rule, the "subject" has its own history of idealist legitimation, whereby certain disciplines and processes are necessarily separated from the conditions of everyday labor. James valorizes point of view as a technical device, precisely because he imagines the "form" of the novel to be not only homologous with but constitutive of an aesthetic "consciousness," the very "center" of fictional relations, that would be the best alternative to the alienating forces of modern industrial societies. The "central consciousness" in James is at once the protagonist (around whom the "ado" of consciousness is organized), the dispersed author (always effaced in order to achieve metonymic realization through character and reader), and the Implied Reader: "In James, . . . the reader (or Implied Author) is in a position to hold private or monadic experience together with an external moral perspective in the unity of a single act of consciousness. Jamesian irony, therefore, unlike the judgments Lewis's narratives sometimes seem to project, unites point of view with ethical valuation in an immanent way."[6] Within nineteenth-century bourgeois culture, "self-consciousness" and the capability of *representing* that self become indispensable tokens of the "right to rule."

The Jamesian "drama of consciousness" is for Jameson a key to the ideological function of the "metaliterary" themes that are so dominant in James's fiction, especially in the later works. What Jameson terms "the ideal of theatrical representation" is James's valorization of the constitutive activity of consciousness, once it has been freed from some illusion of empiricism—from the "reality principle" that haunts James's characters, especially in their efforts to enter the ruling social order and to understand its codes. James's "scenic art," then, effectively transforms the narrativity of the novel, with its traditional emphasis on history and temporality, into the "theatricality" made available to the "spectatorial" consciousness, which receives literary representation as if from the privileged vantage of the theater-goer—at once inside and outside the "dramatic" action. Jameson is thinking here of the essentially "theatrical" quality of Victorian society itself, in which the class contradictions within that society are made to *appear* coherent and structurally unified by way of those "social arts" that would assign individuals their proper "roles" within the drama. Despite what recent cultural critics like Guy de Bord and Jean Baudrillard have said about the uniquely spectatorial and theatrical qualities of postindustrial and postmodern culture, industrial capitalism also "staged" its social drama in the rhetoric of Victorian culture and helped pave the way for the more complex forms of social dramatization in our own postmodern era.

In this view, then, the battle of the Jamesian "fine conscience" with the illegitimate "authorities" of the bourgeoisie becomes James's own means of compensating for a vanished aristocracy with a new, artistic "aristocracy." By the same token, the "hereditary," even genetically encoded "right to rule" claimed by the landed aristocracy is now claimed by those initiates into the "religion" of consciousness, whose "inheritance" is the literary and intellectual tradition so relentlessly "erased" in the gray wash of the modern. In exposing "false consciousness"—generally that of the bourgeoisie (Maud Manningham in *The Wings of the Dove*, for example)—or the impotence of a deposed aristocracy (Lord Mark in *Wings of the Dove* or Prince Casamassima in *The Princess Casamassima*), James emphasizes the *imitative* and *derivative* qualities of his bourgeois characters. By failing to express themselves, by *imitating* the practices of a bankrupt aristocracy, James's bourgeois characters show themselves to be slavish followers, bad artists, and inadvertent reactionaries. Rather than representing in some exemplary way their age, they refuse to assert aggressively their own unique power. Thus Adam Verver in *The Golden Bowl* does not appear to us as the aggressive industrialist who acquired such a fortune, but as an aesthete striving to build in American City some simulacrum of that monument to aristocratic patronage: the European museum. By the same token, Christopher Newman in *The American*, for all his deliberate "Americanisms," uses all of these "democratic charms" in the interests of social climbing. Always trivializing his actual accomplishments as a capitalist, Newman typifies nothing so much as the cynical shape-shifting of the bourgeois entrepreneur; his "innocence" is a deliberate strategy of protean adaptation. For similar reasons, the "vulgar" product manufactured by the Newsomes in *The Ambassadors* is never mentioned, not so much because James considers it basely "material" but because the *Newsomes* do. Thus Mrs. Newsome's patronage of Strether's literary journal, her desire for Chad to be "cultivated" and thus well married are the signs of a bourgeois "leadership" that refuses its own authority for the sake of some imitation of aristocratic pretensions. In his own reading, of course, James identifies just these contradictions as central to bourgeois ideology, thus offering some of the most cogent and sophisticated criticism of capitalism that we have had in modern literature.

The ideological subtext that governs James's formal and technical practices is thus clear enough. Capitalist alienation causes the self-conscious writer to imagine an alternative space, whose "theater" stages precisely those forces that have driven it out of the world, into fiction. Rather than seeing this "corner" as a space of merely powerless stylization, the "impressionistic" novelist *reifies* his own technical strategies, such that they themselves become the fe-

tishes of the artistic "identity" that compensates for the social cor-
ruptions revealed in the narrative. The entire act of the Jamesian
novel, then, is quite traditionally a coming to "self-consciousness,"
but only of the means and techniques by which such self-consciousness has been thematized. Successively dismissing all social
and historical contents, the Jamesian novel leaves us only with the
"value" of its own "style"—the formal rendering of an "impression"
that speaks the psychological truth of the observer, thereby guar-
anteeing that observer's identity.

What such aestheticism accomplishes, against its own better
judgment, of course, is the reinstatement of that individualism
dreamt by bourgeois ideology. And the Jamesian novel does this
work precisely by distinguishing between "masters" and "servants,"
between those capable of equating "being" with "doing" and those
who merely "labor" for others—for some alien, external social "authority." What James attacks so mercilessly in his novels is precisely
that "closed society" of those who "know" (who understand the
social codes), but Jameson argues that James's own aesthetic morality substitutes such ideals as "intersubjectivity" and observational
"knowledge" as props to an increasingly precarious notion of
philosophical subjectivity. Together with the New Critics spawned
by this Jamesian formalism, Jameson includes those other "psychological realists," those neo-Freudians who would offer their own
psychic equivalents to the "literary self-conscious" of the Jamesian
novel: "Jamesian point of view, which comes into being as a protest
and a defense against reification, ends up furnishing a powerful
ideological instrument in the perpetuation of an increasingly
subjectivized and psychologized world, a world whose social vision
is one of a thoroughgoing relativity of monads in coexistence and
whose *ethos* is irony and neo-Freudian projection theory and adap-
tation-to-reality therapy. This is the context in which the remarkable
transformation of Henry James from a minor nineteenth-century
man of letters into the greatest American novelist of the 1950s may
best be appreciated." [7]

What distinguishes James's artistic consciousness, the authorial
"self," from the bourgeoisie's slavish imitation of aristocratic identity
is the artist's acceptance of the utterly fictive bases for any such
authority. Unlike English law and capitalist economics, the Jamesian
novel *never* naturalizes the process of human consciousness. Henry

James is extraordinarily consistent in his dissociation of artistic form from anything faintly resembling "Nature." Even in his most realist pronunciamentos, James insists only upon the relation of art to *experience, life,* or *reality*: "Humanity is immense and reality has a myriad forms; the most one can affirm is that some of the flowers of fiction have the odour of it, and others have not; as for telling you in advance how your nosegay should be composed, that is another affair." [8] Even the "flowers of fiction" mock any naive correspondence of art to nature; already "composed" in a "nosegay," they have grown out of the "myriad forms" of humanity and its different realities. For James, the complexity of social reality and its history reminds us of the compositional forms that expose both as elaborate contrivances, fictions of human construction, albeit with very tangible consequences.

The artist's appeal for the reader to *recognize* the fictive origins of social reality is a common motive and aesthetic rationale for many moderns. Insofar as industrial capitalism repeated the efforts of the landed aristocracy to "naturalize" social reality, it not only "mystified" the real relation of men and women to their social conditions of existence, it also undermined its own legitimacy by imitating the rhetoric of an older order—one that it had attempted to supersede. Artistic identity and authority, then, offered an alternative to this social "repetition-compulsion," and throughout modern literature and thought we find a persistent distinction between "good" fictions and "bad" fictions, the former those that reveal their own terms of representation and, most often, expose the disguises by which the latter assume some "natural" or "conventional" status. The modern writer thus established a kind of literary "third world," some shadow kingdom between the "real" and "fictive," the "natural" and "artificial," in which *fiction* itself could claim its own formal *reality*.

This modernist "anti-terra" offers some very tangible utopian prospects, most of them written into the aesthetic imperatives of reading and writing the modernist text. The implied reader of a James novel is thus committed to recognize the fictive bases of social reality, at least as such society is represented in the James novel. Such a "recognition"—"recognition" scenes of this sort are common structural moments in James's fiction—promises a certain liberation from the constraints of ordinary experience.[9] In the first place, this recognition (or "self-consciousness") encouraged character and reader to question the self-sufficiency of the present and to explore the *historical* (social and personal) forces conditioning any apparently "current event" or "action." That such a "history" is, in fact, a history of representations, of *fictions*, is in no way surprising, given the terms by which such a "consciousness of history" is made available. It is no step at all to the common modernist conclusion that history itself is nothing but a series of complexly interrelated *texts*, individually and collectively calling for their interpretation.

Thus the literary author's capability to work with texts and to write and know by way of the wayward rhetoric of this textual situation gives such an author a special credibility in the modern age—a credibility that this same author often claims has special political relevance. The "historical self-consciousness" offered by literature exposes the fictions of discrete historical periods, nationalities, canonical traditions (in the arts and other disciplines), as well as social conventions of gender, class, and working relations. The modernist's will to *expose* such fictionality involves an appeal to countertraditions, "foreign" cultures, and transnational issues. James's "international theme," for example, is not just an occasion for literary drama; it typifies the modernist's general effort to unveil the fiction of nationality by way of a strategic, literary cosmopolitanism.

The high moderns sought a particular kind of "aesthetic" internationalism, which was prompted in part by their various quests for literary traditions other than those that often had helped shape the nationalism of their countries of origin. The rallying cry, "Make It New," had a repeated undertone: "Look elsewhere." A "world" elsewhere is the figure by which the aestheticism and formalism of the moderns variously has been celebrated and condemned, but this repudiation of American and European nationalism often worked perversely to recover its most contradictory political values.

In the writing of Ezra Pound, such internationalism is carried to an extreme unmatched by any other modern, insofar as it is offered both as a political utopia and as a poetic theory. The historical and cultural *hubris* of Pound's poetry exceeds the sublimest madness of any previous epic poet, because Pound's poetic promises the mythic foundation not only for a new culture but also for a "culture" that would encompass all the different cultures and periods in recorded human history. The utopian "culture" of the *Cantos* is, of course, decidedly multinational only according to the first recognition of modernism: the fictionality and thus textuality of history. James works to achieve this recognition for his characters and his implied readers; in fact, James's art is often nothing but this recognition. Pound, however, *begins* with this modernist assumption, elaborating in complex ways the kind of postmodern utopia implied by such knowledge.

Even in his early poetry, Pound interprets "Nature" in terms that are always informed by poetic or social conventions. "Nature" may be the place of seasonal change and renewal employed in the haiku and tanka, the referent for the Chinese ideogram, the mythic space of Greek classicism, the ordered cosmos of Western medievalism, the resources misused by capitalist usury, and the like. Students of Pound are often confused by his apparent appeal to some "natural ground," especially in his adaptation of Fenollosa's theory of the Chinese written character or his earlier theory of the poetic "realism," and his Symbolist conception of an "artificial" nature: a contrived, fabricated space *constituted* by poetic discourse. From the apprentice poems of *Personae* to the final *Cantos*, however, Pound remains true to the idea that "Nature" is the effect of a certain textuality. In "'Blandula, Tenella, Vagula,'" he writes:

> Will not our cult be founded on the waves,
> Clear sapphire, cobalt, cyanine,
> On triune azures, the impalpable
> Mirrors unstill of the eternal change?[10]

And virtually answers this question in Canto CXVI:

> But the record
> the palimpsest—a little light
> in great darkness—cuniculi—An old "crank" dead in Virginia.[11]

The "palimpsest" of history as textuality produces its own internal "light," its own natural "illumination" shines only through the "underground passages" or "mine shafts" (*cuniculi*) cut through history by Pound's poetic practice, his strategic intertextuality. "History" itself is always already the "natural ground," but it appears chaotic without the organization or illumination of poetic form. As it cuts passages, finds resemblances, and contrives certain "influences," poetry claims to make history visible. Pound repeatedly metaphorizes his poetry as a form of *energy*, which regathers actions scattered through history into the energetic nodes or clusters of the image, ideogram, or strong personality. Pound poetically gathers the limbs of Osiris or, in the passage from the *Cantos*, revives the political authority of Jefferson, who otherwise is simply "an old 'crank' dead in Virginia."

The modern author is thus not simply an anatomist of social fictionality but a masterful manipulator of such textuality. The very fact that Pound can and does move the texts of history into new and unexpected contexts, violating thereby conventional boundaries, testifies to their figural and fictional qualities. At some level, intolerant readers of Pound are quite right: there is a sense of purely *virtuoso* performance in the *Cantos*. But beyond that sheer performance, that shameless *display* of learning, Pound builds a monument of his own to those "authors" who engage history by learning to read and use the figurative, connotative potential of otherwise denotative texts and historical "records." The "hero" of the *Cantos* is an amalgamated "character," who draws upon the virtues of Homer, Confucius, Malatesta, Dante, Adams, Jefferson, Mussolini, and Pound himself, among many other so-called "thrones," to claim some sociopolitical authority for poetry and art.

Pound's "thrones" serve as "vortices" that draw together into a "character" (or ideogram) the force of a transnational, transindividual, and ultimately transhistorical ideal for literature.[12] Pound's "thrones" are similar to the "strong personality" Jameson interprets as central to Wyndham Lewis's writings: "The ideal of the 'strong personality'—too complex to be resumed under the current term of 'elitism'—is in fact the central organizational category of Lewis's mature ideology, and the primary 'value' from which are generated all those more provocative, yet structurally derivative ideological motifs and obsessions of racism and sexism, the attack on the Youth Cult, the disgust with parliamentary democracy, the satiric aesthetic of Otherness, the violent polemic and moral stance of the didactic works, the momentary infatuation with Nazism as well as the implacable repudiation of Marxism."[13] Insofar as this "negative" determination of the "strong personality" or the "throne" is "self-conscious," as I think it must be understood in application to the Pound of the *Cantos*, then it is conceived as the "negation of negation," the effective cancellation of an ideological *ressentiment* that has marginalized artistic representation. In this regard, the archetype for Pound's "throne" is the satirist.

But as Jameson makes clear in his treatment of such *ressentiment* as the "weakness" of contemporary culture, it is possible only by virtue of the artist's own *ressentiment*—his own reaction to the time, change, and becoming that have resulted in his contradictory situation. Pound's "thrones," which have for so many critics the virtue of providing some means of understanding the "productive" logic of the language machine of the *Cantos*, end by miming the very will to authorial power they were designed to supplant. *Thrones de los cantares* (1959), specifically 96–109, focus on *philology*, as Kenner argues in *The Pound Era*.[14] The cast of characters gathered under the category "thrones" constitutes Pound's peculiar etymology of the qualities of the effective leader; each is explicitly a product of a certain textual history, even Pound's contemporaries, such as Douglas and Mussolini. And each of Pound's figures metaphorized as a "throne" may be said to "incorporate" the diversity, divergence, and contradictoriness of human language and its *history* in an intertextuality that represents the higher reality of Pound's poetic *histoire*.

The "throne" or "strong personality" derives *his* (decidedly a patriarchal figure for Pound) authority from his recognition of a world of dizzying textuality and his willingness to accept his social responsibility to find some channel or passage to action amid these prior interpretations. Whatever limited "freedom" he may claim comes from just this knowledge that the essential figurality of language makes *any* social representation manipulable, adaptable to some new purpose. Unlike the antihero of modern fiction or Pound's own poetic double, Hugh Selwyn Mauberley, the "throne" claims his right to rule on the basis of his awareness that the textual condition demands decisive action:

> JEFFERSON was guyed as a doctrinaire. It is difficult to see what doctrine covers his "Embargo" unless it be the doctrine that when an unforseen emergency arises one should try to understand it and meet it.
>
> The truth is that Jefferson used verbal formulations as tools. He was not afflicted by fixations. Neither he nor Mussolini has been really interested

in governmental machinery. That is not paradox, they have both invented it and used it, but they have both been more deeply interested in something else.[15]

In the *Cantos*, Jefferson is frequently characterized as a master of language, a *bricoleur* capable of patching together a solution to a present problem from the rhetoric of the past.[16] What distinguishes such "leadership"—what Pound elsewhere terms the "right reason" of Mussolini—from "fixation" is its reliance on a certain *critical* function that carves a passage or channel for action within the welter of different interpretations:

> The DUCE sits in Rome calling five hundred bluffs (or thereabouts) every morning. Some bright lad might present him to our glorious fatherland under the title of MUSSOLINI DEBUNKER.

In the immediately following paragraphs, Pound answers the criticism that his poetry is derivative:

> An acute critic tells me I shall never learn to write for the public because I insist on citing other books.
>
> How the deuce is one to avoid it? Several ideas occurred to humanity before I bought a portable typewriter.
>
> De Gourmont wrote a good deal about breaking up cliches, both verbal and rhythmic.
>
> There is possibly some trick of handing out Confucius, Frobenius, Fenollosa, Gourmont, Dante, etc., as if the bright lad on the platform had done all of their jobs for himself, with the express aim of delighting his public.[17]

This is hardly free-association; Pound links Mussolini as debunker with his own poetic practice *and* with that short-list of literary and scholarly "thrones" to whom Pound here pays allegiance.

What justifies this manipulation of history's language is, of course, the use to which such rhetoric is put, and that use is always contrasted with the *usury* and *ownership* of capital:

> Ownership? Use? there is a difference.
> The temple ⎍⎍⎍⎍ is not for sale.
> (Canto XCVII, 678)

The only "currency" that promises use rather than a system of exchange that encourages "accumulation" is language. The "temple" in whatever cultural figuration—from the Greek temple to Malatesta's *tempio* to the Confucian body— is always already a poetic temple, an altar to language. The "throne" in the "temple" is thus the legitimating figure for the proper use of language, and this throne figures proper use as both critical *and* decisive in the same gesture that allows the "strong personality" to *make laws*—that is, to respond to local circumstances by adapting the language of history. The linguistic constructs of Pound's "thrones" hold out the promise of some poetic economy and discipline that might avoid the sheer *usury* of historical drift and waste: the sheer accumulation of historical "surpluses." Thus the "energetics" or *synergy* of Pound's poetry in the *Cantos* is offered quite literally as an alternative to the waste, dispersion, and fragmentation of the various material economies that culminated in Western industrialism and its "monetary system." The poetry claims to *produce* what more material manufacture has failed to yield: culture and its principles of order.

With extraordinary prescience, it would appear, Pound anticipates the postmodern economy by way of the textual cosmos of the *Cantos*. This is, of course, only *apparent* clairvoyance, because Pound's strident *predictions* are in large part wish-fulfilling fantasies that could be realized only by way of independent economic and political changes. Even so, it is remarkable how often Pound identifies his "thrones" with a coming of age whose economy would be based on the production of culture and its representation, thereby superseding the material economies of industrial capitalism. His criticism of Marx, when it is not just crankily directed at what Pound judges to be Marx's economic naiveté, concerns Marx's fixation on purely industrial economies:

> The fascist revolution was FOR the preservation of certain liberties and FOR the maintenance of a certain level of culture, certain standards of living, it was NOT a refusal to come down to a level of riches or poverty, but a refusal to surrender certain immaterial prerogatives, a refusal to surrender a great slice of the cultural heritage.

> The "cultural heritage" as fountain of value in Douglas' economics is in process of superseding labour as the fountain of values, which it WAS in the time of Marx, or at any rate was in overwhelming proportion.[18]

For Pound, Mussolini's Italian fascism "is the first revolution occurring simultaneously with the change in material bases of life." [19] The "immaterial prerogatives" of the "cultural heritage" are quite obviously what Pound's "critical reading" of history offers us in the *Cantos*. His identification with "thrones" whose authority is at once poetic and political, rhetorical and legal, prefigures more than just his desperate desire to claim some power for the artist in an age that increasingly has little use for artistic and mythic wisdom. Pound's poetic "throne" fabricates a certain identity and authority that would become well suited to lead the postmodern age and its economies. Power is for such a figure an effect of rhetoric, but not simply an *act* of rhetorical performance. It includes the critical capacity to turn the language of the past, the language of history to certain contemporary purposes, and for that work the postmodern leader must operate critically, creating "passages" in such history that will lead, however tortuously, to *his* situation. In this way, the "author," understanding himself to be nothing but a potential effect of language, "positions" himself so that such language will *speak him* into being.

In a purely reflectionist theory, Pound's *Cantos* express well the historical disorder, the "sea-wrack," generated by the fragmenting and alienating forces of modern European industrial society. From the standpoint of Jameson's "ideology of form," Pound's *Cantos*, like Lewis's futurist experiments in the novel and prose satire, deconstruct the traditionally legitimating functions of the aristocratic epic or the realistic novel. Yet what they have deconstructed is not ideology, but merely literature's presumed independence from ideology, thus revealing the secret reason for art's *secondary*, derivative status. Under the circumstances, Pound vainly struggles to invent his "own" ideology—his own precarious balance of political, historical, artistic, psychological, and hermeneutical forces. As sublimely absurd as it is for me to claim that an author "invents" his own ideology, it is nonetheless a vainglory characteristic of modernism at its limit: that point at which it recognizes that its own experimentation is already anticipated by, even necessitated by, historical currents.

Pound's cosmopolitanism, unlike James's or Lewis's, already carries within its cultivated voice the echo of its daemonic double: the "communication" of the Western tradition to every corner of the globe by force of words or arms; the insistence that its chaos might be redeemed by "two gross of broken statues,/For a few thousand battered books," as Pound himself parodies this cultural colonialism in *Hugh Selwyn Mauberley*. With the breakup of the European colonial empires, nation-states faced a "legitimation crisis" that required something like a "paradigm-shift" from the material economy to the rhetorical economy of postmodern culture. As Jean-Francois Lyotard has argued, postmodernism involves the *delegitimation* of those master-narratives that had propped up industrialism.[20] The very different *uses* to which Pound puts the traditional epic "master-narratives," ranging from the *Odyssey* and Greek mythology to Jeffersonian republicanism, in the *Cantos* help delegitimize them. By taking cultural expressions out of their material, historical contexts, the moderns transformed such narratives into abstract, ahistorical "verbal assemblages," which could be used to create a poetic space, a "world elsewhere," for poetic authority with no necessary obligation to the historical networks from which these "stories" had been stolen. Even for those most critical of modernist literary theory and practice, the self-conscious "borrowings" of the modern poet have seemed harmless enough, mere signs of the poet's defensive bid for power in an increasingly scientific age. As such, modern literature could be condemned for its vainglory, for its actual impotence, for its nostalgia, and for its sad withdrawal from the exigencies of a changing world. The utopian dream of Pound's *Cantos* was decidedly not realized by Mussolini's fascism; instead, it was achieved paradoxically by precisely those "sensitive kindly professors who have never affirmed anything in their lives, who are possibly too cultured to make an affirmation, or too polite to risk stating an opinion that might jostle their colloquitor. . . ."[21] Indeed, with a certain self-contempt, we might recognize the "cosmopolitan" dream of Pound's poetics not in some social utopia but in the academic reality of the international conference, the use by exchange of scholarly papers, and the "community" of scholars sustained by such difficult modernist writings as the *Cantos*.

There is, however, another side to this story, which unfortunately does not redeem the "scholarship" in part spawned by the herculean and protean literature of high moderns like Henry James and Ezra Pound. The apparent anarchy of competing discourses, none of which makes any pretense at representing a "material" reality, has become one of the distinguishing characteristics of postmodern culture, at least in the definitions of Baudrillard and Lyotard. The shift from industrial to postindustrial society is accomplished by the change from material to immaterial products. Such a basic economic change offers a perverse "solution" to what classical Marxists judge the ineluctable problem of capitalism: the alienation of labor-power from itself, consequent commodity-fetishism, and the ultimate class struggle that such internal divisions would occasion. Once the "object" of labor is shifted from a concrete product to an immaterial one, such as "information" or "service," then "alienation" loses the status it holds in classical Marxism. In industrial economies, capitalist rhetoric may be designed primarily to *mask* the real sources of alienation, thus generating competing discourses, such as philosophy and psychoanalysis, which stake their respective claims to understand the causes of individual alienation—causes that are always figured as prior to or *beyond* the actual economic conditions. Nevertheless, such mystification not only can be exposed but will inevitably reveal itself as such as the worker continues to work at his problem. In postindustrial economies, however, there is no conflict between referent and representation, precisely because there is nothing but representation. The product *is* the process, and every worker has apparent "access" to what is produced according to his or her level of *competency* in the technologies involved. The "machine" is not glorified or anthropomorphized; it is nothing but a "machine," which *serves* the operator according to his relative mastery of its rules. James's valorization of "experience" as "the very atmosphere of the mind," that is, a purely mental category that depends upon intellectual capabilities, is effectively realized in postmodern culture. Postindustrial societies thus can relegitimate class distinctions by elaborating the elementary distinction between those who *can* and those who *cannot use* the information produced. The great myth of telematics, as Lyotard has argued, is that information becomes accessible to everyone and that the privatization of life occasioned by and historically intensified by nineteenth-century capitalism may well vanish as the media for two-way communication (from the telephone to the computer telephone modem) become affordable enough to be integral parts of individuals' domestic as well as commercial economies. By the same token, the very division between "domestic" and "public" spaces, between the family and job, promises to disappear as the same technology that makes it possible for individuals to work at home may also be employed to perform basic domestic chores.

I need hardly argue how insidious these claims to telematic egalitarianism are; each of us knows in his or her own way that this *apparent* and *promising* unification of all those social practices alienated from each other under industrial capitalism—domestic from commercial life, labor-power from its product, the individual from social governance and authority, etc.—are merely redistributed in some new myth of information that promises democracy while maintaining the old class distinctions. As Lyotard argues cogently, the apparent "egalitarianism" of the new information age merely disguises the hierarchical relations served best by the new technologies: "No money, no proof—and that means no verification of statements and no truth. The games of scientific language become the games of the rich, in which whoever is wealthiest has the best chance of being right. An equation between wealth, efficiency, and truth is thus established." [22]

Lyotard offers *paralogy* as an alternative to the "efficiency" criteria currently employed to judge scientific knowledge: "It is necessary to posit the existence of a power that destabilizes the capacity for explanation, manifested in the promulgation of new norms for understanding or, if one prefers, in a proposal to establish new rules circumscribing a new field of research for the language of science." [23] Lyotard's "solution" is, in fact, a reversion from within postmodern culture to modernist literary values. His "new" science might resist the equation of truth, efficiency, and capital (their *synonymity?*) by approximating the alternative rhetoric of artistic, figurative expression. Indeed, in keeping with his fundamental Kantianism, Lyotard relates paralogy, the differend, and other strategies of what poststructuralists have termed heterogeneity and dissemination to "the quintessential form of imaginative invention" and that which characteristically deconstructs a consensus criterion for knowledge.[24] His utopian alternative would rely on something like a strategic "dissensus," which itself would be the standard for measuring the *use* of knowledge. Every claim for knowledge would be tested by the competing claims it provoked and the previously "unthought" that it would help bring into the culture's cognitive field. This paralogical method of thinking accords well, of course, with Lyotard's well-known definition of the "postmodern" as "the presentation of the unpresentable," and it resembles nothing so well as modern art's effort to maximize its signifying potential. Thus the claims for "connotative richness," "plurisignification," "infinite interpretation," and "dissemination" that are made so often for the works of high modern art have been translated into the predicates of Lyotard's ideal postmodern culture.

What Lyotard seems to ignore or conveniently "forget" is the degree to which modern art and aesthetics paved the way for the postmodern cultural situation of our current "information age." James's self-conscious author/reader and Pound's "throne" prefigure more than just the competent scholar; they prefigure the promoter, advertising executive, and television or film producer, each of whom must assess the marketability of his product in terms of its ability to situate itself in relation to competitive products. When those "products" are understood to be nothing but "representations," then the task of marketing becomes equivalent to the problem of discovering some "voice" or "style" for the avant-garde artist. The normal function of this immaterial economy, in short, is the production of that which will appear to be "new," even as postmodern culture acknowledges that pure novelty, utter originality, is impossible. What is marketable as "new" is some recontextualized version of the old, achieved by means of a critical reading of (a self-consciousness regarding) what has lost its figurative freshness. In modernist culture, the artist distinguished his work from that of popular culture by insisting that the latter was composed of nothing but cliches, mere conventions that had become unreflective or purely instrumental. In postmodern culture, popularity depends upon endless novelty, the repeated critique of cliches, and the recycling of old stories in new contexts.

For Lyotard, the solution to what he terms "technocratic terrorism," by which he means the reinstatement of the old, industrial class system according to the new criterion of performative efficiency, is the "differential or imaginative or paralogical activity" that would measure efficiency and performance according to the production of new "ideas, in other words, new statements." [25] As Jameson points out in his Foreword to Lyotard's *The Postmodern Condition*, this appeal to a poststructuralist mode of disseminative knowledge merely reproduces one of the guiding assumptions of industrial capitalism: "The dynamic of perpetual change is, as Marx showed in the *Manifesto,* not some alien rhythm within capital—a rhythm specific to these noninstrumental activities that are art and science—but rather is the very 'permanent revolution' of capitalist production itself: at which point the exhilaration with such revolutionary dynamism is a feature of the bonus of pleasure and the reward of the social reproduction of the system itself." [26] Jameson's argument seems confirmed by the fact that our postmodern economies have merely intensified and renewed the basic philosophical aims of capitalism. Whereas James and Pound might have envisaged something "beyond" industrial capitalism—be it James's utopia of artistic sensibility or Pound's dystopia of fascism, the West's postindustrial economies of "information," "service," and "representation" have enabled capitalism to transform itself from a system of material production to one of immaterial circulation and distribution. By refiguring the "authority" of such production from the "natural rights" of the aristocrat and "rational ingenuity" of the capitalist to the theatrical self-consciousness of the modern artist, modern writers like James and Pound helped transform the contradictions of modern culture (late industrialism and colonialism) into the productive resources of a postmodern economy. The "death of the novel," the withdrawal of poetry behind academic walls, the gradual disappearance of "high" literary forms ironically may not toll the triumph of science over art, but simply declare the perverse realization of the modern artist's dream. The old forms of modernist art—novel, poem, play—have helped dream the postmodern world into existence and are reproduced in the lives we are compelled to lead.

Notes

1. Anton Kaes and I offer a more extensive treatment of this argument about the reactionary "modernism" of American literature in the past decade in "Das Ende der Avant-garde? Tendenzen der gegenwartigen amerikanischen Erzählprosa," *Zeitschrift fur Literaturwissenschaft und Linguistik* 36 (Fall 1979): 13–26.

2. In his Foreword to Lyotard's *The Postmodern Condition,* trans. Geoff Bennington and Brian Masumi (Minneapolis, 1984), xviii, Fredric Jameson characterizes the deliberate *artificiality* of postmodernist architecture in terms that are appropriate for our literary discussion here: "This is a rich and

creative movement, of the greatest aesthetic play and delight, that can perhaps be most rapidly characterized as a whole by two important features: first, the falling away of the prototypical vocation and the terrorist stance of the older modernism and, second, by the eclipse of all of the affect (depth, anxiety, terror, the emotions of the monumental) that marked high modernism and its replacement by what Coleridge would have called fancy or Schiller aesthetic play, a commitment to surface and to the superficial in all the senses of the word."

3. Philip Roth, "Writing American Fiction," *Commentary* 31 (1961): 224.

4. Geoffrey Hartman, "Language from the Point of View of Literature," in *Beyond Formalism* (New Haven, Conn., 1970), 353.

5. In *On Moral Fiction* (New York, 1978), 71, Gardner uses Gass to exemplify the special concern of experimental writers with language in and for itself: "The more time one spends piling up words, the less often one needs to move from point to point, argument to argument, or event to event; that is, the less need one has of structure." Gardner clearly judges Gass's "language games," his fictional "logical positivism," to be substitutes for the sorts of philosophically credible arguments conventionally offered by fiction.

6. Fredric Jameson, *Fables of Aggression: Wyndham Lewis, The Modernist as Fascist* (Berkeley, 1979), 55.

7. Fredric Jameson, *The Political Unconscious: Narrative as a Socially Symbolic Act* (Ithaca, N.Y., 1981), 221–22.

8. Henry James, "The Art of Fiction" (1884), in Morris Shapira, ed., *Selected Literary Criticism* (Harmondsworth, Eng., 1968), 85.

9. Isabel Archer's "vigil of searching criticism" in ch. 42 of *Portrait of a Lady,* Milly Theale's contemplation of the "kingdoms of the earth" from her Alpine ledge in the beginning of *The Wings of the Dove,* Lambert Strether's "little study in French ruralism" when he confronts Chad Newsome and Madame de Vionnet in *The Ambassadors,* are all versions in that central recognition in James's fiction in which *fictionality* itself reveals itself to the central consciousness.

10. " 'Blandula, Tenella, Vagula,' " *Selected Poems of Ezra Pound* (New York, 1957), 13–14.

11. Canto CXVI, from "Drafts and Fragments of Cantos," *The Cantos of Ezra Pound* (New York, 1970), 795.

12. Pound adapted the term "throne" from the Thrones in Dante's *Divine Comedy,* who "are the angels in control of the seventh sphere," as Carroll F. Terrell notes in *A Companion to the Cantos of Ezra Pound,* vol. 1 (Berkeley, 1980), 143. Terrell also points out that Dante associates the Thrones with rubies and "later with a description of the surrounding brilliance of gleaming water and light." Pound associates his own historical "thrones" with the radiant light and diaphonous form that he uses elsewhere for poetic form and energy.

13. Jameson, *Fables of Aggression,* 110.

14. Hugh Kenner, *The Pound Era* (Berkeley, 1971), 532.

15. Ezra Pound, *Jefferson and/or Mussolini* (London, 1935), 62.

16. The textualist pose of Pound's John Adams is as explicit as that of his Thomas Jefferson, as Thomas Cody is demonstrating in a doctoral dissertation on Pound's *Cantos*, which he is completing under my direction.

17. Pound, *Jefferson and/or Mussolini*, 35.

18. Ibid., 127.

19. Ibid.

20. Lyotard, *The Postmodern Condition*, 37–38: "The decline of narrative can be seen as an effect of the blossoming of techniques and technologies since the Second World War, which has shifted emphasis from the ends of action to its means; it can also be seen as an effect of the redeployment of advanced liberal capitalism after its retreat under the protection of Keynesianism during the period 1930–1960, a renewal that has eliminated the communist alternative and valorized the individual enjoyment of goods and services." Lyotard goes on, however, to "locate the seeds of 'delegitimation' and nihilism that were inherent in the grand narratives of the nineteenth century" (38).

21. Pound, *Jefferson and/or Mussolini*, 59.

22. Lyotard, *The Postmodern Condition*, 45.

23. Ibid., 61.

24. Ibid., 60.

25. Ibid., 65.

26. Foreword, ibid., xx.